A CHANCE TO MAKE A DIFFERENCE . . .

A ROLE NO ONE ELSE CAN FILL . . .

A TIME OF LIFE THAT CAN BE THE VERY BEST OF ALL

# *FROM AGE-ING TO SAGE-ING*

"A totally different understanding of what aging can be. . . . The author's zest is itself the best proof of his thesis, which is that a person can live joyfully, fearlessly, and richly till the very end. Those who are old and those who hope to someday be old can learn much from him."

—***Jewish Bulletin***

"Not only can it prepare the young and middle-aged adult for the role of sage and mentor, but, just as important, it can improve their current quality of life. . . . Perhaps a better title for this book would have been 'From Sage-ing to Age-ing,' heralding a process that commences with birth and continues through one's lifetime, reaching its apex at the end."

—***Midstream***

"A practical, probing, and inspiring book."

—**Marion Woodman, author of *Addiction to Perfection***

*more . . .*

"This fine book provides an extraordinarily rich contextual framework for understanding and catalyzing a significant evolutionary shift in the way we respond to aging in America."

—**Ram Dass, author of *How Can I Help?***

"Both balm and inspiration . . . a discerning and perceptive guide."

—**June Singer, Ph.D., author of *Boundaries of the Soul: The Practice of Jung's Psychology***

"A tremendous work, stunning in the depth and breadth of its view of aging."

—**Allan Chinen, author of *Once Upon a Midlife: Classic Stories and Mythic Tales to Illuminate the Middle Years***

"Wonderful wisdom on growing old gracefully."

—**Sam Keen, author of *Fire in the Belly: On Being a Man***

# *From* AGE-ING *to* *Sage-ing*

*A Profound New Vision of Growing Older*

Zalman Schachter-Shalomi
and Ronald S. Miller

GRAND CENTRAL
PUBLISHING

NEW YORK BOSTON

Grand Central Publishing
Hachette Book Group USA
237 Park Avenue
New York, NY 10017

Visit our Web site at www.HachetteBookGroupUSA.com.

Printed in the United States of America

First Trade Edition: December 1997

10 9 8



**Library of Congress Cataloging-in-Publication Data**
Schachter-Shalomi, Zalman
From age-ing to sage-ing : a profound new vision of growing older
Zalman Schachter-Shalomi and Ronald S. Miller.
p. cm.
Includes bibliographical references.
ISBN 978-0-446-67177-4
Aged—Attitudes. 2. Old Age— Psychological aspects. 3. Self-actualization (Psychology) in old age. I. Miller, Ronald S.
II. Title
HQ1061.S3165 1995
305.26—dc20 94-33014
CIP

*Cover design by Suzanne Noli*
*Book design by Giorgetta Bell McRee*

To my mother, Chayah Gitl Schachter,
and my sister, Ada Tamar Scharfman,
whose transit occurred during the writing of this book.

—Zalman Schachter-Shalomi

To my loving wife, Karen, my best friend and soulmate,
and our son Jason,
our special scholar-athlete and sage-in-training.

—Ronald S. Miller

# Contents

# ACKNOWLEDGMENTS

I would like to express my deepest appreciation and gratitude to:

Ronald S. Miller, whose insights, scholarship, and in-depth interviews with participants of spiritual eldering workshops brought sparks of creative originality to this book. Crafting words with the deft touch of spiritual sensitivity, he mothered the book as I fathered it. We stimulated and potentiated each other, guided by the spirit that wanted to be incarnated in the book.

Eve Ilsen, my wonderful partner, who constantly reminds me that physical health and the aesthetic dimension are integral aspects of spiritual eldering.

Barry and Debby Barkan and the staff of the Live Oak Institute for inspiration, friendship, and permission to use the Elder Creed in our workshops and in this book.

Lynne Iser for her organizational expertise at the Spiritual Eldering Institute.

Dr. Jean Houston for providing guidance and the practical tools that help people of all ages develop extended consciousness.

Gay Gaer Luce whose pioneering work at the SAGE (Senior Actualization and Growth Exploration) Project provided a solid foundation upon which to build.

Phillip Mandelkorn for transcriptions of conversations we had when the spiritual eldering work was in its incipient stages.

Omega Institute for sponsoring its groundbreaking conscious aging conference in May 1992.

Rabbi Jeff Roth, who as executive director of P'nai Or Religious Fellowship prepared the organizational space to bring this project to fruition.

Susan Saxe, good friend and executive director of Aleph, the Alliance for Jewish Renewal, the umbrella organization that oversees the Spiritual Eldering Institute.

Livia Szekely and the staff of Rancho La Puerta in Tecate, Mexico, for nourishing body and soul during the writing of the book.

Shrimati Ma Jaya for her inspiration, blessing, and her amazing work with AIDS patients.

A brief but by no means exhaustive list of other friends, colleagues, and teachers who influenced me in writing this book include Professor Martin Buber, Rabbi Schlomo Carlebach, Dr. Ken Dychtwald, Gerald Heard, Dr. Joan Halifax, Rabbi Abraham Joshua Heschel, Dr. Sheldon Isenberg, Pir Vilayat Khan, Maggie Kuhn, Murshid Samuel Lewis, Dr. Helen Luke, Dr. David Morgenstern, Dr. Claudio Naranjo, Ram Dass (Dr. Richard Alpert), Swami Satchidananda, Grand Rabbis Joseph Schneerson and Menachim Schneerson, Dr. Howard Thurman, and Dr. Edith Wallace.

—Zalman Schachter-Shalomi

I would like to express my heartfelt appreciation to:

Zalman Schachter-Shalomi, a compassionate elder and dear friend whose vision of spiritual eldering inspired me to write from my creative depths. By sharing with me the triumphs and challenges of his own eldering process with unaffected honesty and sincerity, he has served as a model of the wise, vigorous, fully functioning elder I hope to become one day.

My lovely and talented wife, Karen, for her constant love and unflagging support during the book's genesis, and our son, Jason, who again witnessed firsthand the magical process by which a book is birthed.

Sarah Jayne Freymann, our literary agent, who believed in this project from the very beginning and whose unqualified support helped turn a promising idea into a completed book.

Joann Davis, our editor at Warner Books, whose understanding of spiritual eldering and keen literary skills have contributed to the book's clarity and readability.

Jeremy Tarcher, the literary matchmaker who was instrumental in bringing Zalman and me together as partners.

Gloria Krasno for her encouragement at the beginning of the project.

Dr. Jag Deva Singh, who provided many insights about how to enrich the retirement years by applying the Indian model of human development to Western society.

Carol Segrave, a visionary gerontologist, who helped deepen my understanding of the economic, political, and psychological problems associated with aging in the United States.

Joseph Chilton Pearce for his insights in brain-mind development and human evolution.

The many wonderful participants at Zalman's spiritual eldering workshops who are quoted throughout the book.

Among the faithful friends who offered support during the writing process, I would like to thank Gwen Snyder (book midwife extraordinaire), Claude Balestra, artist J. McNeil Sargent, Jim O'Meara, Drs. Celia Dominguez and Brunilda Nazario, and Debbie Cooke. They graced my life with a generous supply of love and encouragement that went beyond the call of duty.

—Ronald S. Miller

# *From* AGE-ING *to* *Sage-ing*

# Introduction

I was approaching my sixtieth birthday, and a feeling of futility had invaded my soul, plunging me into a state of depression that no amount of busyness or diversion could dispel. On the surface, I had much to be thankful for. During the preceding decade, I had worked tirelessly and joyously in a pioneering movement to renew Jewish spirituality in the contemporary world. As a rabbi schooled in Kabbalah, the mystical wisdom of Judaism, I had broadened my base of operations by studying with Sufi and Buddhist teachers, Native American elders, Catholic monks, as well as humanistic and transpersonal psychologists. Besides serving as a professor of religion at Temple University in Philadelphia, I was speaking at national conferences and giving retreats at leading growth centers on the need for an ecumenical approach in renewing Western religion.

Yet while my public life was bustling with activity, beneath the surface, away from my teaching and pastoral work, something unknown was stirring in my depths that left me feeling anxious and out of sorts whenever I was alone. To avoid these upsetting feelings, I threw myself back into my work with a renewed resolve not to yield to the depression. But despite my best efforts, I could not keep up the hectic pace that had marked my previous decades of work. At night, looking at myself in the mirror in unguarded moments, I realized that I was growing old. Feeling alone and vulnerable, I feared becoming a geriatric case who follows the predictable pattern of retirement, painful physical diminishment, a rocking-chair existence in a nursing home, and the eventual dark and inevitable end to my life.

New questions began assailing me at these times. With an extended life span guaranteed by medical advances and our health-conscious lifestyles, could I convert my extra years into a blessing rather than a curse? What does one do with one's extra years? Were there exemplary long-lived people, patron saints of the elder years as it were, who could serve as inspired role models whom I could emulate? For all the earlier phases of my life, I had models to inspire and guide me, but when it came to growing old, there were no good models, codes of behavior, scripts, or social expectations to shape and give meaning to my life. As a rabbi and spiritual leader, I was supposed to provide answers to other people, but as I confronted my own aging process, I didn't know how to answer the new questions that life so insistently was bringing to my attention.

To deal with my unanswered questions, in 1984 I took a forty-day retreat at the Lama Foundation, an ecumenical retreat center located near Taos, New Mexico. I lived in a rustic cabin overlooking the Rio Grande where I spent most of my time in solitude, praying, meditating, writing, studying, and taking long walks. I was on a Vision Quest, an ancient shamanic rite of passage in which the seeker retreats from civilization, goes to a sacred place in nature, and cries for a vision of his life path and purpose.

After a few days, when the surface noise of my mind died down, I realized that I was sloughing off an old phase of life that I had outgrown. At the same time, to my great surprise and wonderment, I was being initiated as an elder, a sage who offers his experience, balanced judgment, and wisdom for the welfare of society. As I followed the intuitive promptings that came from within, I instinctively began harvesting my life, a process that involves bringing one's earthly journey to a successful completion, enjoying the contributions one has made, and passing on a legacy to the future. To initiate the process, I asked myself, "If I had to die now, what would I most regret not having done? What remains incomplete in my life?" As a first tentative step toward harvesting my life, I devoted an entire day meditating on my children and praying for their welfare. I wrote each one a heartfelt letter expressing much of the "mushy" stuff that frequently remains unexpressed between parents and children. I also set new priorities for my professional life and personal relationships.

When I returned from the retreat, I had a new spring in my step and a buoyancy in my heart. Having been to the mountaintop where I had glimpsed a vision of elderhood, I set about slowly at first, then with increased momentum, to bring my vision down to earth. Fueled by a sense of urgency and excitement, I did extensive reading in gerontology and life extension. I consulted with well-known consciousness researchers, such as Jean Houston and Gay Luce, who were doing remarkable work in developing the potentials of older adults. I applied the teachings of spirituality and transpersonal psychology to the issues of aging. Most of all, I studied my own eldering process, piecing together from my own quest the tools that lead to successful life completion. From this exploration, in 1987 I founded the Spiritual Eldering Institute, which sponsors nondenominational workshops that provide the emotional support, along with the psychological and spiritual tools, to help people become elders within our modern culture.

Giving these workshops across the country, I have witnessed firsthand how people are searching for a new approach to aging. Most of us have grown up with a deep-seated fear and loathing of old age. Our youth-oriented culture, while touting aerobically perfect bodies and lifestyles as life's *summum bonum*, focuses obsessively on the physical diminishments associated with old age. In the popular imagination, old age means wrinkled skin and chronic disease, rather than the wisdom, serenity, balanced judgment, and self-knowledge that represent the fruit of long life experience. Fortunately, our culture's limited, one-sided view of aging is undergoing a profound reconceptualization in our time. We are the first generation to apply the insights of humanistic and transpersonal psychology and contemplative techniques from our spiritual traditions to the aging process itself, giving birth to what some people call the conscious aging movement.

There are profound demographic forces pushing us in this direction. When the Social Security system was first designed, long-range planners conceived our life span to be no more than the biblical threescore and ten. Now, because of nutritional, medical, and economic advancements, our life span has increased to such a degree that the elderly represent the fastest growing segment of the population. What gerontologist Ken Dychtwald calls the Age Wave is coming on like a tidal wave. Consider the following facts:

In 1776, a child born in the United States had an average life expectancy of thirty-five. In a little more than two centuries, thanks to medical breakthroughs, public health campaigns, and lifestyle changes, Americans have more than doubled that figure to seventy-five. By the middle of the next century, the National Institute of Aging projects that life expectancy will be eighty-six years for men and nearly ninety-two years for women.

One hundred years ago, only 2.4 million Americans were over sixty-five, making up less than 4 percent of the population, according to Ken Dychtwald and Joe Flower, authors of *Age Wave*. Today there are more than 30 million people over that age, representing 12 percent of the population. The U.S. Census Bureau predicts that by the year 2000, 35 million Americans—or about one seventh of the population—will be over sixty-five. "Throughout most of recorded history, only one in ten people could expect to live to the age of sixty-five," write Dychtwald and Flower. "Today, nearly 80 percent of Americans will live to be past that age."

As the trend toward increased longevity continues, the baby boom generation—the 76 million Americans born between 1946 and 1964—will reach retirement age early next century. This health-conscious generation will inherit a reinvigorated approach to aging that has become popular within the past several decades. Until recently, because of negative images and expectations shared by our culture, people regarded old age as a time of waning vigor, lowered esteem, and social uselessness. But the senior boom, with its interest in lifelong learning, healthy lifestyle practices, and political activism is helping to reverse the demeaning ageist stereotypes that give old age a bad name. Gerontologists no longer regard the "inevitable declines of nature"—such as reduced physical strength and mental acuity—as necessities of nature. Rather, they view these conditions as the result of a sedentary lifestyle that is reinforced by negative aging stereotypes that condition us to expect physical and mental decline in our later years.

Across the country, people are casting off the negative images and expectations that sentence older adults to the junkheap as social outcasts. In its place, they are hoisting the banner of what gerontologists call "successful aging," an activity-oriented approach that promises increased physical vigor, continued intellectual growth, and meaningful work during the elder years. This new image represents an improvement over the stereotype of the bent, shuffling older adult consigned to a life of social isolation and futility. But it does not go far enough. As the baby boomers approach their elder years—indeed, as all older adults make the transition into what sociologists call the third age—they need a psychospiritual model of development that enables them to complete their life journey, harvest the wisdom of their years, and transmit a legacy to future generations. Without envisioning old age as the culminating stage of spiritual development, we short-circuit this process and put brakes on the evolutionary imperative for growth that can be unleashed by our increased longevity.

We don't normally associate old age with self-development and spiritual growth. According to the traditional model of life span development, we ascend the ladder of our careers, reach the zenith of our success and influence in midlife, then give way to an inevitable decline that culminates in a weak, often impoverished old age. This is *aging* pure and simple, a process of gradually increasing personal diminishment and disengagement from life. As an alternative to inevitable senescence, this book proposes a new model of late-life development called *sage-ing*, a process that enables older people to become spiritually radiant, physically vital, and socially responsible "elders of the tribe."

Sages draw on growth techniques from modern psychology and contemplative techniques from the world's spiritual traditions to expand their consciousness and develop wisdom. By expressing this wisdom as consecrated service to the community, they endow their lives with meaning and avoid becoming economic and psychological burdens on their loved ones and on society. This ongoing process, which I call *spiritual eldering*, helps us consciously transform the downward arc of aging into the upward arc of expanded consciousness that crowns an elder's life with meaning and purpose.

In putting forth a new model of spiritual elderhood, I am not only reviving an ancient and venerable institution that has enriched civilization since time immemorial, but taking it a step further. As part of the emerging approach to late-life development, the contemporary sage draws on three sources: models of the traditional tribal elder whose wisdom guided the social order for thousands of years; state-of-the-art breakthroughs in brain-mind and consciousness research; and the ecology movement, which urges us to live in harmony with the natural world. These forces converge in the sage, whose explorations in consciousness are giving birth to an elderhood that is appropriate for the modern world.

Throughout most of history, elders occupied honored roles in society as sages and seers, leaders and judges, guardians of the traditions, and instructors of the young. They were revered as gurus, shamans, wise old men and women who helped guide the social order and who initiated spiritual seekers into the mysteries of inner space. Beginning with the Industrial Revolution, with its emphasis on technological knowledge that often was beyond their ken, elders lost their esteemed place in society and fell into the disempowered state that we now ascribe to a "normal" old age. Today, as the Age Wave crests all about us and we confront existential questions about the purpose of our extended longevity, we are searching for new myths and models to ennoble the experience of old age.

The model that I'm proposing does more than restore the elder to a position of honor and dignity based on age and long life experience. It envisions the elder as an agent of evolution, attracted as much by the future of humanity's expanded brain-mind potential as by the wisdom of the past. With an increased life span and the psychotechnologies to expand the mind's frontiers, the spiritual elder heralds the next phase of human and global development.

Until recently, the techniques for spiritual eldering were unavailable to the public. But as the consciousness movement grew in popularity during the 1960s, 1970s, and 1980s, the once-hidden teachings of yoga, Zen and Tibetan Buddhism, shamanism, Sufism and Kabbalah (the mystical teachings of Islam and Judaism) entered mainstream Western culture. The same period witnessed the growth of humanistic psychology (with its emphasis on an expanded human potential), transpersonal psychology (which uses meditation as a therapeutic tool), and the brain-mind revolution, which uses contemplative techniques and the latest technology to expand our vast mental potential.

Spiritual elders use the tools from these disciplines to awaken the intuitive capacities of mind associated with inner knowledge, wisdom, and expanded perception. By activating their dormant powers of intuition, they become seers who feed wisdom back into society and who guide the long-term reclamation project of healing our beleaguered planet. Once elders are restored to positions of leadership, they will function as wisdomkeepers, inspiring us to live by higher values that will help convert our throwaway lifestyle into a more sustainable, Earth-cherishing one. They also will serve as evolutionary pathfinders offering hope and guidance to all those searching for models of a fulfilled human potential.

According to the new picture of aging presented in this book, extended longevity calls for the development of extended consciousness to help offset the physical and social diminishments of old age. Part One, consisting of the first three chapters, provides the conceptual understanding and historical perspective to help you begin your journey into elderhood. Part Two, covering the next four chapters, presents psychological and spiritual tools for transforming your life, such as meditation, life review, and journal writing. Besides using these contemplative tools, you will learn how to broaden your understanding of time, living with the intimations of eternity that are part of elder consciousness. You also will learn about how to approach death consciously as an opportunity for spiritual awakening. Part Three, covering the last three chapters, focuses on becoming a mentor; healing the family, the community, and the planet through elder wisdom; and creating the social structures for elderhood to emerge as a significant force in the near future.

I sincerely hope that *From Age-ing to Sage-ing* will help you recontextualize aging as the anticipated fulfillment of life, not its inevitable decline, a badge of success rather than a mark of failure. The book affirms, despite all the invalidations of our youth culture, that elderhood is a time of unparalleled inner growth having evolutionary significance in this era of worldwide cultural transformation. Because spiritual eldering is a call from the future, I invite you to accompany me on this pioneering journey into our unmapped potential. Whether you are young or old, I urge you to undertake this journey not only for your own personal well-being, but for the health and survival of our ailing planet Earth. Together, we will help give birth to a new civilization of unprecedented human development, spearheaded by spiritual elders working with people of all ages to create a peaceful and harmonious global society.

# *Part One*

# THE THEORY OF SPIRITUAL ELDERING

## Chapter 1

# *The Vision of Spiritual Eldering*

To you who are taking your first steps into the unexplored territory of spiritual eldering, I say, "Bravo!" Whether you are a retired person, someone in midlife, or a younger person contemplating your future, I salute you all as pioneers in search of a more fulfilling old age. Contrary to conventional thinking, aging is a great success, a result of strength and survivorship. Aging doesn't mean diminishment or exile from the ranks of the living. As the period in which we harvest the fruits of a lifetime's labor, it gives us the panoramic vision from which spiritual wisdom flows.

Like mountain climbers who have scaled a high peak, we have achieved a vantage point in old age from which to observe the path of our ascent and to appreciate the personality that we have created with discipline and devotion. We can survey the struggles for career, marriage, and financial security that occupied much of our time and see why they were all so necessary. Putting the puzzle pieces together, we can glimpse the larger patterns that crown our lives with deeper meaning. To you who stand triumphantly at the summit, I say, "You made it!" And to you who are still climbing the mountain of life's promises, I say in all sincerity, "Keep climbing. You have so much to look forward to in aging."

Obviously, this attitude smacks of heresy in our youth-oriented society. Everywhere you look, old age suffers from a bad reputation. Because of negative images and expectations shared by our culture, people enter the country called "old age" with fear and trembling. Feeling betrayed by their bodies and defeated by life, they believe they're condemned to lives of decreasing self-esteem and respect. As citizens of this oppressed nation, they expect to suffer from reduced vigor, enjoyment, and social usefulness.

Today, there's a growing movement to rebuild this country into a healthier, more positive place. Advocates of this movement are beginning to replace dehumanizing images of old age with new ones that restore the honored elder to Western society. Elders are *not* "senior citizens" who get gold watches at retirement, move to Sunbelt states, and play cards, shuffleboard, and bingo *ad nauseam*. In the words of Maggie Kuhn, founder of the Gray Panthers, a national alliance of older and younger adults committed to positive social change, they are not "wrinkled babies, succumbing to a trivial, purposeless waste" of their years and their time.

Then what are elders? They are wisdomkeepers who have an ongoing responsibility for maintaining society's well-being and safeguarding the health of our ailing planet Earth. They are pioneers in consciousness who practice contemplative arts from our spiritual traditions to open up greater intelligence for their late-life vocations. Using tools for inner growth, such as meditation, journal writing, and life review, elders come to terms with their mortality, harvest the wisdom of their years, and transmit a legacy to future generations. Serving as mentors, they pass on the distilled essence of their life experience to others. The joy of passing on wisdom to younger people not only seeds the future, but crowns an elder's life with worth and nobility.

As explorers of the unmapped country called "old age," we rarely find entries in our guidebooks under the heading "elder." However, under "elderly" we find numerous articles on topics such as retirement and loss of role identity, purposelessness, emptiness, infirmity, depression, and fear of death. Who would volunteer to enter such a country? Over the ages, our tour guides—the world's playwrights, philosophers, and religious traditions—have rarely painted a cheerful picture of aging. So before we can transform our conventional aging script and make our journey more triumphant, we must look squarely at what we find so distasteful about growing older.

For example, in the famous speech in *As You Like It* outlining the seven ages of man, William Shakespeare describes old age as "second childishness and mere oblivion/Sans teeth, sans eyes, sans taste, sans everything." We find an equally distressing picture in the Bible. In Ecclesiastes 12:1–5 (my translation), there is the following lamentation about senescence: "Then come the creaking days. Years creep up in which one feels like saying, 'I have no taste for them.' For the sunlight darkens in the eyes; dimmed is the light of the moon and stars; and the vision is patchy like a cloudy sky after the rain. The hands and arms, the guards of the house, begin to tremble. And the legs, like battle-tired soldiers, are unsure in their step. The grinding mills, the teeth, are fewer, and the windows of the mind fog up.... The back is bent and the urge to mate is weakened as a person walks to his eternal home." In her well-known book *The Coming of Age*, French philosopher Simone de Beauvoir sums up our dilemma: "[T]he vast majority of mankind looks upon the coming of old age with sorrow or rebellion. It fills them with more aversion than death itself."

With expectations like these, no wonder we dread old age. Our culture worships youth for its unbounded potential and despises old age as a terminal illness. Because we believe that growing older means physical and mental diminishment, many of us shuffle into an inactive, withdrawn, and depressed old age. Now add to these diminishments the grim prospect of being warehoused in a nursing home as part of a useless and redundant population. No wonder we wake up at 2 A.M., toss on our bed, pace the bedroom, and ask ourselves, "What have I got to look forward to?" We have very real nightmares about aging. We fear being institutionalized in nursing homes, losing our autonomy, and becoming emotional and financial burdens on our loved ones.

## AN ALTERNATIVE IMAGE: SAGE-ING

Now let's replace these negative images of aging with a more joyous vision that I call *sage-ing*. To begin with, this means changing many of our negative and limiting notions about growing older. Aging itself isn't the problem. It's the images that we hold about it, our cultural expectations, that cause our problems. To have a more positive old age, we must change our aging *paradigm*, the model or blueprint that determines the quality of our experience. Much like software that we insert into the active memory of a computer, the program that we run dictates whether we will have a fearful, unattractive old age or a creative, fulfilling one.

If my elder program reads, "waning physical and mental powers and social uselessness," then when I press the "enter" button of my biocomputer, that's what prints out in my experience. My body will be programmed for an inactive, sexless life of sensory deprivation. If I complain to my doctor of decreased energy, along with minor aches and pains, she might well observe, "Well, what do you expect? You're getting old." If everyone in my family dies before age sixty, I might feel guilty about breaking the family "age trance" and comply with my programming by conveniently getting a heart attack in my late fifties. On the other hand, if I expect to have a long life, filled with physical vigor and social usefulness, my programming acts as an inner blueprint for building this more hopeful future.

"Each of us has . . . an 'elder within,' made up of all the images we possess about later life," write Ken Dychtwald and Joe Flower in *Age Wave*. "Many of these impressions were formed during our youth and are based on our experiences with our grandparents and their friends. The often unconscious impressions and expectations we carry form the foundation for our future.

"If the images of these 'elders within' are negative, then living longer could become an extension of the unpleasant and unrelenting decline of all that is joyous and full in life. If these images are positive, if our 'elders within' are healthy, involved, active, and full of life and learning, then the gift of extended life might hold the promise of a dramatic and unprecedented expansion of our opportunities for growth, adventure, wisdom, experience, and love."

As a first step in changing our aging paradigm, listen to the following definition of an elder. It was formulated by Barry Barkan, a futurist and gerontologist who founded Live Oak Living Center, a humanistically run nursing home, in El Sobrante, California:

"An elder is a person who is still growing, still a learner, still with potential and whose life continues to have within it promise for, and connection to, the future. An elder is still in pursuit of happiness, joy, and pleasure, and her or his birthright to these remains intact. Moreover, an elder is a person who deserves respect and honor and whose work it is to synthesize wisdom from long life experience and formulate this into a legacy for future generations."

According to psychologist Gay Luce, author of *Longer Life, More Joy*, elderhood "is a time to discover inner richness for self-development and spiritual growth. It is also a time of transition and preparation for dying, which is at least as important as preparation for a career or family. Out of this time of inner growth come our sages, healers, prophets, and models for the generations to follow."

As these two proponents of conscious aging imply, elders refuse to follow the well-trodden path marked "aging." Instead, they trail-blaze unmarked paths that lead to an exciting and fulfilling future. These pioneers represent a new shoot on the Tree of Life. As members of humanity's vanguard who devote the afternoon of life to developing their full human potential, they look upon aging as a developmental process whose goal is an ever-widening expansion of consciousness and a growing sense of unity with life. In the words of philosopher Jean Houston, they are lured by the prospect of their becoming, harbingers of the possible human.

People don't automatically become sages simply by living to a great age. They become wise by undertaking the inner work that leads in stages to expanded consciousness. The elders I have in mind refute the notion that older people are closed-minded, set in their ways, slow, and often senile—"old dogs who can't learn new tricks." They can and do undertake new learning by using growth methods from our contemplative traditions and exciting breakthroughs from brain-mind research.

Elders mine the riches of our spiritual traditions using meditation, relaxation techniques, and breathing exercises to awaken their intuitive abilities. They use techniques developed by brain-mind researchers, such as body awareness, brain hemisphere coordination, and memory enhancement, to extend their vast, untapped physical and mental potentials. Drawing on recent developments in humanistic psychology, especially the use of journal writing for inner development, elders also engage in life review, a process that enables them to grasp the larger patterns of their lives. Together, all these tools in our new mind laboratory help us alchemically convert our cleverness and street smarts into the philosopher's stone of wisdom.

At what age do we become sages? To answer this question, we first need to make a distinction between "elders" and the "elderly." Elders go through a process of conscious and deliberate growth, becoming sages who are capable of guiding their families and communities with hard-earned wisdom. The elderly, on the other hand, often survive into their eighth and ninth decades plagued by a gradually mounting sense of alienation, loneliness, and social uselessness. Suffering from reduced capacities and an erosion of self-esteem, these people age without sage-ing.

Our culture designates us as elderly when we pass certain significant thresholds on the aging continuum. At age fifty-five, for example, we may join the American Association of Retired Persons (AARP) and begin qualifying for senior discounts. At age sixty-five, the traditional retirement age, many people begin drawing Social Security benefits. These age thresholds simply mark us as senior citizens, an honorific title that belies our nonessential participation in the workplace, family life, and the social and political spheres. According to age-related stereotypes, the elderly withdraw from active participation in the world, pursue innocuous hobbies, travel, and reminisce about the past.

By chronological standards, old age and senior citizenship begin at around age sixty in our society. Usually by this time, we experience loss of skin elasticity, changes in hearing and vision, reduced energy levels, a more sluggish metabolism, and a host of other physical diminishments. Although we must do all that we can to remain fit, I believe that coming to terms with these physical diminishments is a major developmental task of old age that helps awaken the elder state of consciousness, with its promise of expanded mental potentials, spiritual renewal, and greater social usefulness. If we consciously embrace our aging in the late fifties and early sixties, we can avoid becoming elderly and initiate the process of becoming elders. In this way, the breakdown of the youthful self can lead to the breakthrough of the emerging elder self.

Elderhood, then, is a state of consciousness that arises in the context of physiological aging, usually making its presence felt around the traditional retirement years. At this time, the psyche issues a call for us to engage in life completion, a process that involves specific tasks, such as coming to terms with our mortality, healing our relationships, enjoying our achievements, and leaving a legacy for the future. Although this call surfaces from time to time throughout the life cycle, it generally becomes a significant force in the elder years. Sometimes, however, it announces itself most insistently when a younger person faces a life-threatening illness such as cancer or AIDS. Such a person must compress into a relatively short period of time a gradual process of maturation that usually occurs over a period of years and decades.

When I use the term "elder," I refer to those who are just beginning their inner work as sages and to those who have completed significant steps in this ongoing transformative process. For these people, growing older is not necessarily a bad joke that God plays on us. By an act of faith, they can say, "For the benefit of who we are and what we may become, it's good to experience old age." This attitude enables us to harvest our lives, to bless all that we have lived through—the triumphs and the tragedies, the realized dreams and the bitter disappointments, the acts of love and the shock of betrayal—and to convert this rich experience into wisdom.

If we compare our lives to dramas with various themes and dramatic plot lines, then old age is the time when the meaning of the play becomes clear to us. Or to use another metaphor: Up to now, we have gone shopping in all the world's markets, gathering the ingredients for a cake. To become an elder, we must stop rushing madly about, learn to get quiet, mix all the ingredients together meditatively, bake the cake, and allow it to rise in its own time. In this way, elderhood represents the crowning achievement of life.

## ELDERHOOD: A GREAT SUCCESS

Elderhood offers us the wonderful opportunity to complete our lives triumphantly, but how many of us accept the offer? Most people want to arrest their youth at one point—say at forty-two, in the prime of life. But we cannot arrest the process of life without stopping it, so we experience a deep sense of frustration when we fail at this impossible task. We *are* failures in remaining middle-aged, but we are *not* failures in becoming sixty-five, eighty-five, or older. With our longer life spans and the widespread availability of psychospiritual growth techniques, we can shape ourselves into the kind of elders we want to be, enjoying creative, deeply fulfilling lives.

Unfortunately, because our culture does not provide models for growth into elderhood, most people age unconsciously—and uncomfortably. To illustrate the point, let me tell you about a high-powered businessman I knew some years ago.

Howard was an executive vice president of a multinational electronics corporation on the East Coast who retired after a long and successful career. An outgoing man with a Type-A personality, he had a good marriage and three grown children. Now that he was sidelined in the game of life, this former corporate mover and shaker suffered from an agonizing diminishment of his being. Even though he was reasonably healthy and financially secure, Howard grieved the loss of his work status. What could replace it? What kind of future did he face?

Like many men and women, Howard stumbled into retirement as something that happened to him, rather than something he consciously planned for. Because he had defined himself almost exclusively in terms of his work role, he was devastated when retirement removed his primary source of self-worth. Howard had no preparation in developing a contemplative life, because the aging model he subscribed to encouraged him to focus strictly on productivity in the workplace. According to this model, he was supposed to constantly prove his worth by rushing around, meeting deadlines, and competing with younger men and women on their turf.

Like a good workaholic, he planned on extending the activity level and productivity of middle age into elderhood. Toward the end of his life, as in the climactic scene of a cowboy movie, Howard hoped to ride off on his horse into the sunset and to die in the saddle, as it were. Once retired from the workplace, however, there were no good guys to defend and no bad guys to shoot, no glorious sunsets to ride toward and no new conquests on the horizon.

"I'm growing old," this once-vigorous man confided to me over lunch one afternoon. "Despite my best attempts to fill my days with what they euphemistically call 'meaningful activities,' I feel that life is on an inevitable downhill trajectory. Suddenly, with all this free time, my mind is flooded with memories of relationships that went sour and regrets over roads not taken. I feel a dull ache inside me, almost as if someone is calling to me, but I can't make out what he's saying. I'm depressed a lot and I can't sleep at night. Often during the early morning hours I find myself pacing around the house, wondering what all this hard work was for."

Now consider Suzanne, an old friend and retired city planner from Boston, whose circumstances are similar to Howard's. She didn't wait for old age to accost her unexpectedly like a burglar in the night. Just as a woman prepares for childbirth by practicing breathing exercises that are appropriate for each phase of the process, so Suzanne prepared for the predictable challenges of elderhood before she retired. I call this approach the *psychoprophylaxis* of eldering. It keeps us from getting infected by the viruses of unfinished business, unlived life, and an unknown future (issues that are covered in chapter 4).

Like Howard, Suzanne could have walked blindly into retirement. She could have focused obsessively on her waning physical powers, the loss of her work identity, and regrets over the past. But in her early fifties, she enrolled in a spiritual eldering workshop where she discovered old age as an achievement to savor, a success to enjoy. Later, with the help of psychological and spiritual counseling, she moved consciously into elderhood as an anticipated stage of growth, rather than as a punishment for having outlived her usefulness.

Over the course of several years, Suzanne practiced meditation on a regular basis. She also kept a journal to clarify the stages of her inward journey. These introspective practices helped her process feelings of fear, despair, and confusion that often accompany this disorienting life passage. Suzanne also met periodically with trusted friends and intimates who were involved in eldering work. In an atmosphere of trust and unconditional acceptance—what I call "spiritual intimacy"—she could confront her fears and move through them. She looked unblinkingly at the eventual death of her husband, Al, who suffered from terminal cancer; the prospect of living alone as a widow; her growing invisibility in society as a postmenopausal woman with grown children; and unsettling feelings she had about not completing her life work. As she faced these issues courageously, she released deep-seated tensions in her body and became healthier and more radiant.

With the help of therapy and her support group, Suzanne plunged headlong into life review. She revisited the past to assemble the puzzle pieces of her life in search of "the pattern that connects." She relived decisions made at crucial turning points that she later regretted because of a lack of maturity and foresight. She also relived painful relationships that forty years later still left a bitter taste in her mouth.

Suzanne did not return to the past to punish herself for the indiscretions of youth and midlife, but to *recontextualize* her life. Essentially, this means using the panoramic vision that comes with old age to reframe our so-called mistakes and failures, mining them for the unexpected success and wisdom that were their fallout. As she worked on recontextualizing her life, Suzanne began putting to rest the "what if"s and "should have"s of a lifetime. In this way, she began feeling more peaceful and self-accepting.

Suzanne also wrestled with the inevitability of her physical death. With the increased insight and serenity that come from inner work, she eventually developed a more accepting, less fearful relationship with her mortality. Having embraced her finitude and having grieved the former stages of her life, Suzanne began formulating a legacy to leave her grandchildren. Besides narrating her life story on videotape for family members, she started a neighborhood tree planting group to beautify the urban environment and to reduce global warming. Today she is passionately dedicated to the future, serving as an Earth steward who considers the impact of her decisions on future generations.

"We can spend our time in elderhood comparing notes with friends about bodily breakdowns and disappointments about how life has turned out," Suzanne once observed. "But if we refuse to give way to useless complaining and if we avoid spending our time in amusements that distract us from contemplative work, we can choose to face the challenges of aging head on. It's not easy, but it has brought me the peace I could only dream about in my youth."

Inner work such as Suzanne's has more than just personal significance. It provides people in midlife and young people as well with viable models for elderhood. Let me tell you about Meryl

Nadell, a fifty-four-year-old social worker at Jewish Family Service in Scotch Plains, New Jersey, who came to a spiritual eldering seminar suffering from the middle-age blahs. "Before the workshop, when I looked in the mirror, I saw the tired face of an aging woman," Meryl confided. "Living another thirty or forty years seemed more like a sentence than a reward for living. In despair, I lamented, 'What will I do with myself?' "

In the seminar, she encountered vibrant elders in their sixties, seventies, and eighties engaged in the process of soul making. Here were older people who didn't just sit in rocking chairs and reminisce about "the good old days." They exercised and meditated, clarified their relationship with God and the cosmos, risked being open with relative strangers, owned up to very human failings, and repaired important human relationships—all in the context of creating a more fulfilling future for themselves. This soul making staggered Meryl, whose stereotypical picture of aging dissolved in the space of a few days. In its place there arose the possibility of spiritual eldering, with its wonderful preview of coming attractions.

"Being with elders who were claiming their inner wisdom gave me positive models for my own journey to greater wisdom," she shared with an infectious enthusiasm. "In our twenties and thirties, we're starved for models who can demonstrate what a fulfilled adult life looks like. In the same way, we need models of competent, caring, wise women and men to show us the potential of old age. After spending time with these brave, inspiring older explorers, I now look in the mirror and say with pride, 'This is what a fifty-four-year-old face looks like!' And I can't wait to discover what to do with the next thirty or forty years!"

So now a choice confronts us. If we choose to grow older like my friend Howard, the retired business executive, we will continue subscribing to our culture's notion of aging as unavoidable breakdown and obsolescence. But if we choose to "sage" like my other friends, Suzanne and Meryl, we can pioneer a path into the yet unexplored terrain of spiritual eldering. We start our journey by revisioning old age as the culminating stage of our spiritual development.

"One ought to enter old age the way one enters the senior year at a university, in exciting anticipation of consummation," writes Abraham Joshua Heschel in *The Insecurity of Freedom*. "The years of old age may enable us to attain the high values we failed to sense, the insights we have missed, the wisdom we ignored. They are indeed formative years, rich in possibilities to unlearn the follies of a lifetime, to see through inbred self-deceptions, to deepen understanding and compassion, to widen the horizon of honesty, to refine the sense of fairness."

## A BIBLICAL VIEW OF THE LIFE CYCLE

To approach elderhood as Heschel suggests, I find it helpful to adopt a biblical perspective and think of every seven years as one month of the life cycle. Let me explain why.

Living as they did close to nature, biblical writers observed that the rhythm of organic time is inherent in all life. It pulses through the procession of the four seasons, the waxing and waning of the moon, the daily alternation between day and night, and still faster rhythms of digestion and heartbeat. Looking from a larger perspective, these writers observed seven-year cycles in nature that I believe coincide with periods of growth in the human body and psyche. Even though life doesn't unfold like clockwork, but within general patterns that affect the unique events of our lives, let's see how these seven-year periods relate to the life cycle.

The first period, January, represents infancy and early childhood. In February puberty arrives, with the awakening of sexuality and the transition into adolescence. At the end of March, when you are twenty-one years old and on the verge of first adulthood, the winter months are over and spring begins.

By April you are twenty-eight, and you start cleaning up the emotional and intellectual debris that you have acquired from your parents, educators, and friends in building an adult personality. Pruning away certain goals and mind-styles, you retain what seems workable and proceed to the new challenges of the thirties. By May, at age thirty-five, most people have settled into a career and family life. By June, at age forty-two, they essentially have finished the task of establishing their social identity and their place in the world. They have "arrived." Now they can create the magnum opus of their lives.

At this point in the summer, says Swiss psychiatrist Carl Jung, the morning of life is over and the evening has begun. Jung noted that after midlife, when the rising sun has established its position at the zenith and begun its descent toward evening, people should begin spending more time contacting their inner selves. We begin *individuating*, becoming and expressing the unique selves that we are. This curriculum of life's second half involves more than the completion of our biological imperative. It involves the evocation of soul and spirit.

In *Passages About the Earth*, philosopher William Irwin Thompson describes the June, July, and August phases as periods in which mind, body, and heart are unified. He characterizes the middle years up to age forty-nine not so much for the joyous performance of skill, but "as the stage of responsibility, of mastery of institutions, of leadership." The individual, coming into the fullness of power, exercises it as the dean, administrator, or politician. Between ages forty-nine and sixty-three, as we grow beyond our drive for personal power, a full, deeper humanity emerges. Now we are concerned with the custodianship of the institutions themselves. The developing elder serves as judge, president of the university, corporation, or nation.

As we approach the October, November, and December of our lives, the time for harvesting arrives. This involves reflecting on our achievements, feeling pride in our contribution to family and society, and ultimately finding our place in the cosmos. Unfortunately, we have no model of elderhood to encourage such harvesting. So we either fall into disuse through retirement, or else we strive valiantly but foolishly to compete with younger men and women in the July, August, and September periods of their lives. We cling to the unrealistic dreams of our youth culture and recoil from the door marked "elderhood" looming before us. If we viewed elderhood as the crowning achievement of our lives, we would open the door with reverence and anticipation. Prayerfully, we would say, "Oh, my soul, you are growing something special and good inside me. How can I give it the proper sunshine and nourishment to ensure that it grows to health and vigor?"

However, instead of welcoming their inner life, most people continue clinging to their worth in terms of material productivity and money. We are used to models of heroes who die in the saddle, rather than developing contemplative skills in later life. To remain "productive," to have an "active life" is how we perpetuate the myth of remaining frozen in our prime years. But the secret gets out. As we age and enter the October, November, and December of life, we cannot afford to remain addicted to the habits of rushing and conquering that we acquired during earlier phases.

Modern men and women, who define themselves according to the values of the workplace, have a particularly hard time breaking their addiction to productivity. But women also suffer from what philosopher Susan Sontag calls the "double standard of aging." Where men's self-worth hinges on employment, women's age status depends on events in the reproductive cycle. Society rewards women in the first half of life for youthful appearance and sexual desirability. It devalues them in the second half when physical beauty begins to fade and the onset of menopause signals entry into older adulthood.

How often do we hear stories about postmenopausal women whose "nests are empty" (whose children have grown up and moved out of the house) and whose husbands have deserted them for younger women? This all-too-common example underscores one of the darker sides of this double standard. Even with all the tricks of the cosmetic trade, including face lifts and tummy tucks, women who identify primarily with their physical beauty cannot remain competitive in the youth market. But if women can learn to surrender the seductiveness of youth and to value themselves by other than adolescent standards of beauty, they can explore the dignity of "elder beauty" and reclaim the right to age without stigma.

When as older adults we identify obsessively with our work role or with a youthful appearance, we find ourselves in conflict. The deep psyche wants us to harvest our lives, while our surface self keeps us obsessed with staying in the saddle. Split this way, we lament, "Why can't I do what I used to?" If we stay stuck and make ourselves deaf to the call to elderhood, we easily can fall prey to depression and withdraw from life in bitterness and defeat.

How can we break our addiction to staying in the saddle? Here is the Bible's prescription: We labor in the fields for six years, and we dedicate the seventh as a sabbatical year unto the Lord. During six years the Earth is active and productive, bringing forth fruits, and during the seventh year the land lies completely fallow. In other words, during our productive years we build our careers and raise our families. Now, during a well-earned Sabbath period, we can catch our breath and listen meditatively to where our inner promptings are leading us.

Imagine the ecological wisdom of this principle! Imagine living according to organic time, respecting the natural cycles of birth, growth, maturity, decay, and regeneration that we find in nature. Instead, we modern people live by commodity time, the "time is money" ideology that has dominated our thinking since the Industrial Revolution. In this approach, we parcel out our lives in the packaged blocks of time that govern industry, banking, business, schools, and television. We conform to uniform, industrial rhythms of activity that cater to corporate convenience rather than the promptings of our inner life. The game of commodity time, which is good for making money, ignores our organic relationship to nature. In agriculture, for example, we don't let the land lie fallow to restore itself after crops have been harvested. We heap pesticides and herbicides on the depleted topsoil to force the earth to bring forth fruits, whether it can sustain such growth or not.

In a similar way, we force the "elder earth" to bring forth fruits, whether it's desirable or not. We do this by encouraging older adults to emulate the activity level and productivity of middle-aged people, in effect extending middle age into elderhood. How much better if we lived according to organic time and let the "elder earth" stand fallow for a time. This means stepping out of commodity time and listening attentively and respectfully to our own organic needs. Living according to the ebb and flow of our inner nature, we can cultivate a contemplative attitude, harvest a lifetime of achievement through a well-earned period of retreat and reflection, and then decide on a new curriculum for the last season of our lives.

## THE ART OF BEING

Our culture, which is influenced heavily by the Puritan ethic, gives us little instruction in how to enjoy the fruits of our labor. Society schools us obsessively in the art of achieving. We become mavens in running after desirable goals, such as sex, jobs, status, and wealth. But we remain woefully unschooled in the art of being, which involves enjoying and celebrating our achievements. It also involves finding a sense of "enoughness" from within, rather than chasing after satisfaction from the outside, always as "more"—more pleasure, possessions, or exciting relationships.

Because our busy lifestyles leave little room for inwardness, we need the help of the world's contemplative traditions in harvesting our lives. The spiritual technologies that come from yoga, Zen Buddhism, Kabbalah, and contemplative Christianity give us the tools to expand our consciousness, connect with our inmost essence, and cultivate the calmness and self-knowledge that breed wisdom. Meditative practices from these traditions help us find contentment from within so that we are not overdriven by excessive goal orientation. They also enable us to break our attachment to the social persona we have exclusively identified with. We then have the freedom to reclaim and develop aspects of the self that we abandoned earlier in life to become successful in the world.

"In modern gerontology, successful aging basically boils down to achievement and activity, which are the hallmarks of Western culture," observes Harry Moody, deputy director of the Brookdale Center on Aging at Hunter College. "The contemplative traditions can help us revision retirement in terms other than the 'productive aging' so characteristic of our time. From this perspective, we can think of aging as a kind of 'natural monastery' in which earlier roles, attachments, and pleasures are naturally stripped away from us. What then can emerge is a miraculous sense of discovery, an extraordinary energy that transcends 'doing' in favor of 'being,' and a clarity of consciousness that comes from spiritual growth. These are gifts of a contemplative old age, precisely because the young are too busy to cultivate the quietness and inwardness from which mystical experience is possible."

As Moody points out, we sacrifice much in becoming responsible adults. To maintain our places in society, we put our inner lives on hold, devaluing contact with the sacred in favor of mastering the skills needed in the everyday utilitarian world. Elderhood gives us the opportunity to reconnect with the sacred dimension of life. We can divest ourselves of demanding, often restrictive social roles, and, in a sense, "take the universe back in." We can loosen the sash of our tight-fitting costume, breathe more deeply, get new bearings, and seek a homecoming with our inner nature. We need this kind of inwardness to guide us through the maze of choices that confronts us.

Throughout most of our lives, we knew what was expected of us. From our student days in school to the time we marry, start a family, and launch our careers, we usually follow a fairly predictable life course. Now, in retirement, the tectonic plates of our lives are shifting, and we are bereft of certainty. There seem to be hardly any respected authorities or guides to offer incontrovertible answers, the security of the "one true way" that helped us construct a life when we were younger. We have more options now than ever before, a prospect that we may find overwhelming.

Should we start a second career, go back to school, volunteer in charitable organizations, or pursue hobbies that have always attracted us? Should we move to a different part of the country or travel around the world? Should we deepen our spiritual awareness or drift along on a sea of memories and deferred dreams?

Whatever we do, we don't want to give up our hard-earned autonomy for the sake of others. If I've spent an entire lifetime living according to other people's expectations, following their stairway to success, putting their needs before my own, then disowning my own inclinations could prove disastrous. In elderhood, therefore, the big question remains: "When will you finally start living for yourself?" At this time in life, when we become the most individualized, we are entitled to pursue our own paths to fulfillment, without conforming to external goals and standards. Although it's risky to follow our own inner prompting and intuitive leads, the rewards for becoming an elder far outweigh the liabilities involved in clinging to the well-worn path of aging.

A case in point is Florence Ross, who is a curriculum director and adjunct professor of humanities at Nova University in Fort Lauderdale, Florida. A lifelong peace activist and former medical researcher and fund-raiser, Florence at age seventy-four is pursuing a Ph.D. in conflict resolution at Nova to sharpen her skills as a mediator. She recently attended one of my spiritual eldering seminars where she recognized to her great astonishment and delight that she was an elder "in every sense of the word," a discovery that has given her life a new sense of dignity and purpose.

"As an elder, I stand taller now, knowing that I make a difference in the world by mentoring young people and leaving a legacy for the future," she said. "People in their twenties, thirties, forties, and even older approach me all the time, eager to share their struggles, their quests for identity, and their triumphs with someone who is committed to their psychological and spiritual well-being. I care for my mentees as if they were my own children, and this has enriched my life beyond measure. I feel so honored when they write me notes of appreciation or surprise me with unexpected little gifts. Although I don't mean to sound immodest, some of them even say, 'Florence, when I grow up, I want to be like you!' "

In her view, elders have a special responsibility to infuse public life with higher values that stress cross-cultural understanding, social justice, and world peace. To illustrate her point, she tells the story of how she exercised her responsibility as an elder in giving political advice to Mikhail Gorbachev when he was the leader of the former Soviet Union.

In the late 1980s, when President Ronald Reagan was railing against the Soviet Union in his most lurid Cold War rhetoric, calling it the "Evil Empire," Florence and her now deceased husband, Michael, were among 250 citizen diplomats who traveled to Moscow for a summit meeting of Americans and Soviets aimed at improving East-West relations. Although the conference was organized by private citizens, government officials of both superpowers watched the proceedings with great interest. The conference got off to a bad start when officials from the American and Soviet delegations acting as liaisons from their respective governments began hurling accusations and counteraccusations at each other in typical adversarial fashion. Disturbed by this display of political bravado, Florence went to the podium and said to the plenary session of delegates, "I am taking the prerogative of my age to tell the delegates that they are behaving like little boys playing games of one-upsmanship. You should be ashamed of yourselves. Your leaders should fire all of you!"

When she took her seat, Florence sensed that something extraordinary had happened. That evening her comments were broadcast on Soviet television. The next day American newspaper and television correspondents reported the incident. In a show of solidarity that transcended political differences, the women of Moscow dubbed Florence the "Grandmother of the World" and displayed her photograph in the windows of department stores. Wherever she went—whether in shops, restaurants, or museums—people would bow to her and shower her with little gifts and mementos. Several high-ranking Soviet officials even told her in private how much they appreciated her act of political candor and daring. Like the citizen diplomats, they, too, wanted to end their country's adversarial relationship with the United States.

But the best surprise of all occurred at the closing session of the conference. In summing up the proceedings, the moderator read a specially drafted message to Mrs. Florence Ross from Secretary Mikhail Gorbachev, "who appreciates her advice and will consider it in his deliberations."

"Perhaps in some small way my action helped contribute to the climate of increased tolerance and understanding between the United States and the former Soviet Union," she says. "I've always spoken out for the humanitarian causes I believed in, but now that I'm growing into my full stature as an elder, I plan to speak out more often and more authoritatively. I know what I'm talking about! At my age, because I'm no longer in doubt about my deepest identity and beliefs, I can speak publicly in the political sphere and privately to my mentees with an inner authority that serves as my credentials. And because I'm committed to nurturing the health of the community and the environment, I feel that I can make a contribution to the welfare of society."

Although Florence's story demonstrates how elders can work to change society, please don't think that you have to write letters to world leaders to qualify as an elder. Attaining elderhood is not like buying a garment in a department store in which "one size fits all." After their postretirement sabbaticals, some elders may choose to launch second careers in the marketplace, perhaps as emeritus teachers or corporate mentors. Some may work in the social and political arenas to heal inner-city tensions or to improve our educational system. Others may devote themselves to ecological issues, acting as defenders and lovers of our beleaguered planet Earth. Still others may choose to work within their families, facilitating the transmission of values between grandparents and grandchildren so often missing in our isolated nuclear families.

Whichever path you choose, please remember that elderhood is a state of great success. You have paid your dues to society by fulfilling the demands of career and parenting. Instead of being retired to uselessness, you now can graduate into the global function of seership, involved in the larger issues of life, the wider cultural and planetary concerns. You can earn the respect and recognition you deserve by becoming a sage, charged with the evolutionary task of feeding wisdom back to society and guiding its future development.

Sages bear witness to the enduring values that transcend individual conflicts and selfishness. Unlike younger people who make decisions based on short-term consideration, sages bear witness to long-term evolutionary trends that cover great sweeps of time. Given the authority to exercise leadership through their advisory capacities, they can inspire our society to give up its shortsighted, quarterly "bottom-line" mentality in favor of spiritual values that will help create a more sustainable, Earth-cherishing lifestyle.

As the possibility of becoming a sage takes root in your heart and mind, I hope you sense what a glorious future awaits you in old age. No longer will you dread the evening of life as a time of unremitting suffering and futility, but as an opportunity for continued growth in consciousness and service to humanity. What a vista, what a wonderful adventure, what a miraculous window of opportunity awaits us in old age! And so I say, *L'chaim* (To life!) to all you possible sages on the way to your new vocations!

# Chapter 2

# *Becoming the Possible Sage*

From childhood to late adulthood, we're like railroad trains that follow highly regular stretches of track to predictable destinations. Then, as elderhood approaches, we reach the end of the line, only to discover that management hasn't had the foresight to lay any more track. We must get off the train and walk—but to where? What is our next destination?

Jungian analyst June Singer wrestled with this issue when she reached her seventieth birthday, the biblical threescore and ten years. Having moved through the sequence of life stages described by modern psychology, she entered a strange netherworld where there were no clearly marked stages. At this age, she thought, "One is supposed to be dead in the head. One isn't supposed to cause anybody any more trouble. As an old woman, you should take your place as a granny, utter an occasional wise statement, and get your hair fixed every week so people will remark, 'But you don't look over seventy!' "

Fortunately, Singer never bought into these cultural stereotypes. While on the surface things remained tranquil, her depths stirred with so many unanswered questions that often she found herself lying awake at night. During the day she sometimes drifted out of waking consciousness into a space of profound mystery where the unknowable cried out for attention.

"There are more and more elders like myself," she says, "who have completed their allotted time and chores and who ask themselves, 'Why am I still here? To what purpose?' Stirring with passionate energy and concerns, we make space in our lives for embracing the spirit, refining the crucible of our self, and distilling its contents. In a time when the outer light begins to fade, we need to attend to the fire from within."

Another Jungian analyst, Florida Scott-Maxwell, described her puzzling encounter with old age in a journal, *The Measure of My Days*, which she began writing at age eighty-two. "I thought [age] was a quiet time," she writes. "My seventies were interesting, and fairly serene, but my eighties are passionate. I grow more intense as I age . . . Inside we flame with a wild life that is almost incommunicable. In silent, hot rebellion we cry silently, 'I have lived my life, haven't I? What more is expected of me?' "

In elderhood, Scott-Maxwell writes, we sometimes experience "a swelling clarity as though all was resolved. It has no content, it seems to expand us, it does not derive from the body. . . . It may be a degree of consciousness which lies outside activity, and which when young we are too busy to experience."

When we enter old age, these two psychologists tell us, we should expect to live with passion and mystery. Our spirits will be questing rather than resting. Our consciousness will grow rather than slow into doddering decline. We can use our extended life span to develop extended consciousness—what philosopher Gerald Heard calls "second maturity"—or we can lapse by default into second childhood, which we associate with a sort of fatuous senility. We can use our leisure for trivial pursuits, or we can progress to second maturity using the contemplative tools of spiritual eldering. Only by growing beyond first maturity's tasks of ego development, career, and parenting can we sufficiently answer the questions, "Why am I still here? What more is expected of me?"

# THE PROMISE OF SECOND MATURITY

The notion of first and second maturity comes from Gerald Heard's thought-provoking book, *The Five Ages of Man*. Human consciousness, he writes, has evolved through five epochs of world history. We recapitulate these stages in our personal lives as we grow from infancy, through adolescence, and into first maturity. When we arrive at elderhood, we have the possibility of taking a quantum leap into second maturity, with its task of spiritual realization.

In Heard's first stage, the *pre-individual*, we are one with nature and the tribe without having a sense of individuality. Pre-individuals conform to tribal codes and rituals but can't initiate any self-motivated action. This phase, which we observe in preliterate, primitive cultures, corresponds to infancy, when we have a completely dependent relationship with our mothers.

In the second stage, the *proto-individual*, we rebel against our suffocation in the womb of the Great Mother and take our first brash, heroic steps to establish a separate identity. By their acts of will and courage, the great heroes of classical literature, such as Ulysses and Heracles, show us the struggles involved in forging a personal identity. The heroic age of Mediterranean classical cultures corresponds to childhood.

After the heroic age comes the *ascetic* or *mid-individual* era. After saying "No!" to everything in a fury of self-assertion, we feel like reforming ourselves. So with a desire for self-improvement and a passion for self-transcendence, people turn inward, using contemplative tools to master themselves. Western society took this inward turn during the Middle Ages as droves of people fled the world in search of their souls in monastic communities. The ascetic phase corresponds to adolescence, when we search for our identity and often work on self-improvement.

During the fourth, or *humanic*, era, which begins with the Renaissance in Western Europe, we turn our gaze away from the heavens and focus on the physical world. Harnessing the empirical methods of science to our growing sense of individualism, we set out to master the world and improve the social order. What begins as a promising idea gets out of hand at the end of the humanic era. As spiritual knowledge is debunked, we become preoccupied with unlimited material progress and consumption that threaten our planet with ecological havoc. The fourth era, the one in which we live, represents first maturity.

Now, at this point in the world historical drama, the curtain is rising on the exciting fifth act. In Heard's view, the longevity of today's elders is helping evolution give birth to humanity's higher potential, the *post-individual* of second maturity. "In this century a new age group has appeared that is above and beyond the first maturity age group," he writes in *The Five Ages of Man*. "But they are utterly untaught, their education is completely neglected, their part is unwritten, their pattern of behavior unprovided, their contribution unknown." Heard believes that when people in second maturity achieve group solidarity and claim their role as society's seers and sages, they will usher in an epoch-making, post-individual age.

With Heard, I believe that post-individuals are appearing everywhere on the world scene, giving birth to an unprecedented era of human development. The elderly population condemned to the junkheap in the humanic era will play a crucial role in humanity's leap to the next evolutionary level. Why? In earlier ages, when people barely reached age forty or fifty, they didn't have enough time to ripen through the four stages that precede second maturity. People went to the grave like unripe fruit on the vine. Now, with our extended life span, we can use the extra time available in elderhood as evolution's springboard into the post-individual phase.

"The years beyond sixty, the years of our second maturity, may be evolution's greatest gift to humanity," says Jean Houston, director of the Foundation for Mind Research in Pomona, New York, and author of *Life Force*. "No longer needing to compete and to be acceptable, likeable, and all those other things considered respectable in society, people are finally uncaged in their elder years, free to release energies and capacities that the culture restrained in them when they were younger. The energies that people release after age sixty-five are not really new at all, but exist in a state of latency within the mind-body system. When we don't have to devote a large percentage of our time in fulfilling social obligations and meeting other people's expectations, we can unleash these energies and harness them for self-awareness, spiritual development, and creativity."

How can we identify a person in second maturity? Post-individuals balance the inwardness of the ascetic era with the outwardness of the humanic. They do this by expressing their spiritual realization in the everyday world of work, family life, and politics. Viewing the world as sacred, post-individuals honor the planet and its multitude of species as a single living entity. Pre-individuals felt this oneness with nature in our ancestral past, but post-individuals fall in love with our world having a fully developed self-consciousness. Post-individuals also value cooperation rather than competition, stewardship rather than acquisitiveness. Above all, they remind us of our connection to the spiritual realm and the need to grow beyond our addiction to materialism. Let me tell you about a few of these pioneers.

In his late sixties, Joseph Chilton Pearce, author of *Evolution's End*, lectures tirelessly to audiences worldwide about how 3 billion years of evolution lie within the neural structures of our brains. "We are the culmination of a huge evolutionary process," Pearce says. "If we unfold and develop our potential, we open ourselves up to an incredible higher order of being. But if we continue to deny the real intelligence manifested through the heart and rely only on our intellect, evolution will fail in its task."

By the heart, Pearce means the longing we feel for our next stage of development—what Heard calls post-individuality. The heart blossoms briefly in adolescence when we sense that something tremendous is supposed to happen. Feeling uniquely selected for some great task or ultimate challenge, says Pearce, adolescents always gesture toward the heart when speaking of the secret, unique greatness in themselves that seeks expression. Unfortunately, our materialistic culture provides few vehicles for them to convert their spiritual idealism into practical reality.

By the time we are adolescents, he explains, we have developed the brain structures that relate us to the physical and social worlds. If we then are given a nurturing environment and are exposed to self-actualizing adults who evoke our potential by modeling a higher human development, we would experience a brain growth spurt around age fifteen that would link the human brain with the Spirit that transcends it. Unfortunately, these conditions rarely exist in our commercially driven, secular society. Our brain-mind potential also remains undeveloped because sexuality opens up at the same time that we feel "intimations of immortality." In our confusion, we mistakenly identify our higher evolutionary promptings as misplaced libido, and so the great longing of the heart is usually diverted into social and sexual channels. This longing goes underground and remains dormant during our adult lives but can resurface in elderhood after a detour of five decades. If we can survive long enough and reduce the pull of the passions and preoccupations of our earlier years, we can complete the developmental process that is normally interrupted by the exigencies of life and reconnect with the higher intelligence that we abandoned in adolescence.

"Old age is an intensely exciting time of exploration and return, of adventure and spiritual discovery," Pearce says. "If this is old age, give me more of it! Sure, the body starts getting tired and breaks down, but the mind gets sharper and sharper. The real challenge of old age is to risk all habitual frames of reference and to open the mind to another field of possibility that lies beyond the physical. Having gained a foothold in the inner world, we then can encounter death with calm anticipation rather than horrifying fear."

George Leonard, author of *Mastery*, is another pioneer in second maturity who experiences elderhood as evolution's crowning achievement. Elderhood gives us the chance not only to perfect the skills we've acquired over a lifetime, but to learn new ones. In fact, lifelong learning fulfills the deep-seated purpose of our species. "Human beings are learning animals," he says, "and whenever we stop learning, we defeat evolution's master plan for us."

Leonard believes that a spiritual practice when pursued on a regular basis can strengthen an elder's commitment to continued learning. He views practice as positive activity, involving mind, body, and spirit, that we pursue not for any desired outcome, but for the sake of the activity itself. Practice includes the traditional disciplines of yoga, Zen, and Aikido, the martial art he's practiced for several decades. It also may include gardening, jogging, pottery, painting, or journal writing.

According to Leonard, Morihei Ueshiba, the founder of Aikido, did not really reach his peak as a martial artist until he was seventy years old. Before then, his practice relied on physical strength. But as he aged, he surrendered his reliance on sheer physical mastery and developed the power of *ki*, a vital life energy generated through spiritual discipline that manifests as physical presence and strength. Opponents who attacked him in ritual Aikido encounters typically described "entering a cloud" and contacting a "giant spring" that turned them around and flung them through the air upside down. Generally considered one of the greatest martial artists who ever lived, Morihei continued improving in old age, giving his most spectacular demonstrations in his eighties.

"Elders such as Morihei, who serve as models for continued growth, give us something to aspire to in old age," Leonard says. "I'll be seventy soon, and I'm bristling with anticipation about improving my practice. Even though I have a black belt and teach Aikido, I pursue it as a student by studying with a younger teacher and learning new techniques. Following the example of Morihei, I can't wait to see what amazing things await me as I continue 'staying on the mat' and practicing!"

Having a practice with an unlimited potential evokes our deepest learning capacities, he adds. "As we continue our ceaseless explorations of consciousness, we may advance one mile toward our destination, only to see it recede two miles toward the horizon. But this doesn't discourage us at all. In fact, we feel exhilarated, because a practice with limitless possibilities keeps us open to a life of constant learning."

Now consider Anne Dosher, whose mission in second maturity combines spiritual vision with compassionate social action. Dosher is a community psychologist who helped start a network of agencies that serves runaway and homeless youth in San Diego County. She is the elder member of the Community for Sacred Ecology, a nonprofit group of women who practice Native American forms of Earth-based spirituality in the San Diego area. On the eve of her sixty-fifth birthday, while on a retreat with members of her clan, she had a spiritual experience that served as her initiation into elderhood. Unable to sleep that night, she was lifted into an altered state of consciousness and wrote a series of verse chants that became the clan's creation story. Suddenly her community began treating her as a spiritual elder. But what did that mean?

The year after her initiation, at a national retreat for youth service professionals in Vermont, Dosher took the first tentative step to find out. She decided not to hide behind her professional persona and knowledge. Abandoning her role as keynote speaker, she gave a series of fireside chats, speaking authentically from the heart about essential values, including spiritual connectedness. As she spoke spontaneously from her authentic self, something wonderful happened. She rediscovered a sense of inner knowing, a heart knowledge that links us to nature and each other, which she possessed as a child but lost on the way to success in the academic and professional worlds. As she shared herself in spiritual intimacy with this group of professionals, she watched their armor drop. Miraculously, bonds of sacred community were forming in a place where it was least expected.

Since then, she has carried this sacred sense of community building into the government planning sessions that she leads, doing what she calls "ensouled work." Her planning activities always stem from a long-term, compassionate vision of a safe future for San Diego County's older citizens, children, and minorities. Her insistence that those entrusted with the welfare of local institutions work, speak, and make decisions from the heart has earned her the honorary title "Guardian of the Community."

"As elders of the tribe, we have the responsibility to keep the consciousness of the whole at all times," Dosher remarks. "When younger people turn to their elders, they have a yearning for something more. This yearning prompts us to search within for the source of spiritual connectedness. Out of this search comes wisdom, which is knowledge informed by values, which we can transmit to the generations that follow us."

As these three pioneers point out, eldering is a vast unexplored territory, filled with promise and risk, questing and growth. During this time, we can explore our depths, continue a course of lifelong learning, and take our wisdom out into the world. To approach the door marked "elderhood," we must leave the realm of the known and familiar at a time when society enjoins us to rest and conserve our energies. We also must remain faithful to the hard-earned sense of individuality we have forged through a lifetime's effort. Because individuality reaches its peak in old age, I can't prescribe how you should approach the door, when you should open it, and what you'll find on the other side. Drawing on the disciplines of psychology and spirituality, I can only offer general guidelines to help you in your eldering work. I encourage you to consult with your own inner Self about how to adapt these guidelines in your life.

## TAKE CHARGE OF YOUR LIFE IN ELDERING

In speaking of our growth potential, why do I use the verb "to elder"? Eldering for me is a process word, a verb that connotes change and movement. It doesn't connote the unchanging frozen state of a noun. When we call someone a "senior," for example, this noun points to a static, lifeless condition. It's as if a state called "senior" has been attained and all further organic growth had ceased. But when I refer to someone as "eldering," the "ing" of the word refers to a state of growth and evolution, a process with endless possibilities. Eldering implies that we take active responsibility for our destiny in old age, living by conscious choice rather than social expectation.

Many of us can't say, "I live," and keep the verb in the active tense. In truth, we can only say, "I'm being lived." If we looked back on our lives with complete honesty, many of us would conclude, "I was lived by my parents; I was lived by my teachers; I was lived by society." Post-individuals, however, can say for the first time in their lives, "I live in the active form and determine my future." We're not always elders; sometimes we're aging, crotchety, somewhat elderly people. But at any moment in the battle between the forces of aging and eldering, we can become conscious, snap out of the hypnotic trance induced by society and our own inertia, and do the inner work of eldering.

To elder skillfully, we draw on the immense tool chest of practical methods from the world's spiritual traditions. But here a serious question arises. Why do we call this work "spiritual eldering" and not "religious eldering"? *Religious* eldering points to a sectarian approach. It provides people with beliefs, practices, and rituals that all too easily separate some believers from others. *Spiritual* eldering implies an inner search for God, a self-directed flowering of the spirit that unites all people in a common quest, no matter what their affiliation. In this approach, people practice ways of life that promote a direct, inner experience of the divine.

Conventional religion often fulfills people's need for social belonging. How different this is from spiritual eldering, which deals with developing contemplative skills, harvesting one's life, leaving a legacy for the future, and preparing for death. It's the difference between seeking safety and comfort, on the one hand, and reducing the ego and opening to the Spirit, on the other. The religious elder says, "I want to be saved. I want to remain safe and secure in my religious identity. I don't want to feel the anxiety of facing the unknown." The spiritual elder says, "I want to work on myself, even if that means facing past and present anxieties. I want to be generous, pure, and clean in facing the Spirit. I want to live the truth as I see it."

Religious eldering needn't differ from spiritual eldering when done right. Because religions were originally inspired by their founders' spiritual revelations, they carry within their traditions the seeds of higher consciousness. However, most religions today have lost touch with the white heat of transcendental realization that gave birth to their traditions. Stressing an intellectual assent to doctrine, they have become institutionalized, relying heavily on verbal prayer, sermons, and scripture reading. I call this approach oververbalized and underexperienced because it requires worshippers to rely primarily on secondhand descriptions of spiritual revelations rather than on their own direct inner experience.

Most religions today do not provide people with the meditative disciplines that allow intuitive insight and the deeper impulses of spiritual eldering to emerge. Without access to their intuitive depths, people cling to the "brand names" of their religions (Christian, Jewish, Buddhist, Muslim, Hindu), rather than acknowledging the generic core of transformative practices that they share in common. To a person interested in spiritual eldering, the brand names of various religious packages matter less than the generic spiritual technologies that awaken our higher faculties.

## A CONTEMPLATIVE MIND GYM AVAILABLE

In the past, the technologies for spiritual eldering were simply unavailable to the general population. As part of our culture's *esoteric* (or hidden, mystical) teachings, they lay hidden away in the cloisters of Western monasteries and Eastern ashrams, where spiritual directors and gurus usually transmitted their wisdom to special adepts. During the past three decades, many of these once-secret teachings have come out of the closet. Now, wherever we look, we're flooded with books, tapes, and seminars about Eastern mysticism, contemplative Christianity, Kabbalah, and many other of the world's wisdom traditions.

Today we have an extensive array of contemplative tools for doing inner work. We have bodywork to improve our posture and give us better body tone. We have therapies to help us clear hidden memories, overcome phobias, and work on forgiveness and self-acceptance. There are centering prayer, transcendental meditation, mantra meditation—in fact, a whole tool chest of contemplative techniques from the East and the West. There is also the emerging field of electronic mind expansion using goggles, sound, and light to focus the mind. We even can play recordings of prayers, mantras, and guided visualizations on our Walkman to induct us into higher states of consciousness.

As you can see, we have a smorgasbord of techniques for spiritual eldering. Buddhists call these *upaya*, the skillful means that induce transformations of consciousness. Fortunately for us pragmatic Westerners, we have separated these technologies from their sectarian contexts. Many of these contemplative techniques have been tested in laboratory experiments and their healthful results made known to millions of people.

In *Quantum Healing*, for example, Dr. Deepak Chopra, an endocrinologist who advocates holistic approaches to medicine, reports on an experiment performed in 1980 by Harvard psychologist Charles Alexander, who taught mind-body techniques to eighty-year-old residents of three old-age homes in Boston. Residents practiced either a relaxation technique, transcendental meditation, or a set of word games to sharpen mental skills. Follow-up tests showed that meditators scored highest on measures of improved learning ability, low blood pressure, and mental health. When Alexander returned to the old-age homes three years later, he found to his surprise that while one third of the residents had died, the death rate was zero among the meditators.

From this and other similar experiments, Chopra speculates that we may be able to rejuvenate cellular activity and retard the aging process through contemplative practices. "Aging involves a large element of choice," he writes. "Operating at the usual level of superficial, confused thinking, we speed up the aging process in our cells, but as we move to the silent regions of the transcendent, mental activity stops, and apparently cell activity follows accordingly. If this is true, then aging can be programmed from different levels of awareness."

If meditation can improve the lives of eighty-year-olds in old-age homes, imagine the benefits for elders who began practicing it earlier in life. Such an idea, considered fanciful only several decades ago, has become a distinct possibility today. Soon younger people won't dismiss the pronouncements of their grandparents as quaint and gratuitous nothings. They will regard those whom they had previously dismissed as "old folks" to be agents of human evolution! And these pioneers of consciousness will soon be more numerous than you might imagine.

In previous ages the spiritual elder represented a unique flowering of the human spirit, a rare, nonrepeatable event. In India, there was one guru and many disciples. Among the Russian Orthodox, there was one *staretz* (literally "an elder," a sage who functioned as a father confessor and spiritual director) and many monks. Among pious and ecstatic Hasidic Jews, there was one *rebbe* (wise and beloved master) and many Hasidim.

Those rare individuals who flowered into spiritual elderhood had peak experiences or revelations, like Moses on Mount Sinai or Buddha under the bo tree. Their experiences became our common property through the practices of our religious traditions. Over the centuries, however, only a handful of individuals achieved these ecstatic states of consciousness for themselves. Now, experienced as we are with Eastern and Western meditative practices, we can begin exploring these experiences for ourselves on a large scale. As a great domestication of the spirit takes place in modern life, millions of people have the knowledge, techniques, and cultural support to make spiritual eldering a significant force for social change.

## THE BRAIN-MIND REVOLUTION

The key to spiritual eldering lies in awakening our immense brain-mind potential. Most researchers in the field speak glowingly about our glorious mental endowments but sadly report that we use no more than 10 percent of our capacity. I believe that with our increased longevity, evolution is giving us the opportunity to ripen new areas of the brain. Imagine the joy and the freedom in accessing even 10 percent more of our seemingly limitless potential!

Like Gerald Heard, I believe that the next phase of evolution will unfold our intuitive capacities, making us more permeable to the sacred in daily life. By intuition, I mean the faculty of mind that transcends reason and bypasses normal channels of sense verification. While we use analytical reason to comprehend the physical world, we use intuition to explore the nonphysical realms. Intuitive experiences include mystical perception, creative inspiration in art, discovery and invention in science, as well as extrasensory perception. Intuition works in a nonlinear way, bringing together vast fields of knowledge and perception simultaneously. It leaps ahead of our slower-moving logic to show us the "big picture," often through direct inner knowing. Reason works in a linear, step-by-step fashion, helping us understand that picture by analyzing its various parts.

To become complete human beings, we need a balance of both functions. While we need intuition to leap into the unknown, reaching toward new visions in art, science, and religion, we need logic to evaluate our intuitive insights and inspirations. In the words of psychologist Frances Vaughan, author of *Awakening Intuition*, "If we're only intuitive, we're likely to be dreamers. If we're only rational, we may find life to be disillusioning and dispiriting. But if we combine both faculties within ourselves, we can live as effective visionaries in the world."

As elders begin applying mind-body techniques to awaken their intuitive abilities, they will break through to new levels of creative expression. By using relaxation, visualization, guided imagery, and other techniques, they will transform the creative enterprise from a rare phenomenon reserved for only a handful of gifted artists, scientists, philosophers, and mystics to a learned skill available to large numbers of people.

There are historical precedents for this creative breakthrough. Despite the mistaken belief that old age is a time of diminished creativity, history reveals that a number of people have produced works of enduring beauty and significance in their later years. For example, Giuseppe Verdi composed *Otello* at age seventy-three and *Falstaff* when he was approaching eighty. Thomas Mann wrote *Dr. Faustus* and *Confessions of Felix Krull, Confidence Man* after age seventy, while Picasso was producing masterpieces into his nineties. Architect Frank Lloyd Wright began his most creative work at age sixty-nine; philosopher Alfred North Whitehead published his most influential works after age sixty-five; and the mind of scientist-visionary Buckminster Fuller was teeming with creative innovation at age eighty.

While not everyone can become a Verdi or a Picasso, increasing numbers of elders can cultivate their intuitive abilities to explore new avenues of thought, receive creative inspiration, solve personal problems, or improve decision-making abilities. As older adults begin mining their intuitive depths, they will discover practical ways of harnessing the creative imagination in the workplace, in their leisure activities, and in their relationships. As a result, they will help dispel the damaging cultural myth that considers creativity the exclusive prerogative of younger people.

"Freer air blows for many men and women in their later years," writes John McLeish in *The Ulyssean Adult: Creativity in the Middle and Later Years.* "The stakes are less, intimidating jailers are gone, or in the steady process of maturing, new reserves of courage together with wisdom and compassion have brought them to open fields of change and experiment. . . . Thus the creative life is not only as possible for men and women in the later years as when they were much younger, but in important respects often *more* possible."

Besides stimulating our creative abilities, intuition also connects us organically to our environment, reweaving us into the fabric of nature. It enables us to sense our unity with Gaia, our Mother Earth, the living planet that sustains and nourishes us. Since the eighteenth-century Enlightenment in Europe, with its emphasis on rationalism to the complete exclusion of intuition, we have been ripped from the bosom of nature. We have lost a sense of organic connectivity to our environment and to our communities, making us feel alienated in the midst of our technological affluence. When we awaken intuition, we experience a perceptual homecoming that reconnects us to life. With this perception, elders recover an ancient, deep reverence for the Earth as a living organism with whom they lovingly identify. Because elders with an awakened intuitive sense feel the assault on the Earth's ecological integrity as a personal affront, they defend the planet as if protecting the life of a loved one.

## INTUITION AND OUR TRIUNE BRAIN

To understand how evolution has prepared elders to awaken intuition, we need to understand something about the triune (or three-part) structure of the brain. While we used to think that the brain's structure was singular, Dr. Paul MacLean, chief of the Laboratory of Brain Evolution and Behavior at the National Institute of Mental Health, compares it to an archaeological site with three distinct layers. Each layer, which represents a stage in evolutionary development, adds unique neural capacities and behaviors that together make us functional human beings.

The oldest and most primitive part of the brain, which scientists call the *reptilian* brain, deals with our most basic survival needs. It instinctively urges us to say, "I want to live. I need food, shelter, a roof over my head, and someone to reproduce with." When we're operating in the reptilian mode, we revert to being territorial and habit-driven, defending our turf with dinosaur-like tenacity. The next area, the *limbic* brain, which we also share with mammals, relates us on a feeling level to the social world. When the limbic brain is in force, we enjoy singing, dancing, and taking part in rhythmic, ritualized activity that makes us feel part of the herd, so to speak. We enjoy gathering with people in community and celebrating our togetherness, whether in religious worship, at rock concerts, or at athletic events. The third layer, the *neocortex*, adds the ability for learning and using rational thought that are so important in adult life. This part of the brain enables us to develop verbal communication, analytical thought, and problem-solving skills.

We need all three layers of the brain to build a workable life, but evolution isn't content with our present level of development. According to Jean Houston there remains a vast, untapped area of the neocortex associated with intuition that we can develop to extend our mental functioning. "This area of the brain holds the wisdom of the millennia, the dreams of tomorrow, and the capacity for communion with the cosmos," she says. "However, while our brains are gloriously overendowed, we are educated to use only a small fraction of our capacities, making us crippled, limited visions of what we could truly be. In this exciting era of brain-mind breakthrough, we can take our neurological potentials off the shelf and extend our sensory, creative, and problem-solving abilities by developing our latent intuitive potentials."

Echoing this viewpoint, Joseph Chilton Pearce points out that there is a growing belief among contemporary neuroscientists that we severely underdevelop our neocortex and scarcely touch its potential. In his view, this area of the brain contains an untapped neural inheritance with "a quantum leap of additional potential we have not yet developed."

In his recent book *Evolution's End*, an exhaustive investigation into current brain-mind research, Pearce cites a study that illustrates how little of the neocortex we actually develop. Using brain scans, British neuroscientist John Lorber found more than 150 normal, fully functioning people who had virtually no neocortex at all. The test subjects, who all suffered hydrocephalic disease (water on the brain) since birth, used only about 5 percent of the neocortex. Even though their heads were 80 percent full of cerebrospinal fluid, these so-called brainless people had IQs of up to 120; many held advanced degrees and important professional positions; and in general they seemed completely normal. This study, Pearce concludes, bolsters the claim "that we modern humans apparently get along quite well using only a fraction of our [neocortex's] capacity. The hydrocephalics may function as well as we do, since we are using no more [neocortex] than they are, though they are using and developing all of theirs, while we develop and use only a minimum of ours."

The three layers of the brain that we already have developed represent an immense gift on the part of nature. With our current level of cognitive sophistication, we have traveled to the moon and tamed the atom. However, this level of brain-mind development is not sufficient to heal the planet from the ravages of technology. To accomplish this, we need to evolve the intuitive level of the brain, which enables us to overcome our alienation from nature and live in harmony with the Earth. Until now, this faculty of mind was unreliable, since intuitions and peak experiences generally occurred haphazardly as nonrepeatable experiences beyond our control. Now, with the availability of psychotechnologies that domesticate intuition, we consciously can cultivate the higher faculties of mind that awaken the felt sense of oneness with nature that leads to enlightened action in defense of the Earth.

Although safeguarding planetary survival seems like a monumental task, there is an immense fund of brain potential that we can draw upon. Nature has endowed the *frontal lobes* of the neocortex with glorious abilities that we have scarcely investigated. This area of the brain has the capacity for high levels of creativity, empathic understanding, compassion, and intuitive perception. However, it remains a vast unknown for most people who were raised in our scientific culture on a meager diet of skepticism and rational thought. Elders, who are already familiar with the physical, emotional, and intellectual levels of the brain, can now take advantage of their extended life spans to activate a vast new cognitive domain—the intuitive level—by using the contemplative arts. (Young and middle-aged people certainly can awaken their intuition and help preserve the Earth from ecodestruction. But because the evolutionary plan calls for developing latent brain potential in the afternoon and evening of life, elders have a special responsibility to act as leaders in healing the planet and ensuring our continued survival.)

A whole cornucopia of perceptual skills awaits elders when they domesticate the brain's vast potential. Pearce believes that by developing the frontal lobes of the neocortex, we can open up vast new fields of experience beyond the realm of our senses. "The frontal lobes are evolution's latest addition," explains Pearce. "We need the reptilian and limbic brains, along with just 10 percent of the neocortex, to maintain our physical lives in the world. Evolution has been pushing us for ages to develop the other 90 percent of the neocortex. According to Dr. R. B. Ramamurthi, president of the International Congress of Neurosurgery, if we developed the unused portions of the brain, we could explore the 'interior universe,' the inner world that is vast, open-ended, and infinite."

Besides the frontal lobes, other areas of the neocortex hold evolutionary promise. For example, neuroscientists have known for more than half a century that the *temporal lobes* are associated with a variety of paranormal and psychic experiences. In well-documented experiments conducted in the 1950s and 1960s, Wilder Penfield, the father of neurosurgery and author of *The Mystery of the Mind*, used electrical needles to stimulate various areas of the brains of anesthetized patients. (Since the brain has no feeling, after administering a local anesthetic to remove the skull, he could speak at leisure with each fully awake patient while exploring the brain with an electrode.) Penfield found that stimulating by chance certain key areas in the temporal lobes brought about vivid memories from the patient's past as if occurring in present time with full sensory acuteness. Extrapolating from this pioneering work, modern brain researchers speculate that a host of paranormal phenomena, including lucid dreaming and out-of-body experience, occur in the temporal lobes and involve the same brain circuitry as in Penfield's experiments.

As we can see from these examples, when we rise above our semiconscious use of the brain's potentials, marvelous states of consciousness await us. But whether we develop nature's overabundant gifts depends on our extended life span. A simple analogy will explain why. When I lived in Manitoba, Canada, we didn't have many apple trees. If you tried to grow a regular apple, it couldn't ripen because the summer was too short. All we could do was grow crab apples. Similarly, in a short life span, we couldn't grow the intuitive aspect of the mind that's associated with wisdom. We had to settle for the "crab apples," the unripened state of mind that forced us to take our higher potentials to the grave undeveloped. Now, with our longevity as an established fact, we have the potential of growing apples that are both delicious and mature.

To harvest wisdom in this way, we need to format new areas of the brain. What do I mean by "format"? Computers can read a floppy disk and perform various operations only when the disk has been formatted. This refers to partitioning off designated areas of the disk so that information can be stored and retrieved. In the same manner, we have a lot of potential brain capacity, but we haven't formatted 90 percent of its capacity for the storage and retrieval of information and the processing of complex cognitive operations. Accessing this untapped area of the brain holds great promise for our health and continued growth as elders.

By formatting more of the brain, we also can counteract the ravages of brain cell disintegration associated with aging. As Deepak Chopra points out in *Quantum Healing*, people lose more than 1 billion neurons throughout their lifetimes. But they can compensate for this loss by increasing the number of connections linking nerve cells to each other. Just as we exercise to strengthen our bodies, we can exercise the brain-mind through meditation and lifelong learning, thus opening up new neural pathways in the brain.

With more neural connections, we can better handle the complexity of modern life. In fact, we need increased brain-mind development to coordinate the huge influx of information that bombards us daily in our high-tech society. Just as we upgrade computers for greater random access memory, more storage, and better retrieval of information, so elders need to upgrade the number and range of programs that their brains are able to process. Without doing this, elders will continue to be devalued by society as a useless and redundant population. But when they have more memory capacity in their biocomputers, they will better handle the complexity of living in a high-tech, information-rich global society.

"To transmit our know-how to the next generation, we need to change faster than ever before—in fact, even faster than the young themselves," counsels Pir Vilayat Inayat Khan, seventy-seven-year-old head of the Sufi Order in the West and a respected meditation teacher. "If you don't know that you can be a new person, you will continue dragging your old self-image into the brave new world. You will be outrun and pronounced redundant, unable to make a contribution to the inexorable advance of evolution on our planet."

Elders tap into their brain-mind potentials for their own personal fulfillment. By using meditation and mind-body disciplines such as yoga that increase vitality and promote flexibility, they can sharpen their sensory abilities, strengthen memory, and awaken their intuition. With more vibrant, responsive bodies and minds that delight in ever-widening realms of knowledge, they can face the future optimistically, with a sense of purpose and the ability to enjoy their personal lives. But in our era, personal fulfillment and planetary responsibility are intimately linked. Ripening of the brain makes us more able to respond to the economic, social, and ecological problems that have stricken our ailing planet. As seers capable of identifying with the whole, elders can have the breadth of vision to act as defenders of global resources and cultures. Who needs "old geezers" around if all they do is deplete the Social Security system and give back little to society?

But if we honored elders for their moral and spiritual leadership, we would value this form of "invisible productivity" as necessary for our survival.

# THE NEW PICTURE OF AGING

The principal thesis of this book is that extended longevity calls for extended consciousness. If our added years are not matched by an expansion of awareness, life becomes depressive. If I live to be eighty years old but my consciousness gets arrested at the mental age of forty-five, I stagnate at that level and may suffer from what psychologists call involutional melancholy, a haunting sense of despair that asks the existential question, "What is it all for?" Who needs years, maybe decades of such decline?

The emerging picture of aging balances our physical diminishment in old age with brain-mind development that opens up greater intelligence and new skills. When extended life span is not matched with extended awareness, the booster rocket of consciousness doesn't propel the space capsule into orbit around the Earth. We take a nosedive back into the atmosphere, often burning up with an unused payload and an aborted mission. What mission? We have the possibility of becoming enlightened sages in old age if we format unused areas of the brain. Mission control has furnished us with the spiritual technologies that enable us to domesticate intuition and to transcend Earth's gravity. Like crew members of the Starship *Enterprise*, we're ready to go where no one has gone before!

On our pioneering mission, spiritual eldering provides the booster rocket for consciousness. We don't have to move unwillingly into inevitable decline. We don't have to face the prospect of being a burden to ourselves and society. We can become sages in our second maturity, the esteemed elders of the tribe.

And not a moment too soon! Thanks to medical breakthroughs, a healthier diet, exercise, and other lifestyle changes, older people have become the fastest-growing group in the United States. According to *Age Wave*, in the past several decades, the over-sixty-five age group has grown more than twice as fast as the rest of the population. As the "graying of America" proceeds, the National Institute of Aging predicts that by the year 2040, 87 million Americans will be over sixty-five. By 2080, the country may well have 5 million centenarians.

In the midst of this long-term trend, the baby boom generation is coming of age. These are the people who turned on, tuned in, and dropped out; who took part in the greening of America; who lived through the angst of future shock; who studied with Eastern gurus and Native American elders; and who matured into responsible adults without forgetting their commitment to global ecology and social justice.

Although many boomers have grown through meditation, therapy, and political involvement, when it comes to aging they remain fixated on the values of our youth culture. As boomers approach their elder years—indeed, as all older adults make the transition into the third age—they need a psychospiritual model of aging to answer the nagging question: "How will I spend my last years without being an economic and psychological burden on my loved ones and on society?"

Spiritual eldering provides the conceptual model and practical tools for the much-needed transvaluation of aging in Western technological society. Today, a growing number of people are dedicating their elder years to the task of spiritual unfoldment. Because of individual differences, there are no immutable formulas that work for all people. Hence spiritual eldering work is essentially a cultural experiment, a research-and-development job with us longer-lived people as both the scientist-researchers and test subjects. As the idea catches on, this work promises to restore older adults to positions of reverence and authority as we seed our culture with prototypes of the "possible sage." At this critical time in the history of our planet, we can scarcely imagine the benefits that spiritual eldering holds for healing the family, renewing political life, and restoring the Earth to ecological health.

# CHAPTER 3

# *Elderhood: Past, Present, and Future*

Several years ago, while traveling in India, the spiritual teacher Ram Dass visited a friend who lived in a village in the Himalayas. "You're looking so old!" the Indian man said to him. "You're so gray!" At first Ram Dass reacted to these statements with a Westerner's typical horror. Calling someone "old" in America is like labeling that person a leper. But in India, he realized, being old was an achievement that entitled one to respect and recognition. "When I quieted down and looked beyond my conditioned dread of aging," Ram Dass said, "I realized that my friend was congratulating me on becoming an elder. He was saying, 'How wonderful that you've arrived at old age!' "

In some places in the world today, people cherish a wrinkled face and even look forward to their first gray hairs. In the village of Vilcabamba in the Ecuadorian Andes, where people have exceptionally long life spans, some elders exaggerate their age to gain greater respect. In India, men and women look forward to old age as a time to detach from the obligations of work and family life to seek knowledge of the inner Self. The Japanese, who regard old age as a source of prestige, celebrate a national holiday called "Honor the Aged Day." Native Americans think of their elders as wisdomkeepers whose contemplative skills help safeguard tribal survival.

Because elders in these cultures have respected roles, they find it easier to engage in life harvesting. In our society, by contrast, older people are exiled from the world of economic productivity and cut off from their historical role as elders of the tribe. No wonder they have little aptitude or training for harvesting their lives.

By harvesting, I mean gathering in the fruits of a lifetime's experience and enjoying them in old age. When we harvest, we consciously recognize and celebrate the contributions we have made in our career and family life. We also appreciate the friendships we have nurtured, the young people we have mentored, and our wider involvements on behalf of the community, the nation, and ultimately the Earth. Harvesting can be experienced from within as quiet self-appreciation or from without through the honor, respect, and recognition received from family members, relatives, colleagues at work, and mentees.

For example, harvesting takes place when friends and family members sponsor a celebration dinner for a retiree, honoring her achievements with gifts, reminiscences, movies, and videotaped interviews by loved ones that highlight her contribution to their lives. A teacher who implants humanitarian values in his students receives a harvest when they acknowledge him as the source of their inspiration to serve in the Peace Corps. When a young person sends his mentor a note of appreciation that says, "Your love and support have helped change my life," that, too, is an act of harvesting. Sometimes harvesting comes through the words of appreciation we receive when helping our adult children through difficult life transitions, while other times it takes the form of financial help, gifts, and unsolicited acts of kindness that make us feel honored and appreciated.

Harvesting shows us that we have made a difference in the world. We sense that our lives have meaning; that we have contributed to others; and that we are worthwhile human beings. When we are young, we invest our time, energy, and aspirations in endeavors that we hope will bear fruit as the successes of life. But when we arrive at the harvest season, we rarely receive the expected return on our investment because we have not been schooled in the high art of enjoying our achievements. Many of us are rich without knowing it, because we have not permitted ourselves to examine and take delight in the successes that we planted in the past. When we harvest our lives, we receive returns on our investment in the form of inner riches. We see that our work wasn't in vain; that our relationships have brought forth rich fruit; that our struggles for meaning and value have been worthwhile; and that even our failures, stumblings, and ill-conceived actions unwittingly have led to unexpected successes and to a wisdom that is beyond any price tag.

A Hebrew chant points to the dilemma of many elders who have not learned this process of life enrichment: "We have plowed; we have sown seed; but we haven't yet harvested." When older people tell me about the children they have raised, the careers they have mastered, the great historical changes they have witnessed, I often say, "Wonderful! Now, have you harvested the fruits of a lifetime? Have you served as a mentor to young people? Have you received the respect you deserve from your family and your community?" How sad when they answer, "Well, I invested mightily in my youth, but I never received anything back. I never thought that completing my life was even possible. Besides, my religion teaches me that harvesting is supposed to take place in the next world, not this one."

To these people, I would like to announce some good news: Evolution is now making it possible for harvesting to crown our efforts in *this* world. As a new paradigm of aging replaces the old one, we will not have to exit life feeling incomplete, like unfinished works of art. In the emerging picture of aging, we reach the summit of life in the October, November, and December of our lives as we enjoy the fruits of the harvest and replant the seed for the next crop.

The old paradigm of aging grows out of a spiritual worldview that has dominated our culture for the past several thousand years. This approach, which separates spirit and matter, rejects the body, sexuality, and the natural world. It places our hopes for salvation in another dimension, free from the messiness of everyday life. Life here is filled with suffering, a vale of tears, while true happiness lies in the world to come. Our spiritual task, then, is to rise above this fallen world through a vertical escape path called "spiritual life." In the past, spiritual practitioners in the East and West undertook rigorous disciplines to disengage themselves from the world, hoping through prayer and good works to win a place in heaven, free from this "inferior dimension of existence." Proponents of this strictly vertical escape path hoped to leave the world behind and enter the realm of pure Spirit.

Harvesting received short shrift in the old paradigm. Part of the reason had to do with people's short life spans. Until this century, it was rare in many parts of the world for people to live beyond their childbearing years. After people raised their children, they had nothing to look forward to but preparing for death and the afterlife.

Our major Western religions—Christianity, Judaism, and Islam—buttressed this expectation by conceiving of life as a vestibule, a preparation for the true life of paradise. People experienced the stages of childhood, youth, maturity, and old age as a preparation for death and eternity, a pilgrimage to God. Because a healthy old age didn't fit in the picture, neither did harvesting and bringing life to completion. Why harvest life here when you need to prepare for the world to come?

The new paradigm of aging grows out of a spiritual orientation that came to birth in the 1960s, 1970s, and 1980s. It draws on spiritual renewal in Judaism and Christianity, Earth-based Native American spirituality, feminine spirituality and Goddess religion, and the ecology movement. In the emerging view, because there is no separation between spirit and matter, we view God as no less in matter than in spirit. The divine manifests in leaves, worms, rivers, mountains, clouds, and galaxies. In this approach, we learn to redeem "fallen" nature and to live in greater harmony and reverence with all creation. Consequently, we also view sexuality as something wonderful, holy, and worthy of sacred celebration.

According to Buddhist scholar Joanna Macy, the new spirituality that grows out of this orientation does not focus only on our hopes for salvation in a transcendent and immaterial spiritual realm. It balances otherworldly concerns with a here-and-now approach that experiences the divine as immanent, embodied in all forms of physical existence. The new spirituality considers the world of matter as divine and worthy of love as the transcendent realm. Rather than fleeing this so-called inferior world, therefore, we are charged with the task of transforming, protecting, and beautifying it.

As part of this rapprochement between heaven and earth, says Macy, proponents of the new approach are learning "to fall in love with our world" by recognizing the sacredness of the senses, body, sexuality, and the natural world. "As we learn to spiritualize matter, humanity can begin to heal its alienation from nature and live in greater harmony with the Earth," she observes. "In this way, the new spirituality can help us protect the world from ecological destruction."

This shifting attitude has profound implications for eldering. Because we now live for decades beyond our parenting years, we can discover new myths and meanings for old age that our shorter-lived forebears never dreamed of. Because the new spirituality encourages us to have a more loving and respectful relationship with the physical world, we can use our awakening consciousness as elders not to transcend the Earth, but to heal it. And because we can enjoy the fruits of our labor, we can show young people what a fulfilled life looks like.

How wonderful that we can enjoy the fruits of a lifetime "on this side," rather than only in the world to come! Before, we used to say, "You can't get a reward for your good works in this world." It had to be postponed for the afterlife. Now, without diminishing the value of the other world, the new paradigm gives us a foretaste of the joy to come right here. What pleasure awaits us as we pass on our wisdom to succeeding generations through mentoring and through recording our oral histories on audio- and videotape.

Harvesting in this manner has more than just personal significance; it has planetary implications. Scientists recently have begun relating to the Earth as a living organism called Gaia. Our planetary life support system is not just a huge dead rock hurtling through space. It's a living, breathing planet whose governing intelligence sustains all life forms in a web of organic interconnectedness. This same vibrant planet also has become a global village linked by instantaneous electronic communication. Author Peter Russell calls this enormous system for data storage and retrieval that links all peoples and nations the "global brain." Human beings are like individual nerve cells of the global brain, the greater intelligence of Gaia.

From this perspective, harvesting has a purpose that transcends personal motives. When we recount our life stories and mentor young people, we transfer the contents and meaning of our experience into the global brain, raising the overall level of our cultural environment. In this sense, harvesting helps refine all that we have done into its highest essence, so that our individual lives serve as blessings for future generations.

Our life stories cry out to be uploaded to the hard drive of the planet, the global brain, poured back into civilization to help it become more civilized. If we value our experience and the wisdom we have gained, we grieve at the prospect of their being lost with the body's decay. When we grasp the overarching pattern of our lives—the remarkable coincidences referred to as divine providence, the interweaving of people and events that contributed to our destiny, the difficult passages that matured us in the crucible of life experience—we lament that the wisdom gained from this rich harvest will be lost when the physical body disintegrates. As Dr. Elisabeth Kübler-Ross points out, the dying person grieves not only his own death, but the loss of the whole world. For elders, this grief becomes compounded by the prospect of losing the dimensions of consciousness that we have developed and the learning that we have gained.

Hence the nagging question in elderhood: "Are you saved?" When you are working on a computer, sometimes you type a whole page and there is a power outage. If you have not saved your work in the computer's memory, all is lost. In the same way, a lifetime asks the question: "Are you saved?" In the new approach to aging, each of us must write into the global awareness what we have learned in our lifetimes and what we have become.

## A SYMPHONY IN THREE MOVEMENTS

The new model of aging is like the last movement of a symphony that evolution has been orchestrating for countless generations. In the first movement, which precedes the Industrial Revolution, elders have honored roles in society as spiritual leaders, political advisors, and teachers of the young. In the second movement, which begins with the Industrial Revolution and its emphasis on the production and consumption of material goods, elders lose their esteemed place in society. They become victims of *gerontophobia*, an irrational fear of advanced age based on disempowering cultural stereotypes.

In the third movement, people begin searching for new myths and models to ennoble the experience of old age. Drawing on therapeutic and contemplative techniques from humanistic psychology and the world's spiritual traditions, they initiate a major cultural shift to revive elderhood in the modern world. This search for more meaningful roles in old age is in part a response to our evolution from an industrial economy to a postindustrial information and service economy, which has changed our understanding of what constitutes productivity. Because we have come to value the intangible contributions of creative minds, continued productivity for elders in this era means more than sheer physical output in the workplace. It means making available the wisdom, balanced judgment, and guidance that can help our technological culture have a healthier relationship with the natural world.

Let's look briefly at each of the three movements to discover not only our past, but our exciting future.

In the first movement, which runs from prehistory to the Industrial Revolution, elders are woven into the fabric of social life. They serve as political leaders and judges, sages and seers, guardians of the traditions, and teachers of the young. Because of their age and experience, they transmit the great myths, rituals, and special knowledge needed for culture to continue from one generation to the next. In this way, they serve as bridge builders from the past to the future.

They qualify for this role, observes social gerontologist David Gutmann, by exchanging secular for sacred power. Elders have passed through the "parental emergency" in which they sacrifice inner development for the practical necessities of raising children. As their physical strength begins to wane, they give up the secular reins of the tribe to its younger members and begin cultivating inner power. Exercising this power for the welfare of the group, they become shamans, healers, and priests.

Elders also serve as bridge builders between the generations. "Elders are necessary to the well-being of all age groups, particularly the young," writes Gutmann in *Reclaimed Powers*. "To usher the child successfully through the long period of helplessness, human parents also need to be nurtured. In need of special kinds of parenting themselves, these parents receive uniquely important support (beyond mere babysitting) from the older men and women of their communities."

In Gutmann's view, elders have the evolutionary task of safeguarding healthy and effective parenting. Besides transmitting values from one generation to another, they also protect the evolutionary potential of the neocortex, the locus of new learning. To transform brain potential into creative intelligence, he argues, children need the input of both the biological parents and the extended family during the long period of childhood dependency. By instructing the young and encouraging their appetite for new learning, elders serve as "wardens of our precious human heritage" who help ensure "the successful transformation of cortical possibilities into executive capacities of the human ego." Without this influx of loving instruction, children's learning potential may wither on the vine. As Gutmann concludes, "We do not have elders because we have a human gift . . . for keeping the weak alive; we are human because we have elders."

Anthropologist Joan Halifax, who has studied with tribal shamans and medicine people around the world, agrees with this assessment. In her view, elders in traditional societies show us the developmental possibilities of old age. These mature individuals, who have distilled wisdom from experience, have become innocent, clear-seeing, and compassionate.

"Elders function like old cobblers and dressmakers, sewing us back into the fabric of creation," she says. "Through their compassionate relatedness to all of life, they reduce our sense of alienation by helping us rediscover our sacred roots. And they do this without suffering from the disease of deadly earnestness. Elders have a wild, almost prankster-like quality that enables them to see the humor in every situation."

Elders play a number of roles in tribal society that ensure the health of its members, Halifax explains. Elders serve as storytellers who spin webs of enchanted verbal magic that help people understand their place in the cosmos. "When elders tell us stories, we see through our superficial picture of reality into the deeper meaning of life," she says. "These sacred stories reconnect us to our depths, revealing our origins, hopes, and destinies."

As council chiefs, elders settle tribal disputes. As initiators, they guide adolescents through rites of passage that prepare the youth to assume adult responsibilities and to carry on the traditions of their culture. As visionaries and seers, elders serve as conduits between the divine realm and the mundane world, making the abstract truths of spirituality accessible to the community by embodying them in their everyday behavior. Elders also serve as sacred ecologists who preserve the world's beauty and harmony. Finally, they serve as psychopomps who escort the soul in the afterlife. (In modern language, we would call such people death counselors.)

The absence of many of these roles in modern Western society may explain why elders feel so empty and why our families and communities suffer from so much social fragmentation.

"The wisdom that we need to solve our problems lies encoded in the depths of our unconscious minds," Halifax points out, "but it must be evoked by elders who reveal our potentials. Without realized models to evoke our archetypal depths, we are literally lost in the world. We have no map; we have no guide; we have no song; we have no Ariadne's thread to lead us out of the labyrinth. Throughout history, elders have served as beloved pathfinders, beckoning us to enter the province of old age in anticipation of growing strength and usefulness to society."

## ELDERHOOD IN THE ANCIENT WORLD

The image of the tribal elder described by Halifax left its imprint on the cultures of the ancient Near East and the Mediterranean world. For example, if you were alive in ancient Israel and someone called you *zaken* ("an old man"), you would not feel offended. In fact, you would feel honored. The word indicated not only advanced age, but respect associated with wisdom.

Elders in Israel wielded enormous religious and judicial power. They functioned as the consulting body of the city, the nation, and the king. They could appoint a leader or king, proclaim war, conduct political negotiations, uphold the Sacred Law, and perform religious ceremonies. In the ancient world, old men were considered the natural leaders of the people. So great was their influence that Moses made many of his important decisions only after consulting with the seventy wise men he appointed as his council of elders.

The Bible is lavish in its praise of elders. It considers gray hair "a crown of glory" and wrinkles a mark of distinction. The Book of Leviticus instructs us in how to honor elders, whether they are scholars or unlettered: "Thou shall rise up before the hoary head, and honor the face of the old man." The Book of Exodus reaffirms this view: "Honor thy father and mother, that thy days may be long upon the land which the Lord thy God has given thee." And the Book of Deuteronomy explains the special role assigned to elders: "Ask thy father, and he will declare unto thee, thine elders, and they will tell thee."

With few exceptions, ancient Israel granted old age status based on the Torah's veneration of elders. But when we move to the Greek world, we find the sad beginnings of the gerontophobia that pervades the modern world. True, the Greeks expected older people to fulfill their civic duties as representatives in the councils of elders. But their advice, which was never more than advisory, went unheeded as often as it was followed.

Since the Greeks valued youthful heroism, physical perfection, and beauty, it's not surprising that they looked upon aging as a catastrophe, a form of divine punishment. "The gods hate old age," says Aphrodite in the *Homeric Hymn to Aphrodite*. Greek literature is filled with stories of young people rebelling against old tyrants and dethroning them in furies of Oedipal hatred. For example, the patriarchal god Uranos is castrated by his son Kronos, who himself is victimized by his son Zeus.

Greek literature reveals how pessimistic people felt about growing old. The poets Homer and Hesiod describe old age using epithets such as "hateful," "accursed," and "sorrowful." In general, poets and playwrights lampooned the elderly as ugly, feeble, and worthy of social rejection. Elders fared no better in the philosophic tradition. One rarely finds the assumption that age automatically brings wisdom. In fact, in the *Rhetoric*, Aristotle rails against old people, accusing them of being cowardly, selfish, suspicious, talkative, avaricious, and ill-humored.

The status of elders improved in ancient Rome, where their wise counsel carried great legal authority in the senate, the city's most respected public institution. (The word "senate" comes from the Latin "senex," which means "old man.") In the senate, elders actively guided public policy following Cicero's maxim, "Young men for action, old men for counsel." However, even with their political influence and their roles as undisputed heads of the household, elders were as likely to be ridiculed for their frailties as honored for their wisdom. Romans generally thought of old age as a time of lost opportunities, of physical and mental deterioration.

In this climate, Cicero, the famous Roman orator and statesman, wrote a unique apology for elderhood, *De Senectute*. This milestone in gerontology counters many of the negative stereotypes of old age. Its prescription for enjoying elderhood, written nearly two thousand years ago, sounds as relevant today as when it was first written.

"We must use moderate exercise, take just enough food and drink to recruit, but not to overload, our strength," Cicero writes. "Nor is it the body alone that must be supported, but the intellect and soul much more. For they are like lamps: Unless you feed them with oil, they too go out from old age.... The fact is that old age is respectable just as long as it asserts itself, maintains its proper rights, and is not enslaved to any one. For as I admire a young man who has something of the old man him, so do I an old one who has something of a young man. The man who aims at this may possibly become old in body—never in mind."

To attain this praiseworthy state, Cicero counsels a lifestyle of sound nutrition, exercise, sensual moderation, an active mental life, and reflection. These more than compensate for the physical diminishments of old age, he writes. Doesn't this prescription for a sane elderhood sound remarkably like today's self-help manuals?

In the Middle Ages, Christian writers gave a new twist to the predicaments of old age. Where the Greeks and Romans had stressed the physical causes of aging, Christian theologians viewed the decrepitude of old age as a divine punishment visited on humankind because of Adam and Eve's disobedience in the Garden of Eden. The fall of man, therefore, had caused the twin evils of old age and illness. "As an image of sin, a symbol of terrestrial decrepitude, subject to God's curse as a consequence of original sin, the old man was entitled to be miserable, ugly, and ill," writes Georges Minois in *History of Old Age*. "More often than not... he did conform to this stereotype.... An old man in good health did not conform with the divine scheme of things."

Given this outlook, men and women thought of physical life as a sacred pilgrimage having as its destination the world of eternity. Yet even though earthly life was devalued, people felt embedded in a transcendent order that gave meaning to all they endured on their pilgrimages. They had an unshakable conviction about their place in the cosmic order, with the promise of salvation in the world to come.

Beginning with the Renaissance, this conviction was assaulted, battered, and eventually overturned. Modern Europeans, dissatisfied with the social stratification of medieval life, began thinking of themselves as individuals having their own unique destinies. According to gerontologist Thomas Cole, author of *The Journey of Life*, they viewed their lives less as earthly pilgrimages to God and more as careers in the shape of a rising and falling staircase or a pyramid of stairs. Seen this way, we ascend the stairs through education; enjoy our productive powers in the work world, attaining our peak at midlife; then descend inevitably into retirement and senescence.

This staircase image, Cole says, has dominated our thinking for the past several centuries. During this same period, as religious authority declined, science became our culture's dominant paradigm. The Industrial Revolution and democratic government gave birth to a world of accelerating technological and social change. Old age was never to be the same.

## ELDERHOOD IN THE INDUSTRIAL AGE

During the industrial era, the second movement of our symphony sounds its mournful tones. Elders lose their honored place in society as the forces of modernization render them increasingly more useless. It's a sad story but it must be told.

In America it begins just before the Industrial Revolution, in the seventeenth- and eighteenth-century colonial era, when old age was highly respected. The Puritans, whose Bible-based belief dominated social thinking, held that old age was a sign of God's pleasure. It was a sign of divine election, a badge of supernatural sanctity that entitled elders to veneration. At New England town meetings, for example, elders occupied the places of honor, rather than the rich. Because literacy was low, colonial Americans respected elders as repositories of knowledge and teachers of traditional values.

They also were respected for their economic power. During this era, most people lived on farms in extended families. In an agricultural society, where wealth and power were equated with ownership of land, parents kept possession of their farms nearly to the end of their lives. In this way, fathers maintained control of their sons by means of economic dependency. They ruled as patriarchs, venerated for their age and wisdom, but also resented and feared for their economic power.

As industrialism took root in nineteenth-century America, young men migrated in droves to the cities. Here they could escape from their extended families and the rule of rural patriarchs. Instead of working their fathers' fields, these new city dwellers had to acquire the technological knowledge and skills needed to succeed in industrial society. Overnight, the knowledge they had inherited from their parents—the same traditional knowledge that had guided civilization throughout the stable, relatively unchanging agricultural age—became obsolete. Soon young people were better educated than their parents, who could no longer provide vocational guidance and instruction. At the same time, extended families came apart, giving way to mobile nuclear families hungry to break free from the constraints of the past.

In a sense, elders were the victims of democratic zeal. Many immigrants came to America to escape from authoritarian Old World traditions, including the tyranny of kings and monarchies. But in their revolutionary zeal to overthrow authority, they dealt the aged a grievous blow. Identifying old people with the "old ways" that were overturned by the American and French revolutions, they vowed never again to submit to such tyranny. Power passed from the fathers to the democratic sons, who valued the new and technological, rather than the old and traditional ways of the past. This shift has created great technological progress but has left elders without meaningful roles.

In preindustrial society, elders had the task of transmitting their knowledge to younger people through the apprenticeship system. For centuries, young men learned their trade by studying with older skilled craftsmen. For example, a master tailor would demonstrate to his apprentice how to sew a seam and how to hem pants; to his journeyman he would demonstrate how to cut garments from patterns. After the student demonstrated a certain level of mastery, the practicing tailor might say, "Look, I think you're ready to make a suit for Mr. Schulz. Here are the measurements. Show the suit to me when it's finished."

Since the Industrial Revolution, this direct, person-to-person transmission has become the mass-produced province of schools, factories, and professionals. We no longer consult our elders for the practical information we need. Often, the professional knowledge they acquire becomes obsolete in the course of their own lifetimes.

So what do you do with an older population rendered useless by an industrial society? Like any other disempowered group, you warehouse elders in segregated ghettos such as nursing homes and retirement communities. Like other ghetto dwellers, elders submit to this isolation as a condition inflicted on them by society. At the same time, many consciously choose to live a segregated lifestyle as a way to strengthen their collective identity and to enjoy the pleasures of retirement living. In either case, the warehousing of elders in segregated communities today is part and parcel of the Industrial Revolution's cosmology, which treats human beings as mechanisms, machine parts in a mechanical universe. Since machines are prized for their functional value, there is little incentive to keep old ones around that don't produce anymore. We don't totally scrap them, however. We simply remove them from the whir and hum of productive life, where in mechanical fashion they rust from disuse.

Segregated in this manner, elders become victims of *ageism*, the discrimination against people based on age. Ageism is every bit as offensive and dangerous as discrimination based on sex or race. It fosters stereotypes that discourage older adults from participating in the work world, in social and political arenas, and in cultural pursuits. According to popular ageist myths, older adults are unproductive, sexless, senile, poor, sick, and inflexible. Old age itself is a chronic, degenerative disease that calls for quarantining victims in segregated housing. While none of these myths is based in reality, they allow society to ignore the suffering of older adults. They also serve as self-protective mechanisms that keep younger people from facing the reality of their own aging and death.

To counteract this ageist nightmare, gerontologists recently have popularized the notion of "successful aging." This notion builds on the Victorian ideal of a healthy, self-reliant old age, free from dependency and physical debility. It also stresses lifestyle changes, such as regular exercise and sound nutrition, along with the relentless pursuit of a "busy, active life," to combat physical and intellectual decline. Magazines like *Modern Maturity* depict people who age "successfully" as healthy, sexually active, productive, and self-reliant. While this is all well and good, it doesn't go far enough. As Thomas Cole points out, successful aging gives priority to physical health as the path to salvation, but leaves out the spiritual dimension.

"Modern gerontology treats aging as a problem of social engineering to be solved through technological means," says Cole. "The one-sided drive to alter, reverse, or somehow control the biological process of aging actually impoverishes its meaning. So-called positive aspects of aging turn out to be disguised efforts to restore youth, rather than attempts to appreciate growing old as a fundamental part of human existence."

It's at this point, poised between the despair of the industrial paradigm and the promise of second maturity, that the second movement of our symphony sounds its final notes. Like the hushed moment before dawn, Earth catches its breath and waits expectantly for the sounds of a new day.

## REVIVING ELDERHOOD IN THE MODERN WORLD

At the opening of the third movement of our symphony, we find ourselves in a state of *tohu v'vohu* between paradigms. These Hebrew words describe a time at the dawn of creation when, according to the Bible, "the Earth was without form, and void; and darkness was upon the face of the deep." It's a time when the old structures have broken down, and the new ones have not yet coalesced into form. In this creative, exciting period, when we are giving shape to the new paradigm, we can impregnate the group mind with our hopes and dreams of a revitalized elderhood.

When the Israelites ended their forty years of wandering in the desert, they sent scouts into Canaan before taking possession of the Promised Land. We have our equivalent of such pathfinders when it comes to eldering. For example, Gerald Heard held up the vision of second maturity at a time when most elders were still in bondage to old-paradigm expectations of being "elderly."

More recently David Gutmann has called for a revived elderhood without the oppressive patriarchal controls that severely limit the freedom of younger people.

"We will have to enlist the elders, who have traditionally been the wardens of culture, to help and guide us in . . . crafting the new myths on which reculturation can be based," he writes in *Reclaimed Powers*. "We owe this redemption not only to our aging parents. We also owe it to the oncoming generations of children."

I believe the time is coming when older people will convene councils of elders to share their dreams, meditations, and visions of a revived elderhood. As this happens, we will collectively dream the myths and create the models that will galvanize social change. Such myths and models aren't delivered to us ready-made. They arise out of the hearts and minds of many people searching and dreaming together. At this moment, midwives from many disciplines are working tirelessly to help give birth to a revived elderhood. Spiritual teachers, social activists, consciousness researchers, media specialists, and many others all are helping in the delivery process. Let's look at some of the sources from which the new model of elderhood is emerging.

## TRADITIONAL SPIRITUAL MODELS OF ELDERHOOD

All the world's spiritual traditions hold up models of realized elders. There are the *roshi* in Zen Buddhism, the *lama* in Tibetan Buddhism, the *sheikh* in Islam, and the *rebbe* in Hasidic Judaism. Each tradition offers a set of practices, handed down through an unbroken lineage, that leads to self-knowledge. While acknowledging the validity of all these approaches, let's consider the Hindu tradition, with its notion of the four *ashramas*, or stages of life.

The four ashramas in Hindu society provide a psychospiritual guide-map of the human life cycle, a developmental model that accounts for our changing psychological needs as we age within a context of lifelong spiritual development. According to this model, people have an important "job" in old age: self-realization and service to society. Indians think of life as a spiritual journey. They view the four stages, each spanning twenty-five years, as necessary way stations in the soul's unfoldment.

In the student stage, *Brahmacharya*, young people acquire the intellectual, spiritual, and moral tools to prepare for adult life. In the householder stage, *Grihasta*, they marry, have children, take part in social affairs, and work hard to acquire wealth. When they enter the forest-dweller or *Vanaprastha* stage, people begin detaching from their families and social identities to devote more time to spiritual studies and meditation. In the final stage of renunciation, *Sannyasa*, they transcend all limited identification with family, religion, race, and nation. As wandering renunciates, they become citizens of the world, devoting their time to self-realization, spiritual instruction, and selfless service to society.

I'm not suggesting that we adopt this model unthinkingly, so that in later life we become wandering ascetics with begging bowls. However, we can adapt the Indian approach to meet our own needs. We can learn to detach from social roles, deepen our contact with Spirit, and practice compassionate action while remaining in our families and communities.

Modern life hardly prepares us for these tasks. If you consider the forest-dwelling stage as the equivalent of retirement, then the typical American life course takes us only through the first three ashramas. But because we don't practice contemplation during our productive years, we face a painful abyss when we retire and move through the largely unstructured third and fourth stages.

What we can learn from the Hindu notion of the four ashramas is to rethink retirement as a spiritual vocation that we prepare for in middle age by cultivating a contemplative outlook. When we contemplate our lives, we place ourselves on a vast continuum of time that takes into account the remote past, the present, and the unfolding future. With such an outlook, we discern patterns of meaning and purpose that might otherwise escape us when our gaze is restricted to the merely momentary occurrences of day-to-day living. Traditionally, the practice of meditation, along with dream analysis, journal writing, and the many forms of artistic expression, help orient us to the larger patterns of our lives.

If we begin practicing a contemplative discipline in middle age, we can keep the "big picture" before our mind's eye as we move into the afternoon of our days. We also can receive nourishment and support from the deeper levels of our being as we gradually begin detaching from our social and professional identities. By doing our inner homework when we are younger, we won't feel so disoriented when the outer props are removed in retirement. We will have the practical skills to begin shifting our identity from the smaller self, which is concerned with personal survival and well-being, to the larger self, which is concerned with the survival and well-being of the planet and the multitude of species it sustains.

## NEW MODELS OF ELDER PSYCHOLOGY

Until the middle of the twentieth century, psychologists paid little or no attention to adult development in the second half of life. Most psychology was youth-centered, dominated by Sigmund Freud's view that personality is set in childhood and remains relatively unchanged throughout adulthood. But then Carl Jung laid the foundations for an adult developmental psychology by expounding the notion of individuation, the process by which we become the complete human beings we are destined to be.

Jung held that the morning of life—the time of youth and first maturity—should be devoted to the conventional concerns of establishing ourselves in the world, marrying, and having children. When the afternoon of life arrives around thirty-five or forty, we cannot live by morning's program. We need to turn inward, Jung counsels, using contemplative tools such as dream analysis and creative expression, to reconnect with aspects of the self that we silenced in constructing our social selves and careers. Increasingly, we should contact the self, the center of the personality that speaks to us in dreams and archetypal images. By paying attention to these messages from within, we receive guidance for our journeys through life. Jung believed that an ongoing dialogue between the ego and Self in the second half of life brings us to wholeness and makes us more uniquely individual.

"A human being would certainly not grow to be seventy or eighty years old if this longevity had no meaning for the species," writes Jung in his famous essay "The Stages of Life." "The afternoon of human life must also have a significance of its own and cannot be merely a pitiful appendage to life's morning. . . . Whoever carries over into the afternoon the law of the morning . . . must pay for it with damage to his soul. . . ."

Jung held that spirituality should take precedence in later life when physical energy wanes and we lose friends and family members. He also believed that having a spiritual goal that points beyond "the purely natural man and his worldly existence" makes for psychological health. What cured patients in the second half of life, he once observed, was cultivating a spiritual outlook on life.

If Jung laid the foundations for a late-life psychology, then Erik Erikson built the ground floor. In 1950, in his classic work *Childhood and Society*, he set out one of the first comprehensive models of the life cycle, the "Eight Ages of Man." Erikson sees life as a sequence of eight developmental challenges, decisive turning points with either positive or negative outcomes. The successful resolution of each step leads to new growth and maturity, while failure results in neurotic behavior and a halt to further maturation. The first six stages describe how we form our personalities in childhood, seek our identities in adolescence, and develop intimate relationships in adulthood. The last two stages of Erikson's theory most concern older adults.

In the seventh stage, *generativity versus stagnation*, we fulfill our need to be needed by being productive and by guiding the next generation through parenting or mentoring young people. Generativity is motivated by our desire to pass on to the next generation what we have contributed to life—either in the form of creative works, learning, emotional nurturance, or the practical tools and values to create an ecologically sustainable world. Success in this developmental task results in the ability to care, while failure leads to self-absorption and a sense of personal impoverishment.

Middle adulthood's generative responsibility involves the "maintenance of the world," Erikson writes in *Vital Involvement in Old Age*, which he coauthored with his wife, Joan, and Helen Kivnick. "It is therefore the responsibility of each generation of adults to bear, nurture, and guide those people who will succeed them as adults, as well as to develop and maintain those societal institutions and natural resources without which successive generations will not be able to survive."

In the eighth stage, *ego integrity versus despair*, we achieve a sense of completeness and self-acceptance that offsets our inevitable physical decline. Success in this task, Erikson says, leads to wisdom, which in part includes an acceptance of our "one and only life cycle as something that had to be and that, by necessity, permitted of no substitutions." Failure at this task leads to despair, a fear of death, and the feeling that time is too short to start another life.

According to Erikson, those who possess ego integrity defend the dignity of their lifestyles against all physical or economic threats. Their strength stems from the development of wisdom, which he defines as "detached concern with life itself, in the face of death itself." Where do we find such wisdom? As the ultimate flowering of human maturity, "It comes from life experience, well-digested," asserts Joan Erikson, an artist and frequent collaborator with her husband, in a *New York Times* article published in 1988. "It's not what comes from reading great books. When it comes to understanding life, experiential learning is the only worthwhile kind; everything else is hearsay."

Erik Erikson's influential theory has helped to dignify the meaning of later life. It also has spawned a great deal of interest in adult development. Recently, for example, psychiatrist Allan Chinen has proposed a new elder psychology based on his study of fairy tales portraying older heroes.

As parables of the human journey through life, fairy tales contain important insights about human psychology, Chinen points out. Most familiar tales, such as "Cinderella" and "Tom Thumb," for example, portray youthful protagonists. These stories reflect the concerns of the emerging personality, such as separating from parents, struggling to find a place in the world, and making commitments to spouse and career. These youth tales generally end with the phrase, "and they lived happily ever after."

Elder tales, on the other hand, symbolize the developmental tasks of the second half of life. They show what happens in the "ever after" when the hero and heroine raise a family and eventually lose their youthful appearance and outlook. "Elder tales do not speak of growing *up*, they deal instead with growing old, and most importantly, with *growing*—psychologically and spiritually," Chinen writes in *In the Ever After*. "[They] offer . . . a new image of maturity, centered around wisdom, self-knowledge, and transcendence."

Elder tales typically begin with the protagonist in a state of isolation and barrenness—not unlike the condition of many older adults in our society. Through miraculous means, which Chinen calls "rediscovering magic," the older man or woman overcomes this depressed state by accepting the inevitable losses of old age, including the loss of health, a spouse, or social position. Dealing with these painful losses clears the way for new psychological and spiritual development as the elder delves into the unconscious to confront issues that may have been repressed since youth. Inevitably on this journey of discovery, elder heroes must come to terms with the dark, unknown side of the personality that Jung called the *shadow*. Although we normally associate this developmental task with younger people, elder tales suggest that self-reformation is an appropriate task for the second half of life.

By reconciling themselves with loss and confronting their shadows, older adults learn to transcend the ego and find their places in human history and the cosmos. In the process, as they break free of society's conventions, elders learn to follow the dictates of their own hearts, a state that Chinen calls "emancipated innocence." Because they have individuated through facing personal evil and abandoning private ambitions, older people can then work for the well-being of the world. Serving as mediators between the transcendent and everyday realms, they become mentors, teachers, and spiritual leaders.

"Because we've ignored the inner life of older people, the elder psychologies that we've developed so far represent only preliminary approaches," Chinen says. "As the Age Wave continues producing larger numbers of long-lived people, we will create more sophisticated elder psychologies that will put spirituality back into American life. As our elders teach us how to find more inner satisfaction, we'll decrease our reliance on consumerism and live in greater harmony with the Earth and its resources."

## NEW MODELS OF ELDER SOCIAL ACTIVISM

We normally think of elders as conservators of traditional values and "the old ways." According to popular wisdom, they love to reminisce about "the good old days" when Packards and Studebakers were top-of-the-line automobiles or when people danced the Charleston and the Lindy. But people like Maggie Kuhn take exception to this stereotype.

"Older people are not just card-carrying members of Leisure World and midafternoon nap-takers," she says vehemently. "We are tribal elders, with an ongoing responsibility for safeguarding the tribe's survival and protecting the health of the planet. To do this, we must become society's futurists, testing out new instruments, technologies, ideas, and styles of living. We have the freedom to do so, and we have nothing to lose."

As risk-takers who can heal and humanize society, elders have five appropriate roles to play, Kuhn says. They are *mentors* who teach the young; *mediators* who resolve civil, racial, and intergenerational conflict; *monitors* of public bodies who serve as watchdogs of city hall and Congress; *mobilizers* of social change; and *motivators* of society who urge people away from self-interest and toward the public good. Following these guidelines, the Gray Panthers work tirelessly to combat ageism in the media. They also lobby for national health care reform and support the movement for alternative sources of energy, such as solar and geothermal.

Like Kuhn, Marty Knowlton is another iconoclast who wages war against conventional images of the elder. In 1975, he founded Elderhostel, a program of education and travel that enables people of retirement age to live and study on college campuses for a week at a time. In 1988, he also founded Gatekeepers to the Future, a California-based organization that encourages elders to form study groups that research future-oriented issues and take action in the political arena.

For example, a group interested in environmental issues might research global warming, ozone depletion, deforestation, acid rain, or the garbage overload. Narrowing its focus to one issue—ozone depletion, for example—the group then might study whether the community has a recycling center to recover ozone-damaging chlorofluorocarbons (CFCs), which circulate inside refrigerators and air conditioners. If no facilities exist to reclaim CFCs and to prevent their release into the atmosphere, the group might speak before a meeting of the local city council and propose creating such a recycling center.

In Knowlton's view, elders can expedite the vast process of cultural change currently under way by learning "to think free of the past." Echoing the spiritual maxim "If you meet the Buddha on the path, kill him," he quips, "If you meet the old, traditional elder on the path, kill him, too!"

In primitive societies, he explains, elders withdrew from everyday life to become the tribe's thinkers and transmitters of culture. They could discharge their duties because in these static, nontechnological societies, there was a clear, almost unvarying trajectory from the past into the future. Nowadays, this way of life is clearly impossible, given the unprecedented rate of change occurring around the world. The elder as conservator of old values must also become the elder as pathfinder to the future.

"We all tend to dwell in the past, whereas our natural element is always the future," Knowlton asserts. "Elders tend to become entrapped by the past, simply because they have more of it clinging to them. If they can learn to abandon old ways of thought and perception, they can become bridge builders to the future. They won't offer us 'the one true way' of an eternally unchanging worldview. Having the experience and intellectual flexibility to embrace the unknown, they will help us create a global society with wisdom and skill."

What a breathtaking future awaits us as elders when we claim our new role as futurists! As Maggie Kuhn says with characteristic feistiness, "Our goal is to use our freedom, our experience, our knowledge of the past, our ability to cope and survive, not just for free bus fares or tax rebates for people over sixty-five, although we need these benefits. We want to work as *advocates* for the larger public good, as public citizens and responsible consumers."

## NEW MODELS IN THE ARTS, MEDIA, AND LITERATURE

Western culture presents us with so few models of vigorous, actualized older adults that most people cannot honestly say, "Yes, I want to be an elder when I grow up." In literature, for example, we rarely find exemplary elder heroes. Homer shows Odysseus, the world conqueror, returning home from his midlife adventures, but we never see him harvesting his life in old age. King Lear, an archetypal elder figure, has a wretched old age once divested of his regal power. His descent into madness and death, according to Jungian analyst Marion Woodman, illustrates the stripping away of social identity that can occur when we lose our place in society through retirement. In contemporary literature, playwright Arthur Miller presents a twentieth-century rendering of this theme with the poignant portrayal of Willy Loman in *Death of a Salesman*.

I'm not suggesting that there are no positive elder models in Western civilization. There are exceptions, of course, but we really have to wrack our brains to come up with them. Even Moses, the exemplary elder in Judaism who lived to be 120, wasn't such a good model. He remained "in the saddle" to his dying day, leading the children of Israel as he had done uninterruptedly for the previous forty years. Had he known about spiritual eldering, he might have relinquished some of his responsibilities to Joshua and enjoyed his elderhood as an "emeritus prophet"!

When we look to television and movies, we find the same dearth of positive elder models as in literature. The media usually portray elders as either senile, doddering, ineffectual buffoons or as wholesome, unwrinkled, white-haired fun-seekers who work hard to recapture the vigor of their middle years so they can keep their places in the youth culture. Most advertisements don't portray older people who have come to terms with the facts of physical aging and psychological maturity. What we find are idealized older people who can still compete sexually, athletically, and financially with young people.

Whether pathetic or idealized, the portrayal of elders on television occurs rather infrequently. The people who typically populate television programs are seldom over forty years old. In *The Fountain of Age*, author Betty Friedan cites a study of characters who were monitored for one week on a prime-time television drama. The study found that of 464 role portrayals, only 7—or 1.5 percent—appeared to be over sixty-four years of age, a figure that flagrantly underrepresents the older population. Friedan cites another study that found only 2 out of 100 commercials to have older characters. Even when older people are depicted on television, observes media specialist Richard Davis in *Television and the Aging Audience*, the portrayals are generally accomplished through stereotyping. "Whether negative or positive," he says, "[stereotyping] is still unrealistic and biased."

Recently, however, we have witnessed the barest beginnings of reconceptualizing elders in the media. Films like *On Golden Pond* and *Cocoon* present sympathetic portrayals of older people's real-life struggles. In *Fried Green Tomatoes*, Jessica Tandy plays an eighty-three-year-old woman who serves as a glorious role model and mentor for a middle-aged woman who lives as an oppressed, co-dependent wife. As the older woman harvests her life by sharing some of its most transformative moments, the younger woman gives up being victimized, asserts her personal strength, and embarks on her own individual life path. Films like this, which show us a representative of mature elderhood, tempt us to say, "I'd like to become like a Jessica Tandy when I grow up."

One way that the media can help change our cultural aging script is by creating television programs that show elders as positive role models who have grown beyond self-concern and who are engaged in creative activity that benefits society. Such programs would eschew casting older people either in the role of narcissistic consumers of public services or as physically and mentally frail people worthy of our pity or contempt.

"In the near future, we might tune in on Sunday evening to a program entitled *Elder Heroes*," says Doug Waldo, who hosted *Seniors Speak Out*, a program for the over-fifty audience that was produced for seven years at KPBS, San Diego's public television station. "The program would feature exemplary elders—the Maggie Kuhns of the world—who are making a difference in people's lives by giving of themselves. Such programs can use mass communications to stimulate public dialogue in an attempt to reassimilate the wisdom of elders in society."

Like Waldo, I believe that new images of the mature elder will appear in books, movies, and television programs as the graying of America proceeds and spiritual eldering finds an established place in society. A new genre of elder art will emerge to reflect the shift in interests and values as we move from a youth-centered culture to one that includes elders. At the moment, most of our art focuses on youth and middle age. We have few fictional, cinematic, and theatrical forms that deal with the plight of older people, in large part because eldering has never been a significant cultural force. As elder art grows in popularity and influence, young people will be exposed to images of older people that stress inner beauty, purpose, and radiance. Rather than having a horror of growing older, we will begin anticipating elderhood as the summit of life.

## ELDERHOOD IN THE NEW PARADIGM

As we create new models of elderhood from our spiritual traditions, psychology, and the media, let's remember that spiritual eldering is part of a greater cultural shift affecting the world. In *The Turning Point*, physicist Fritjof Capra asserts that our one-sided scientific culture is going through a period of rebalancing. A more holistic perspective is emerging that stresses cooperation rather than competition, ecological awareness rather than mindless consumerism, and intuition to complement our obsession with rationalism. We see evidence of this paradigm shift in the social justice and ecology movements and the rise of feminism. We see further evidence in the appeal of humanistic and transpersonal psychology, with their call for an expanded human potential and inner knowledge, and the widespread interest in Eastern and Western mysticism.

Spiritual eldering has benefited from all this exploration. It draws liberally on the breakthroughs in consciousness that we have made in the past three decades. It also depends on the shift from the old, otherworldly spirituality to the new celebrational spirituality that heals the split between spirit and matter and that affirms the sacredness of life on Earth. This attitude enables us to harvest our lives and to bequeath a legacy to the generations that follow us. As we shall see in future chapters, harvesting also has profound implications for the health and survival of our planet Earth.

*Part Two*

# Spiritual Eldering and Personal Transformation

# Chapter 4

# *The Art of Life Completion*

To harvest our lives successfully, we must come to terms with our mortality. I know that in youth-oriented, cosmetically enhanced America, the subject of one's own death is not only unpopular, but as taboo as sex was in the Victorian era. A fantastic conspiracy of silence surrounds the issue of our mortality. Living as we do in a technological culture, we repress the sacred, transcendent nature of death that was experienced by our ancestors.

Seduced by our technological successes, which have given us unparalleled control of the physical world, we hope that genetic engineering, anti-aging chemicals, and bionic research will eliminate death from our midst. In our hubris, we hope that with enough empirical research, we will reduce the mystery of death to a manageable scientific process that we can program and control at will. In this way, we will expose aging and death as genetic errors, cosmic mistakes rectified by our human ingenuity.

As we approach the subject of our mortality, let's be clear from the beginning: Death is *not* a cosmic mistake. Woven into the warp and woof of existence, the presence of death deepens our appreciation of life. It also regenerates our psyches in preparation for harvesting. The more we embrace our mortality not as an aberration of God and nature, but as an agent urging us on to life completion, the more our anxiety transforms into feelings of awe, thanksgiving, and appreciation. A Zen story illustrates this point.

A monk, who is being chased by a tiger, comes to the edge of a cliff. As the tiger closes in on him, the monk notices a vine leading over the cliff and down into a precipice. Quickly, he crawls over the edge and lets himself down by the vine only to discover another tiger waiting for him below. Looking up, he observes a mouse gnawing away at the vine. Just then, he spots a luscious strawberry within arm's reach. The monk seizes the berry and eats it. Ah, how delicious it tastes!

As the story demonstrates, people who face their mortality live out their days with greater zest and joy. Why is this so? As we age, we receive a number of messages, either consciously or subliminally, about our mortality. For example, we may be aware of shortened breath in climbing a steep grade or the need for longer recuperation time after an illness. Usually, we mobilize our psychological defenses to tune out these messages. Slowly, over years and decades, as we expend more energy to keep reminders of our mortality at arm's length, we have less overall energy and awareness available. As a result, our experience of life loses a certain clarity and depth. There's always a nagging "something," a free-floating anxiety, that we try to drown out through frenetic activity, entertainment, sexual conquests, or obsessive concern with the youthfulness of our bodies.

When we de-repress the fear of death, we reclaim the energy that has gone into denial. We feel buoyed up as streams of creative energy course through our bodies, minds, and nervous systems. By facing a subject that usually depresses and terrifies us, we feel lighter, freer, more perceptually and cognitively alive in all our encounters.

"When we confront our mortality, a shift occurs in our attention that makes us more aware of how precious life really is," says psychologist David Feinstein, co-author of *Rituals for Living and Dying*. "We have an enhanced ability to accept ourselves, along with a greater ability to love. We lose the pervasive anxiety that makes us grasp obsessively for power, wealth, and fame. As we discover a deepened sense of purpose and a profound connectedness with other people, we tend to be motivated by higher, more universal values, such as love, beauty, truth, and justice."

In facing our mortality, we also feel more capable of doing the work of spiritual eldering and harvesting our lives. A wonderful humor even emerges when we face death without squeamishness. As Ram Dass playfully reminds us, "Death is absolutely safe. Nobody ever fails at it."

## NEW LIGHT ON THE DEATH INSTINCT

To understand how coming to terms with death facilitates spiritual eldering, let's consider in a new light Sigmund Freud's theory that two primordial forces drive human experience. He named them *libido*, the life instinct, and *thanatos*, the death instinct. Freud considers life as a ceaseless struggle between these two forces. Libido surges with vitality, seeking pleasure and continuity of experience. Thanatos longs to return to an inanimate state of quiescence devoid of all striving and conflict. Libido yearns for sexual gratification and creative activity, while thanatos drives us toward annihilation and the cessation of all activity. In the end, thanatos wins out over libido as physical existence grinds to its inevitable end in the grave, in death and dissolution.

Because Freud's worldview leaves no room for the transcendent—for the soul and spirit—he presents a bleak, materialistic picture of thanatos. He thought of religion as the projection of humanity's infantile need to remain dependent on a great Cosmic Father, a Super Daddy projected onto the cosmos to fulfill our childish desire to remain cared for and protected. Freud marshaled the forces of scientific objectivity to disabuse us of these infantile longings. In this spirit, those who followed in his footsteps regarded thanatos as the psyche's bleakest force operating in us, the Grim Reaper in all his naked terror. Since the theory of the death instinct was formulated, Freudian theorists essentially have dropped the subject because of its anxiety-provoking nature.

While we may reject Freud's materialistic interpretation of thanatos, he correctly grasped that a bipolar energy is at work in the human psyche. Modern psychologists, in service to the youth culture, have focused almost exclusively on one half of the polarity, the life instinct, with techniques that deal with sexual adjustment, personal effectiveness, and career success. However, they have yet to do their homework on the death instinct.

"We live in a time that denies death, that distorts the dying experience by retaining traditional myths," writes psychologist Stanley Keleman in *Living Your Dying*. "What we need is a fresh start, a new myth, a new vision of maturity and longevity. We are not victims of dying; death does not victimize us. But we *are* victims of shallow, distorted attitudes toward dying, which we conceive as tragic."

Yet despite our resistance to death, we are more familiar with it than we might suspect, Keleman contends. "Our bodies know about dying and at some point in our lives are irrefutably, absolutely, and totally committed to it, with all the lived experience of the genetic code. The body knows how to die. We are born knowing about dying."

While we have an organic familiarity with death, our culture, steeped in denial, can only deal comfortably with expansion, activity, achievement, and goal orientation—the realm of libido. But it's extremely uncomfortable, almost panic-stricken when dealing with contraction, quiescence, lack of activity, and inwardness—the domain of thanatos. I propose that to do eldering work, we must meet, embrace, ennoble, and domesticate the death instinct. We must remove the death mask from thanatos and welcome it as our initiator into the larger life. All the world's spiritual traditions teach that within us lies a transpersonal source of love and wisdom. I believe that thanatos is its messenger.

Understood spiritually, the struggle between libido and thanatos is a record of the ongoing dialogue between the personality and the soul or inner self. In this dialogue, what Freud called the death instinct compares quite clearly with Eastern notions of ego transcendence and enlightenment. For example, Hindu yogis strive to break attachment with their desires ("libido") to attain *samadhi*, a transcendental state in which self-consciousness is totally suspended ("thanatos"). Sufis practice spiritual disciplines that lead to *fana*, a blissful state in which all traces of the self are annihilated. Buddhists attempt to extinguish the forces of *tanha*, the instinctive craving for life, and enter *nirvana*, a desireless state of quiescence and equilibrium.

These spiritual traditions teach that there is a natural, inborn reflex in human consciousness that seeks quiescence as a complement to the outgoing energies that anchor us in the everyday world. Just as the centrifugal energies of the psyche whirl us into tempests of outer activity, so complementary centripetal energies urge us inward toward stillness and equipoise. As an outgoing force that is concerned with survival and sheer quantity of experience, libido thrusts us onto the periphery of life, where we multiply our connections with the world by beginning new relationships and projects. As an ingoing force that is concerned with life completion and self-actualization, thanatos takes us away from the periphery, where we become more selective in the relationships and projects that we undertake as we deepen our connection with the inner Self. Happy and wise is the person who can get these two energies to collaborate!

I like to think of libido and thanatos as a bipolar electrical switch in our consciousness with two settings: on/off, life/death, activity/rest. When we are young, the life polarity is in the ascendancy. We crave movement, excitement, sexuality, family and career building, the maximum exertion of our strength and energy in making a mark on the world. When we grow older, the polarity shifts in our consciousness as thanatos begins to assert itself. Quietly at first, then more insistently, we experience decreased energy and vitality and an awakening sense of inwardness. It's not that the craving for activity ceases. But the quality of that activity shifts as the "off" switch takes increasing precedence over the "on" switch. If at this point we honor thanatos by becoming contemplative, our actions become more discriminating, stamped with the seal of our growing sense of individuality.

In fact, we can think of thanatos as the urge for individuation that Carl Jung says asserts itself in the second half of life. "Aging people should know that their lives are not mounting and expanding," he writes in "The Stages of Life," "but that an inexorable inner process enforces the contraction of life. For a young person it is almost a sin, or least a danger, to be too preoccupied with himself; but for the aging person it is a duty and a necessity to devote serious attention to himself."

From midlife onward, thanatos helps us become more contemplative by setting limits on libidinal activity. It replaces quantity of life with an emphasis on the quality of our experience, making sure that we deepen our awareness when our expanding, conquering mode of behavior is on the wane. So where does libido go when we get older? Based on my own inner work as an elder, which involves studying world literature and psychology, observing myself and my peers, and meditating and reflecting on the aging process, I believe that it shifts from genital sexuality to nonbiological forms of generativity such as mentoring and harvesting. We still have a deep relationship with libido; we still transmit our seed, but not as encoded in our genetic structure. While in youth libido goes into preserving our genetic endowment through founding a family, in elderhood it goes into preserving our legacy through writing, teaching, and creating oral histories. On other planes, we are still conceiving and giving birth, but now we are passing on wisdom rather than propagating the species.

With this understanding, I have renamed libido the Beginning Instinct. Libido isn't so much interested in meaning and wisdom. It's more interested in immersing itself in experience, exerting itself, riding the wave of its reproductive energy, and establishing itself in the world. Whereas libido has an inseminating, seed-sowing function, thanatos has a collecting function, bringing together the fruits of the harvest. Because it's more interested in closure and meaning, I have renamed thanatos the Completing Instinct. Thanatos does *not* predispose us to seeking physical death. Rather, it acts as a natural magnet in the psyche, drawing together and arranging in patterns of meaning all that we have begun in our lifetimes.

We first become aware of the Completing Instinct in midlife, when the balance between libido and thanatos begins to shift. Often a crisis ensues, as the energies of thanatos rise up from the unconscious and demand their place in our libido-driven lives. Rather than embrace the emerging energy, however, we usually deny its presence and take strong measures to conquer new libidinal territory to keep the specter of death at bay. So we find a new lover, exercise madly to compete with younger people, redouble our efforts at work to prove our manhood or womanhood, or have cosmetic surgery to look more youthful. In fact, we do anything except come to terms with the invasion of thanatos, which destroys the idols in the sanctuaries of our youthful selves.

Men and women often experience ennui and dissatisfaction at midlife. There's a deadening sameness in their personal relationships, along with an insidious voice that whispers, "Is this all there is?" All these are symptoms of thanatos, which we rightfully subordinated in building our personality and finding success in the world. Now this patient companion is knocking on the door of personality, staking a claim on the owner of the house. "I'm not a one-time visitor here," says the usually unwelcome intruder. "I'll be visiting from time to time on a regular basis. You may put me up in a guest room or hide me away in a corner of the basement. But whether denied or acknowledged, I'll be a permanent part of your life from now on."

If we better understood the role of the Completing Instinct, we could mitigate the extent of the midlife crisis and welcome—rather than resist—the entry into second maturity. However, we have almost no training in relating to our depths. We fail to understand that what's knocking on the door is not some death-dealing opponent, but the agent of our completed self. The intrusion of thanatos marks the first appearance of the enlightened self that dwells behind the mask of our persona, the social identity that we normally take ourselves to be.

In one of the meditations that we do in our spiritual eldering workshops, we journey into the future to meet our completed self at age 120. (That self lives in eternal time, and since past, present, and future are one in eternity, our seeking self and realized self are one, also.) Then we ask, "Will you teach me the special knowledge I need to become a realized being?" Ultimately, no one else, no external teacher or guru, can lead us to enlightenment by insisting that we imitate an imposed set of practices. We must follow the leads, clues, and messages that come from our own realized inner self. That completed self first announces itself at midlife through the upsurge of thanatos.

A man at midlife who welcomes thanatos might call his wife and teenage children together for a family meeting. "Life is giving me the message that I'm in the afternoon of my days, rather than the morning," he might announce. "To respond appropriately, I want you to know that nailing down lucrative contracts and spending long hours at the office on weekends will not take top billing anymore. I want to spend more quality time with my family, taking walks, playing music, even sharing our dreams together. Getting ahead at work isn't as important to me as the precious hours spent with my loved ones."

For midlife women, menopause represents thanatos's first knock on the door. As women move through the grief and loss associated with the end of their reproductive years, if they consciously cooperate with the biopsychological process taking place, they enter a new phase of life. They become *crones*, postmenopausal women initiated into their depths.

According to Germaine Greer, author of *The Change*, crones experience a feminine wisdom and a detached capacity to love uncorrupted by need, "a feeling of tenderness so still and deep and warm that it gilds every grassblade and blesses every fly." More autonomous, less ruled by the need to take care of others and to "fix" human relationships, crones live their own unvarnished truths. They shine the light of consciousness within themselves to uncover feminine wisdom. Throughout history, this special wisdom has been associated with healing, compassion, and a holistic understanding of how to act in harmony with the cycles of nature. In many tribal traditions, postmenopausal women functioned as healers, spiritual leaders, and psychopomps, guides into the postmortem state.

In coming to terms with thanatos, a professional woman in menopause might say to her family, "I've postponed so much of my life out of love for you (for which you don't owe me anything, mind you). Now I feel entitled to pursue my own interests, which include enrolling in college and pursuing a course in astronomy. I also want to make a pilgrimage to certain art museums in Europe and visit some old friends. I want to do all this with your blessing. I would like your permission to be released from the role in which you've always known me so that I can begin living out other roles that are clamoring for expression."

Since most of us don't live as consciously as this man and woman, we work at cross-purposes with thanatos throughout middle age and later adulthood. Then, when old age approaches, because we have ignored the call for transformation along the way, eldering work becomes crisis-oriented. For example, many people rev up libido in old age in the hopes of staying in the saddle. But they often get overtaken by thanatos, almost like slamming against a brick wall. That's because a preponderance of libido makes old age and death painful prospects.

If we are still searching for the "more"—more pleasure, more activity, more conquests, whether sexual or otherwise—we are flowing against the current of thanatos. If we haven't had enough sex, the prospect of giving up this pleasure may strike us as a painful deprivation that we are unwilling to accept. Lovemaking, which is certainly appropriate in old age, can evolve into a form of communion that is less impulse-driven and that enables us to enjoy a deep, tender, and caring love with our partner. But if we cling obsessively to the driving impulses that fueled us in youth and middle age, comparing ourselves to standards of performance that were appropriate then, our mature self, feeling cheated, will experience intense pain as it rebels against thanatos and its greater claims on our dwindling physical energies. If, however, we embrace thanatos, the obsessive demands of libido will decrease, and we can explore new ways of being generative with our partner, our mentees, and the community at large.

If we listen to the inner promptings of our psyches throughout the life cycle, like whitewater rafters, we can ride the waves of thanatos to a successful, joyous completion in old age. But because we usually ignore its presence for so long, we must make up for decades of missed opportunities through remedial work in elderhood. If even then we continue ignoring the call for transformation, we all too easily can suffer from depression and disengage from life in cynicism and despair.

## LIFE WITHIN THE BOX

I call this condition of paralysis "the box." Imagine that every day you take a step toward the Angel of Death. In youth and even during midlife, you feel relatively "safe" on this journey, because the ultimate destination seems so far away. But as old age and journey's end approach, the Angel's features come more menacingly into view, and we are overcome with a primordial terror that makes us recoil from the future. The Angel beckons us to move through the portal of initiation into elderhood, but we refuse the invitation.

However difficult death was to face in middle age, it becomes even more ominous in old age. Because we cannot meet death head on, we get anxious and anesthetize ourselves by shutting down awareness. We start reciting an unconscious mantra, "I don't want to know. I don't want to know. I don't want to know."

We find ourselves in a no-exit trap called *avidya*, or ignorance, by the Hindus, a state of unawareness, fearful contraction, and clinging that denies us access to the future.

People who cannot look ahead as they grow older *back* into the future, inexorably moving onward in time without looking ahead. But what do we see when we back into the future? The past! The specter of previous failures rises up and darkens our vision. We are haunted by memories of broken plans and ruptured relationships, regrets about missed opportunities, resentments and unresolved conflicts—a lifetime of emotional hot spots and "ouches" that have repeatedly marred our enjoyment of life. The "could have been"s of a lifetime rise up before our vision, taunting us with unlived life. Rather than listen to the chorus of voices that indict us with our failures and unlived dreams, we silence them. In effect, we shut down our living connection to the past.

Shut off from the past and future, what's left? The present. But how much of the present do I wish to be aware of? I don't want to be aware of physical limitations, the creaks and pains of diminished mobility, the nagging chronic ailments, or the indignity of frequent calls to the bathroom. I certainly don't enjoy being reminded of my waning sexual energy and my diminished role in the marketplace of life. So by withdrawing from the past and future, I find myself in a contracted state of awareness in the present. Locked in a small box, resisting the flow of time, I inhabit a shriveled-up present, bereft of past and future in a psychic field that mimics Alzheimer's disease.

How do we leave this self-made prison, this box of diminished consciousness? As mentioned earlier, we must free the energies bound up in the denial of death, energies that are tied up in censoring, suppressing, and silencing every and all evidence of our mortality. The costly burden of repeatedly editing out the signals of our mortality weighs us down and leads to depression. Conscious aging, which hinges on accepting the reality of our death, paradoxically frees us and lightens our burden.

Denying death does serve a useful purpose in our earlier years. Throughout most of our lives, the fear of death, like a faithful soldier, has stood guard at the door, defending nature's built-in program: "Save life at any cost." Whenever our lives are threatened, this wonderful biological program triggers the flight-or-fight response. It automatically pumps adrenaline into our bloodstream and prepares our bodies both psychologically and physically to survive, no matter what. This program fortifies us when we go through unforeseen tragedies and reversals of fortune that tempt us to throw in the towel. When faced with a life-threatening injury or illness, we are grateful that the medical establishment, with its emergency room technology and intensive care units, promotes the program of "Save life at any cost."

## ENCOUNTERING OUR MORTALITY

While this program serves us in youth and midadulthood, it interferes with conscious and deliberate eldering. In old age we need to acquire the contemplative skills—such as meditation, prayer, conscious breathing techniques, philosophic clarity—to approach the Angel at the threshold. These skills enable us to encounter him without panic or without falling into unconsciousness. With these tools, we can learn how to affirm the unity of life in death and death in life.

I don't mean to underestimate the difficulty of this task. Whether we believe in life after death or reincarnation, or whether we are agnostics about the continuity of consciousness, "the aging self is summoned to grapple with the approaching darkness," writes Eugene Bianchi, a professor of religion at Emory University, in *Aging as a Spiritual Journey*. "Only through such nocturnal wrestling, as with Jacob and the angel, can the self experience the fullest blessing of the end-time. It is by facing the terrors of our old age, by launching out on the final night sea-journey, that a person finds the courage and insight to be profoundly wise for others in elderhood."

As Bianchi points out, death gradually educates the person who faces it with sincerity. In confronting and rehearsing our own death, we acquire a new orientation in life. Purged of excessive self-concern, we awaken to the splendors of the moment. We delight in the little things of life: children's laughter, birdsong in the morning, intimate conversations with friends over tea.

Released from myopic self-interest brought on by the terror of death, elders can now serve others. Having acquired a broader philosophic perspective and a rootedness in the continuity of time, they can act as custodians of humanity's wisdom. They become future-oriented because they have liberated themselves from the self-preoccupations of youth and midadulthood. Most of all, writes Bianchi, "if they can demonstrate in old age, the most despised time of life, zest, joy, service, and deep meaning can be found, the aged will not only empower themselves again, they will also encourage younger people to reevaluate elderhood, seeing its promise for their future, as well as its problems."

In this same vein, I like what Ram Dass says about making peace with our mortality. He points out that our fear of death stems from a sense of separation from the whole of life. Our zeal for individuality has left us alienated not only from our families and communities, but from nature and its commonwealth of species. What gives aging its intuitive meaning, he says, is a sense of oneness with Earth's life cycles, the procession of the seasons and the alternating rhythms of birth, growth, decay, death, and transformation into new life. Shielded from these awesome mysteries, we identify with our separateness—and come to fear death. Once we recognize that we are part of the whole, our fear of death dissipates immensely.

At this point in the discussion, you may be wondering, "What can I do to stop postponing my appointment with mortality?" In the next chapter, I will present some of the practical techniques we use in our spiritual eldering workshops for opening our awareness to the presence of death. Here I will just point to some of the instruments in our tool chest. These include taking the necessary legal steps to dispose of our estate; doing journal work to call up from memory our earliest encounters with death; becoming more familiar with death by writing our own obituary to see how we would be remembered; and making preparations for our funeral by envisioning who will be present, what music will be played, and what words will be spoken.

These and other exercises inoculate us against fear, panic, denial, and the general unpreparedness with which most people experience their physical end. And amazingly, rather than being a morbid excursion into the downside of our finitude, this encounter with self releases an abundant supply of energy and vitality to push open the door marked "elderhood." Already we feel better because a path to the future has opened. But at this point, we are only permitted a glimpse of the vestibule. To enter the inner sanctuary, we need to review our past in a more healthy light.

We do this by recontextualizing our failures into successes, releasing our backlog of resentments, and reconnecting with the unlived life that we sacrificed on the way to becoming adults.

## COMING TO TERMS WITH THE PAST

Let's start with life review. Gerontologists tell us that one of the major tasks of old age is to reflect on the wealth of our past experience—our personal achievements as well as our unresolved conflicts—in an attempt to understand what life has meant. Psychologist Victoria Fitch calls this process of introspection "a kind of inner cooking or brewing." In her article "The Psychological Tasks of Old Age," she writes, "The flame is the knowledge of mortality, the ingredients are a lifetime of perceptions, experiences, and relationships as yet unprocessed, and the vessel is the human heart."

Yet too often people who lack schooling in the contemplative arts return to the past with the most intense misgivings. They are afraid of the pain involved in becoming reacquainted with their former selves. "I lived through it once, it was painful, and I don't want to resurrect corpses and reopen old wounds, thank you," we tell ourselves.

What frees us from the tyranny of the past is the understanding that time is *stretchable*, not linear, so we can reframe and reshape it using contemplative techniques. If we think that time is linear, an event happens only once, the outcome is irreversible, and there's no way to reenter it with awareness for the purpose of repairing it. But spiritual insight reveals that time is multidirectional. Because it interpenetrates past, present, and future, we can reach back into the past and repair events and relationships that we perceive as failures or disappointments.

Although we live in present time, a part of ourselves is imprisoned in the pain of past relationships where incompletely lived experiences cry out to be healed. As the recovery movement so clearly demonstrates, although we may have left home and its early-life traumas years ago, the wounded inner child still weeps inside of us. By doing the work of inner repair, we can release ourselves from the prison-bound self of a former time. We also can forgive ourselves for the pain that we caused others. Many of us do "hard time" for acts of the past enacted without the benefit of the more enlightened awareness we now have. It's possible, however, to return to the past and to commute the sentence.

Using journal work, interpersonal exercises, and meditation (which will be explored in the next chapter), we can re-vision our failures and find the "pearl within the oyster." The grain of sand in the sensitive vitals of the oyster causes constant irritation. So what does the oyster do? To relieve the pain, it extrudes a substance to cover the sharp edges of the sand, and a shining pearl grows around the irritant.

So, too, have the irritations in our sensitive vitals caused by strained relationships and sudden career changes forced us to cope and mature in unforeseen ways. Through the psychotechnologies of spiritual eldering, we can discover that how we adapted to life's intractable "irritants" produced the real successes of our mature years. We can learn to revisit the joys and sorrows of our lives and say yes to them for the pearls of wisdom they imparted. When we courageously confront the past, we discover how much we have gained from apparent losses. Once we get past our anxiety, we glory in the hidden benefits that accrue from what we took to be painful failures. In this way, spiritual eldering provides the skills to do reconstructive inner surgery on ourselves.

## TURNING FAILURE INTO SUCCESS

Let me tell you a story from my own life to illustrate the power of recontextualization. A number of years ago, I served a congregation in New Bedford, Massachusetts. One of the members of the congregation was mourning the death of his father. Reaching out to this grief-stricken man, I spent a lot of time giving him personal instruction in the ways of prayer. Later, I got him invited to the board of directors, and eventually he became president of the congregation. How did this man repay me for befriending him? He fired me. For years my mind flashed red with anger whenever I thought about this act of human injustice. But because he fired me, I went to Winnipeg, Manitoba, where I served as an academic chaplain at the University of Manitoba and as professor of Near Eastern and Judaic Studies. Eventually, I became chairman of the department.

Finally, I was invited by Esalen Institute, the world-famous growth center in Big Sur, California, to do workshops and to lead High Holiday services in San Francisco. From this evolved the Aquarian Minyan in Berkeley, a New Age attempt to renew contemporary Judaism. If my so-called malefactor had not fired me, I would probably still be in my first pulpit. However, because he did, a series of events was set in motion, which together with other "failures" rerouted my life so that I could help midwife the national Jewish Renewal movement.

In the same vein, consider how Teresa Martin, a sixty-two-year-old retired social worker from Williston, Vermont, recontextualized an apparent "failure" in one of our spiritual eldering seminars. In 1979 she began working as a caseworker at an agency with a treatment program for sexually abused preschoolers and a residential program for pregnant teenagers. By 1986, when Teresa was the acting executive director, the agency went through an internal restructuring. She fully expected to be appointed the full-time director because of her on-the-job experience and her expertise as an authority on child abuse. However, contrary to her expectations, another person was selected for the position and she was rudely and unceremoniously dismissed from the agency.

Emotionally devastated by her dismissal, Teresa went through a period of depression, eventually gathered her forces, and worked at various social service programs until she retired in 1993. Although she was happily married with five children and nine grandchildren, she felt a profound sense of disquiet. How would she spend the remainder of her life? With this question in mind, she enrolled in one of our workshops and discovered to her unexpected delight that what she originally took to be a professional failure could be reinterpreted as an opportunity to reroute her life toward a new vocation as a spiritual elder.

"Being in the company of elders affirmed me at such a deep level that I was initiated into elderhood myself," Teresa says enthusiastically. "As I began to harvest my life, I looked for the hidden blessings within my traumatic experience, and I realized that my professional setback had actually laid the foundation for a new career as a spiritual eldering instructor. With the enlarged perspective that comes with elderhood, I saw that in some mysterious and beneficent way, life was offering me the opportunity to put my social work and therapy skills to work in helping people become elders themselves."

After the workshop, Teresa began taking courses in gerontology at the University of Vermont to prepare for her new vocation. She has designed a course called "Older Women: Surviving and Thriving," which she plans to teach through the university's department of continuing education. She also plans to lead life-review groups at senior centers and social service agencies in Williston.

"For a while, I felt embittered about my destiny, but now I'm grateful that I'm alive, that I live in a loving family, and that I've survived all the challenges of my life," Teresa reports. "Spiritual eldering has given me a renewed sense of purpose that evokes my deepest capacities to serve others. Because I've matured through adversity, I can provide the empathic understanding to people who are riddled with resentment from the past to reframe their so-called failures into successes."

From these two examples, do you see how the broad perspective of time enables us to recontextualize apparent failures? What a blessing! In our spiritual eldering workshops, I lead people through a process called "A Testimonial Dinner to the Severe Teachers." In this exercise you first list all the people who have wronged you in some way. Then, using anterior vision, you invite them back into your life, thanking and blessing them for the unexpected good that resulted from the apparent injustice inflicted on you. This marvelous alchemy converts resentment and pain into gratefulness, acceptance, and inner peace.

In elderhood, each of us needs to reinterpret the facts of our lives from the vantage point of wisdom and understanding. Bartley Crum, a respected lawyer and newspaper publisher, once told me the following story. When Abraham Lincoln was a trial lawyer circuit-riding in Illinois, he listened patiently for six days as his prominent and highly paid opponent presented arguments in a case. When his opponent had finished his presentation, Lincoln rose and said in rebuttal, "Gentlemen of the jury, the facts are facts but the conclusions are all wrong," whereupon the jurors laughed and soon delivered a verdict for Lincoln's client. The opposing counsel, a sophisticated "city slicker," could not understand how his carefully reasoned arguments had failed to convince the jury, so later he asked the rather unpretentious Lincoln whether he had bribed them.

Lincoln replied, "You fancy lawyers with your fine clothes and generous expense accounts stay in the finest hotels and hobnob with high society. I stayed in the same second-rate hotel where the judge and jurors stayed. We never talked about the case outside the courtroom, but yesterday I told them this joke over beer: 'The son of a farmer, a lad with little experience in life, runs breathlessly to his father and informs him that the barn is burning down. How do you know, the father asked? Because the hired hand lowered his pants and the maid lifted her skirts, the boy answered. Son, the father said, the facts are facts, but the conclusions are all wrong.' "

Like the lad in the story, in our immature and half-baked ways, we jumped to conclusions in our youth that we have not yet reexamined in our maturity. Elders need to investigate the facts from the farmer's perspective rather than from the son's. When you are young and vulnerable, you see the world as being either for or against you, and this view is reinforced when people do hurtful things or betray you. When you approach old age and climb the platform of broader understanding, you can reexamine and contemplate your foundational views of the world and recontextualize what happened to you from a more objective, less impulse-driven philosophical position. In this way, you do not have to remain imprisoned in your earlier conclusions about life. With Lincoln, you can say, "The facts were facts, but my conclusions were wrong."

## HEALING OUR RELATIONSHIPS

One of the most powerful tools we have to reformat the template of our being is *forgiveness*. Using time-stretching techniques, we can reach back to repair the places of great hurt—the broken promises, the acts of betrayal, the ruptures and heartaches that come with the territory of intimate relationships, marriages, and divorces. All of us have unhealed emotional scar tissue that keeps our hearts closed and armored against repeated injuries. But the price that we pay for our continued suspiciousness is enormous.

For example, when I refuse to forgive someone who has wronged me, I mobilize my own inner criminal justice system to punish the offender. As judge and jury, I sentence the person to a long prison term without parole and incarcerate him in a prison that I construct from the bricks and mortar of a hardened heart. Now as jailer and warden, I must spend as much time in prison as the prisoner I am guarding. All the energy that I put into maintaining the prison system comes out of my "energy budget." From this point of view, bearing a grudge is very "costly," because long-held feelings of anger, resentment, and fear drain my energy and imprison my vitality and creativity.

In most cases, we don't forgive because we feel that the offending party deserves to learn a lesson, and we arrogate unto ourselves the task of being the instrument of instruction. In our innermost heart, we say, "How can I forgive him if he hasn't shown regret, learned his lesson, and made restitution?" But as our experience demonstrates, the wronging party usually does not apologize. As anger etches its corrosive mark on our soul, we carry an emotional voucher wherever we go that reads, "Accounts receivable." With our vindictiveness anchored in the past, fixated on slights, "ouches," and resentments, we may wait fifty years to collect our due from ex-spouses, business partners, and family members—often to no avail. Imagine how many people and nations exist in this state, waiting to collect their unpaid bills! That's why the Bible proclaims that after seven years comes the Sabbatical Year, in which there is a remission of debt—not just financial, but emotional as well.

The issue of forgiveness has another dimension that we are normally loath to examine. We often fail to account for the role that we unconsciously play in creating dysfunctional relationships and situations. All too often, we don't ask ourselves, "How did my hidden agenda—my expectations, unacknowledged needs, and unresolved emotional conflicts—lead to my getting hurt?" We cannot forgive the offending party as long as we have not taken responsibility for our own contribution to the misunderstanding. By portraying ourselves as victims, we avoid dealing with the pain that we unconsciously inflict on ourselves. Forgiving another's deed against us requires forgiving ourselves for our complicity in the affair.

In our spiritual eldering workshops, we read and meditate on a prayer of forgiveness. Let me share a few lines of it with you: "Eternal Friend, I hereby forgive anyone who hurt, upset, or offended me; damaging my body, my property, my reputation, or people whom I love; whether done accidentally or willfully, carelessly or purposely; whether done with words, deeds, thoughts, or attitudes; whether in this lifetime or another incarnation. I forgive every person; may no one be punished because of me." When we have forgiven others, the prayer continues: "Eternal Friend, help me to be thoughtful and to resist committing acts that are evil in Your eyes. Whatever sins I have committed, please blot them out in Your abundant kindness and spare me suffering or harmful illnesses. May the words of my mouth and the meditations of my heart find acceptance before You, Eternal Friend, who protects and frees me."

Do you see how equally important it is to forgive yourself, as well as the offending party? We would like to think of ourselves as blameless innocents who mysteriously suffer the slings and arrows of outrageous fortune. But part of spiritual eldering work involves facing our shadow, the despised, rejected, unknown inner self who trips us up and sabotages us when we least expect it. By recognizing the shadow, we can forgive ourselves for our human imperfections.

Let's take the hypothetical case of a woman who complains bitterly about being ripped off by an investment scam that promised astronomical—and improbable—returns on her money. "There's no justice in the world," she cries out in pain. "I invested my life's savings and lost it all. How can I forgive this unscrupulous con man?" Without minimizing her losses or sounding self-righteously simplistic, I would suggest that this woman needs to forgive herself, as well as the scam artist. The con man sells his con because the investor who buys into it also thinks that he is gaining an advantage over the other. In this case, the investor, unaware of her shadow con man, gets taken in by her own unacknowledged crook that is projected onto the shady investment broker. Then, because of her own blindness, she rails against the world's injustice. Like this woman, we, too, sometimes fall into traps of our making, and we need to forgive our all-too-human frailties.

The following story illustrates what I mean. A man who complained that there is no justice in the world searched far and wide until he eventually found an elder venerated for his wisdom. "Why is there so little justice in the world?" he asked the sage. The old man led the seeker to a cave filled with oil lamps that emitted light of supernatural beauty. The sage explained that the flame of each candle was a life; the wick was the body; and the spirit, the power that gives life, was the oil. "When they are together and alive, they burn and give off light," the sage said.

Just at this moment, one of the candles went out. The seeker looked at the old man and said, "Did this one just die?" "Yes." Then the seeker continued, "Is my soul, my life, here also?" The sage again nodded yes, then pointed to a lamp in which the flame was not burning brightly and only a small amount of oil remained in the lamp. The sage admonished the man to meditate on the meaning of what he had seen and turned his back as if to leave. At this moment the seeker, noticing an adjacent candle that was full of oil and burning brightly, reached out to pour a little bit of oil into his own lamp. Suddenly the old man grabbed and restrained the seeker's hand and said, "And you, my son, are looking for justice?"

As this story suggests, the outer reflects the inner, and until we come to terms with our unrecognized shadow selves, our efforts to practice forgiveness will remain unfinished. It is important to release the prisoners we have kept locked up behind bars of resentment and anger. But in many cases we need to forgive ourselves for unconsciously creating the situations that have hounded us and destroyed our equanimity. Through an act of atonement, I become one with the person I have wronged or who has wronged me, and forgiveness releases both of us to lives of greater love.

## BREAKTHROUGHS IN FORGIVENESS

I will present techniques for practicing forgiveness in chapter 5, but at this point let me tell you about two people who made breakthroughs in healing past relationships at spiritual eldering seminars.

At seventy-five, Joyce Quinlan works as a senior staff member at Imago, an educational center in Cincinnati, Ohio, that sponsors workshops emphasizing the spiritual dimension of ecology. An educator, counselor, and futurist, she served as a Benedictine nun for thirty years before leaving the convent in her early fifties to explore what she calls "the wider dimensions of Christian spirituality." Since then, she has become a proponent of an emerging ecospiritual outlook that calls for the practice of Earth stewardship based on a recognition of the interdependence of humanity and the natural world.

During a seminar, she addressed the questions, "What grudges do you still carry from the past? What reconciliations still need to be completed?" She thought immediately of her deceased mother with whom she always had an uneasy, distant relationship. When her despondent, severely alcoholic father came home after church one Sunday morning at the height of the Great Depression and put a bullet through his head, she blamed her mother for the suicide. Their already tense relationship deteriorated when the headstrong teenager announced that she was entering the convent to pursue a religious vocation. This decision so infuriated her mother that she cut off all communication for an entire year. Even though she had worked extensively over the decades with therapists and spiritual directors to heal their relationship, she could muster no more than an emotionally neutral feeling for her mother.

Using guided meditation and structured writing exercises, Joyce gently unknotted the protective coverings that shrouded her heart and rediscovered feelings of love for her mother that she had denied for most of her adult life. "I genuinely miss her," she admits. "I feel a warmth and longing for her company that's altogether new to me. It's natural and normal to desire parental closeness even when we've become mature adults, but I never experienced this deep sense of closeness with my mother until I seriously took up the work of spiritual eldering. It's not only helped me forgive her, but myself as well, for my arrogant, stubborn behavior that contributed to our conflicts.

"Now I can face the future without carrying unresolved regrets about my origins," Joyce adds. "The emotional connection with my mother makes me feel more relaxed and peaceful, as if a great emptiness in my soul has been filled. And because I feel more fundamentally accepting of myself, I have a greater capacity to accept other people as they are."

Another person who has discovered the healing power of forgiveness is Jason Gaber, who is doing his eldering work not in his sixties or seventies, but at the age of thirty-six. Jason retired recently from his position as assistant executive director of the Jewish Community Center of San Francisco after learning that he has AIDS. Because of his shortened life expectancy, Jason does not have the luxury of postponing his eldering work. Like other people with life-threatening illnesses, he must compress within several years the psychological and spiritual growth that normally would extend over several decades.

"I took a spiritual eldering workshop when I was HIV positive," Jason says, "and I realized that although older people may have a few more wrinkles, the issues that they and AIDS patients confront are essentially the same. We both need to work on coming to terms with mortality, practicing forgiveness, serving as mentors, harvesting our lives, and leaving a legacy for the future. The spiritual eldering work gives my life purpose and a focus for positive action at a time when I could easily have withdrawn in bitterness and despair."

For Jason, harvesting primarily takes the form of writing articles on Jewish spirituality and his experiences as a social worker. He also participates in a program called "Putting a Face to AIDS" in which he speaks to various Jewish organizations, such as confirmation classes at local synagogues, about what it's like to have AIDS. Throughout the ups and downs of his illness, Jason finds that practicing forgiveness on a daily basis facilitates life harvesting.

"I have a little magnet on my refrigerator that says, 'Holding a grudge can be hazardous to your health,' " he relates. "Part of my eldering work involves releasing grudges and resentments, since at this stage of my life, I can't afford to hang on to them. Because medical researchers have demonstrated that our habitual thoughts and feelings affect the immune system, I continually have to cleanse myself of resentment or else run the risk of further compromising my health."

Before going to sleep at night, Jason practices the prayer of forgiveness that I mentioned earlier. Although he has been out of the closet as a gay man for fourteen years, he still deals with homophobic friends who cannot accept his sexual orientation.

"I have a woman friend who absolutely refuses to accept the fact that I'm gay," he notes. "Often before falling asleep, I visualize her in my mind's eye and send her all my good wishes in the hope that her homophobia will dissolve. I mentally affirm, 'I love you, and despite the stress in our relationship, I hold no resentment against you. I send you compassion and pray that the light of wisdom release you from the narrow picture that you hold of me.' I believe that acts of forgiveness like this strengthen my immune system and prolong my life. Without exaggerating, I can say that forgiveness is a way of life that gives me more life."

## RESURRECTING UNLIVED LIFE

Besides recontextualizing and practicing forgiveness, reconnecting with our unlived life helps carry forward the work of spiritual eldering. What do I mean by "unlived life"? In forging an adult identity, we sacrifice many parts of our ourselves on the altar of family responsibility and parental expectations. To support our families and to achieve financial and social standing in the community, we often stifle and censor the voices of our authentic self. With the dawning of elderhood, these voices begin clamoring for expression in the world.

They may urge us to break out of outmoded lifestyles and to experiment with new ones; give wing to aesthetic interests by reconnecting with the inner artist; throw caution to the wind and travel around the world or take up new sports; explore deeper forms of personal intimacy; or actualize a desire to serve humanity now that the monetary investment in a career has assumed less importance. "As we surrender less authentic appraisals of ourselves," writes Eugene Bianchi in *Aging as a Spiritual Journey*, "we can begin to draw together, from our personal depths, unfulfilled longings and untapped reservoirs of being appropriate to [our] unique self."

In elderhood we may embrace the various fragments of our unlived lives and continue growing toward self-realization. But what if we choose not to? Then our unlived lives are like ringing telephones that we refuse to answer. When I have a headache, my body is ringing the telephone: "Hey, workaholic, you're at it again. Relax and enjoy life." Instead of listening to my body's message, I "rip out the telephone" by taking double-strength pain reliever. Another example: I feel depressed because I have all but extinguished the passion for playing the violin that I traded in youth for a lucrative career as a physician. Now, in retirement, the yearning I have ignored for several decades is clamoring for readmission into my life: "Hey, practical one, it's time to dream again and to appreciate the beauty of life." So what do I do? I "rip out the telephone" by drowning myself in practical activities or in distractions, such as excessive TV watching.

If we would pick up the receiver, we would hear parts of ourselves screaming because they have been betrayed. Voices of the explorer, creative one, inner child, sensualist, and student beg for readmission in the parliament of our being, but we often turn a deaf ear. How many times have I said to the playful one inside me, "Not now, but wait for the weekend and then we'll play." But when the weekend arrives, I bring work home and betray my promise.

When ignored month after month, year after year, this betrayed voice goes underground. When the retirement years approach and the outer pressures recede, leaving me with endless days and nights of unstructured time, what begins to surface is the doleful voice of that ignored inner presence, nearly starved to death for lack of attention. If only I could hear, I would recognize its presence through the prolonged depression I feel. This voice is like a child pulling at me, pleading, "Hey, you promised to play with me and never kept your word."

How many times have you refused to follow your inner destiny, that child tugging at your sleeves with insistence? In becoming an adult, we often silence our inner voice in deference to the litany of outer voices, such as parents and teachers, the "sensible ones" who dictate how we should live and what we should value. Our task in elderhood is to give ear to that voice calling for authentic life and to complete its call to the best of our ability. Much as we get graded incompletes in college for starting but not finishing courses, we also receive incompletes from life itself, which is the metaschool in which we are all enrolled. The question that now confronts us is: How do we pass the course?

One way is to reframe our failures and frustrations, finding within them the seeds of fulfillment, albeit not in the form that we initially expected. For example, if I wanted to be a painter when I was young but became a lawyer because of practical exigencies, I might recontextualize my life by realizing how I expressed my aesthetic impulses in other mediums. Perhaps I created a meditative garden in the backyard of my home that uplifted everyone who enjoyed its serene beauty. Or perhaps as a lawyer I took on cases for artists and museums or served on the board of directors of a local artists' guild. True, in these examples I have substituted the object of my original desire with other ones, but I have given form and expression to my creative impulse, which surely must be counted among life's successes. Recontextualizing life in this manner helps reduce the pressure of unlived life through a shift in awareness that reveals hidden blessings where we thought none existed.

Not all unlived life can be lived. We cannot fulfill all our fantasies, nor should we. Recognizing that we have unlived life does not justify acting in a manner that is inappropriate to our current stage of life. To make up for our perceived losses, we can find appropriate ways to resurrect our unlived life and to express it in meaningful ways. For example, we can resume an interest in painting without the pressure to gain professional recognition. We can have conversations with people we never would have dreamed of knowing earlier in our lives. We can learn foreign languages and travel to countries that have always fascinated us. Most of all, we can loosen the constrictive belt of "should" and "ought" that we have worn all our lives, expanding the repertoire of "acceptable" behavior that we allow ourselves to enjoy.

## A FUTURE OF EXPANDED POTENTIAL

So now we have looked at the preliminary work in spiritual eldering. We have taken the first steps in befriending thanatos, the agent of our completed self and the energy that fuels life completion. We also have assembled the jigsaw puzzle called life review, which is made of three interconnected parts: recontextualizing, forgiving, and reclaiming unlived life. Together they help us reshape the template that organizes our experiences and gives our life its unique character, charm, and meaning.

Most of us have received a number of "hot potatoes" from the parents, educators, religious teachers, and peers who shaped our original template. We have received an inheritance of judgments, fears, and limitations that has severely restricted our freedom. Part of spiritual eldering involves examining the template, changing its form and contents, then healing relationships with parents (living or deceased), children, spouses, ex-spouses, and business associates. This work of inner repair also expands the boundaries of our self and ensures a future of expanded potential.

In its deepest sense, spiritual eldering enables us to complete our lives triumphantly. As our spiritual vision widens, we perceive our interconnectedness with the Earth and all of nature. Relieved of the anxiety that comes from perceiving ourselves as separate, isolated individuals, we are supported by life, rooted in an organic process of which we are integral parts. From this perspective of global awareness, we release feelings of failure and depression. We say gratefully, "I have done my job. I have participated in the grand experiment of life, and I have made a necessary and important contribution to the whole." What a joyous experience! What a fitting conclusion to a life! Accepting the inevitable rightness of how events unfolded, we marvel at the living work of art we have become as the Spirit completes its work through us.

# Chapter 5

# *Tools for Harvesting Life*

While we wrestle with many challenging issues in later life, success in spiritual eldering ultimately depends on answering one simple but potentially life-changing question. Rabbi Zusya of Hanipol, a great Hasidic master, posed that question shortly before his death. "In the coming world, they will not ask me, 'Why were you not like Moses?' They will ask me, 'Why were you not what you, Zusya, could have been?' "

In the same way, each of us must grapple with the question, "Why was I not what I could have been?" If we compare our lives to an unpolluted stream, then in the normal course of living, the waters of self get muddied with many foreign substances. The inner work of spiritual eldering helps precipitate out many of the contaminants, enabling us to return to the clarity of our true natures. We become individuated, living not as Moses, the Buddha, Jesus, or Mohammed, but as the precious, unique, nonrepeatable experiments of the universe that we are.

Let me tell you about a group of people who in pursuit of this goal gathered for a five-day seminar, "From Age-ing to Sage-ing," in the summer of 1992. It took place at Omega Institute, a retreat center in Rhinebeck, New York, that provides the woodland beauty and seclusion that are ideal for doing inner work. The group consisted largely of elders, although we had participants in midlife and young adulthood. People came from a broad spectrum of backgrounds and professions, including social workers, therapists, financial planners, retirement counselors, educators, engineers, and homemakers.

In Omega's peaceful, rural setting, we created an atmosphere of spiritual intimacy, a trusting, accepting environment in which we could tell our stories to each other and share our dreams. We affirmed the success of aging; explored the origins of our diminished images of old age; and undertook a joyous life review, with an eye toward transforming feelings of resentment into gratefulness and serenity.

By week's end, through the gentle alchemy of community building, several people made dramatic breakthroughs and were initiated into the state of elderhood. Others, in less dramatic fashion, received nourishment for their continued journeys. Still others, trapped in the "box" of no future and no past, wrestled with issues of mortality and social uselessness. These people took significant steps in extricating themselves from their painful state of paralysis.

A case in point is Helen Hopkins, whose spirit was suffocating in a senior retirement community in Ontario, Canada. Helen had retired nine years earlier after serving as security manager for a large chain of Canadian department stores. When this active, outspoken woman moved into an institution having more than three hundred people, she quickly learned about the loneliness, depression, and segregation that elders are forced to endure.

"Playing bingo and cards with your peers is no equation for personal happiness," Helen lamented. "People live in anxiety and depression in retirement centers, avoiding all mention of death, often hiding behind their apartment doors in secrecy and fear. After years of living in this deadening way, I decided to sit quietly, read my books, and wait to die, like everyone else in the building. When my daughter dragged me to this workshop, I had a jolt of recognition: 'My God, that's me in the box, without a future, just feeling sorry for myself about getting older.' I decided that I had to get out of the box and get on with my life."

Because she was taking her first growth seminar at age seventy, Helen participated in the gentle interpersonal exercises with understandable caution. For ice-breakers, people sat with partners and shared memories about their first encounters with aging. Later they talked about their first awareness of sickness and death. In the workshop's nonjudgmental, supportive atmosphere, Helen felt safe and loved enough to begin opening up to complete strangers. Soon she was making friends with them as her emotional armoring melted and fell by the wayside. The more she opened up, the more people encouraged her to value not only her past achievements, but her potential for growth in the present and the future.

One morning Helen was so touched by the unaccustomed encouragement she was receiving that she left the meeting room and went to a nearby garden where she broke down crying. Despite all attempts to control "making a fool" of herself, her tears kept watering the earth with years of withheld anger, along with feelings of powerlessness and self-invalidation. When finally her tears had ceased, she felt lighter, happier—and more alive. Returning to the room, she carried herself with an awakening sense of dignity and pride.

"Being here has opened a new window on the world for me," Helen later shared enthusiastically with the group. "After years of living in a graveyard, I'm discovering just how alive I am! When something happens now that touches my soul, I don't just put a gag over my mouth and politely squelch my feelings; I jump up and respond. And I see quite clearly that I have to be around people who are alive.

"When I return home, I'm going to share my discoveries about spiritual eldering with members of my senior club. I may go back to school to complete my education or organize elders in local retirement centers to write letters to the government protesting violence on television. Whatever I do, I can never use 'I'm too old' as an excuse for remaining stuck in fear and inertia."

## FOURFOLD MODEL OF THE SELF

Obviously, we cannot extricate ourselves from the "box" of restricted living in a five-day workshop. But we can start. The question is, "Where do we start?" The Kabbalah provides a useful conceptual model to answer this question. Like other holistic systems, it teaches that we express ourselves on four levels: the physical, emotional, mental, and spiritual. Kabbalists say that the healthy person strives to integrate all four levels of his being. Carl Jung speaks of this same quaternity when he attributes four functions to human personality: sensation, feeling, intellect, and intuition. To restore ourselves to wholeness, therefore, we must clarify the outstanding issues of each level and weave the four strands of our being into a harmoniously functioning unity.

We begin on the physical level with exercises that relax the body and make it more flexible and energetic. On the emotional level, we engage in life review, reframing past mistakes and betrayals. On the mental level, we do our philosophic homework, addressing life's perennial questions, such as "What is the meaning of my life?" and "What is my relationship to God?" On the spiritual level, we acquire contemplative skills to develop the extended consciousness from which harvesting can proceed. Let's look at each of these four levels.

Work on the physical level starts with the recognition that by exercising and practicing certain mind-body disciplines, we can retard and in some cases reverse the so-called inevitable declines of aging. We age largely because of habitual attitudes of body and mind that weigh us down with undischarged stress. Many of the chronic, degenerative diseases of old age, such as heart disease, cancer, and arthritis, are in part lifestyle-related. They result from repeated stress reactions to chronic tensions, rather than from old age itself. People suffer more from the negative effects of a sedentary lifestyle, poor dietary habits, and maladaptive ways of handling stress than from the aging process.

Having a sedentary lifestyle, for example, not only raises stress levels, but accelerates physical deterioration. As Jean Houston points out, lack of physical activity keeps our muscles overcontracted, deforms skeletal alignment, inhibits the movement of joints, and reduces blood flow to the brain. Thankfully, we can still educate the body for greater awareness and improved use. As we discharge stress, breathe more deeply, and reorganize muscle patterns, we can lift body and mind to new levels of enhanced performance.

In spiritual eldering work, we consider the reduced level of physical health and vitality normally associated with elders as the result of cultural programming. Because we expect to be socially useless after a certain age, our expectation triggers physical changes in the body that lead to reduced health and vigor, as Deepak Chopra points out in *Ageless Body, Timeless Mind.* We can, however, change our expectation of gradual breakdown by reprogramming our beliefs about old age to create a more vital, healthful experience.

In his book, Chopra cites a seminal study by psychologist Ellen Langer at Harvard University that demonstrates how aging can be reversed through changes in self-perception. During a week's retreat at a country resort, the subjects of the study, who were seventy-five or older and in good health, were encouraged to think, look, act, and speak as if they were twenty years younger. Participants played music that was twenty years old; wore ID photos from that era; referred to their wives and children as if they were twenty years younger; and considered their careers to be in full swing. The results of this "play-acting" were remarkable, reports Chopra. Compared to the control group (those who acted their age), members of the make-believe group improved in memory and manual dexterity and became more active and self-sufficient. Impartial judges who studied before and after photographs of the men observed that their faces looked on the average three years younger. What's more, participants reported that stiff joints were more flexible, posture began to straighten, and muscle strength improved, along with hearing and vision.

"Professor Langer's study was a landmark in proving that so-called irreversible signs of aging could be reversed using psychological intervention," writes Chopra. "By increasing someone's awareness, bringing it into a new focus and breaking out of old patterns, you can alter aging."

In general, our negative expectations make us age faster than nature intended. For example, popular health books erroneously point out that our aerobic capacity decreases by 10 percent per decade after age 30, along with similar losses in strength, muscle mass, and lung capacity. But these statistics come from population studies of largely sedentary people. Our so-called physical decline stems not from age, but simply from lack of exercise.

Exercise physiologists used to assume that older people cannot build muscle strength or muscle mass after age fifty-five. But a study by Dr. William Evans, a researcher at Tufts University, demonstrated that with twelve weeks of strength training, a group of men aged sixty to seventy-two increased muscle strength two- to threefold and muscle mass by 10 to 15 percent. In an eight-week study of eighty-seven- to ninety-six-year-old women confined to a nursing home, subjects tripled their muscle strength and increased muscle mass by 10 percent. "You're never too old to exercise," Evans and his partner, Irwin Rosenberg, write in *Biomarkers*. "To the contrary, you're too old *not* to exercise.... Exercise is the key to a healthy and rewarding old age."

Fortunately, there's a whole menu of choices for reanimating our bodies and minds. When performed regularly, aerobic exercise, such as walking, jogging, swimming, and bicycling, maintains cardiovascular fitness. Massage, which does wonders for older adults who often experience touch deficits, relaxes the body and increases our sense of trust and self-acceptance. Yoga and T'ai Chi increase flexibility, while deep-breathing exercises cultivate calmness and mental alertness. The Feldenkrais method, a system of movement reeducation, helps repattern the habitual ways that the brain responds to input from the nervous system, while reducing chronic physical and emotional tension lodged in the body.

At our workshops, we practice gentle stretching exercises and massage to promote flexibility and relaxation. Shunning heroics, we are not out to break fitness records or strain the body beyond its proper limits. We exercise as sages in training, performing our regimens in a relaxed, focused, and sensible way to restore the body to limberness and vitality. No matter what our age or physical conditions, exercise not only helps us live with greater ease and grace in our bodies. It also gives us more energy for carrying out the work of spiritual eldering.

On the physical level, then, respect and reverence for the body serve as the foundation for our spiritual journeys. In our workshops, we teach a prayer that expresses the gratitude we feel for the exquisite service performed by our bodies each day. When waking in the morning, we make a mental survey of the body, blessing and giving thanks to our dear old friends: the limbs; the organs of perception, such as eyes and ears; the organs of digestion and elimination, such as the kidneys and bladder; the heart and brain; and the pulse. We end the prayer by saying, "Thank you, body, vehicle of my spirit, for taking me for a wonderful ride one more day." Such a prayerful and grateful attitude goes a long way in enlisting the body's support in eldering work.

## ENCOUNTERING OUR MORTALITY

When we move to the emotional level of our work, two tasks immediately confront us: coming to terms with our mortality and recontextualizing our past as part of life review. Let's begin with our deeply ingrained habit of denying the presence of death.

According to our magical thinking, we mistakenly believe that contemplating death will hasten its arrival. So we banish thanatos, the harvester turned bogeyman, to the unconscious, splitting the bipolar energy of life-death into antagonists. We take sides with the life polarity in a futile attempt to banish death. But as we saw in the last chapter, this strategy only serves to constrict consciousness, robbing us of being present for life harvesting. Hence a major task in spiritual eldering involves acknowledging our fear of dying and looking squarely at the reality of our physical demise.

We do this on a social level by getting our affairs in order legally and financially. As part of our estate planning, we draw up a will. To avoid burdening our loved ones with grief at the time of our death, we make plans for our funeral or memorial service. We also sign a living will, a document ensuring that no heroic measures be taken to extend our lives if we are diagnosed as being terminal and death is imminent. Because a living will is often not legally binding, we also sign a durable power of attorney, which appoints a person to make medical and financial choices for us in case we are comatose or mentally incapacitated. I myself keep these and other such documents in what I call a "God Forbid Book," which is updated every few years to reflect changes in legal and financial status.

Next, as we work on the psychological level, we rehearse our own physical deaths in an attempt to desensitize our automatic fear reactions. This work, which on first sight appears morbid, actually affirms life. It accomplishes this miracle by converting the energy involved in repressing death into greater awareness and vitality for living. By contemplating your *deathstyle*, writes consciousness researcher John White in *A Practical Guide to Death & Dying*, "you automatically enhance your *lifestyle*—not in a material sense, of course, but in the richness and joy with which you experience each passing moment, each relationship, each situation and circumstance, day by day."

In dealing with our fear of death, we also need to gain philosophic insight as to where death figures in the scheme of things. Does it bring consciousness to an end? Does it deliver us to another dimension where consciousness continues? Well-meaning proponents of the world's religions promise us salvation in the afterlife, but with the existential reality of our approaching end in sight, we cannot merely give assent to the testimony of others. We must confront our anxiety and clarify for ourselves whether going through the narrow gate leads to the continuity of life or its complete cessation. We need to acquire the depth of mind that can reconcile our desire for permanence with the reality of a physical universe whose only constant appears to be ceaseless change. How can we find something changeless when our senses reveal that everything at the subatomic and macrocosmic level is in flux? It takes spiritual insight to perceive that within and beyond this universe of ceaseless transformation there exists something permanent that remains untouched by the passage of time. By successfully wrestling with the issue of change and discovering a timeless dimension within their own souls, many people become serene as they approach the portals of their physical dissolution.

To become more accepting of our mortality, we do a number of exercises in our workshops. We sit with partners and explore the origins of our ideas about death by responding to questions such as "When did you first encounter death?" and "What do you most fear about dying?" We deepen our familiarity with death by writing our own obituaries. We also visualize and write deathbed scenarios, orchestrating our final moments according to our own deep sense of sacredness.

In scripting our last moments on earth, we plan for the music we wish to hear; the poems, prayers, or sacred texts that we want recited; the physical surroundings that make us feel most comfortable; and the special people we want present. How wonderful to have the gentle presence of good friends to hold your hand and wish you Godspeed in this last and greatest adventure of a lifetime. (In my case, I would like a friend to keep me focused while I listen to Albinoni's Adagio for Organ and Strings while receiving my last Feldenkrais treatment to gently ease me out of my body.) Rehearsing our deathbed scenarios in this way does more than strip the experience of its terror. It gives us the expectation of approaching our physical end with the same exalted feeling as Richard Strauss's moving tone poem *Death and Transfiguration*. In scripting a beautiful death, we nurture the expectation that we, too, will be transfigured in our final moments.

Contrary to expectations, dealing with death in this way does not depress or mortify people. It enlivens them. However, because we normally put a lid on thanatos, most of us lose connection with this source of creative vitality and we shrivel up. And as workshop participant Pam Mayer found out, we also lose touch with the voice of our own authenticity.

Pam, a highly intuitive woman with a rich inner life, is an adult educator and hospice counselor living in Hanover, New Hampshire. She developed colon cancer in 1987, when she was sixty-seven years old. During the course of her treatment, she realized that cancer was like a messenger from her inner Self, urging her to speak with the authority of her own voice. As oncologist Carl Simonton points out, cancer patients often suffer from the lifelong habit of pleasing others, rather than living their own authentic lives. They suppress their own feelings and values to meet other people's expectations. Pam's illness made her realize how often she said yes when she needed to say no. Her deep encounter with death liberated her from this form of self-betrayal.

"The cancer has not returned in years, but I never want it to leave entirely," Pam admits. "I want it to sit on my left shoulder for the remainder of my life, because the encounter with death gives me the authority to claim my own voice and sing my own song. Elderhood, too, because of its proximity to death and its emphasis on greater individuality, releases me from the fear of pleasing others and gives me permission to be my authentic self. Encountering death has initiated me into states of inner freedom I could scarcely imagine when I was younger.

"I may encounter physical diminishment as I age," Pam continues, "but never again will I experience inner, psychic diminishment. Now that I'm an elder, I'm committed to maintaining a steadfast loyalty to the Self that transcends all outer expectations. I wasted a lot of my life attempting to be like everyone else. Elderhood gives me permission to delight in my uniqueness. I've discovered that as we age, we don't become more like others; we become more like ourselves."

## REPAIRING OUR LIVES

Now that we have looked death in the face and have taken away some of its sting, let's journey into the past for the noble work of life repair. We generally avoid this journey because we come face-to-face with a chorus of self-recriminating voices that tempt us to reject ourselves and to disparage our achievements. They torture us with accusations, such as "If only I had done otherwise" or "Why didn't I listen to reason?" We heap scorn on ourselves using language usually reserved for our vilest enemies. Often we preface our insults with this opening statement: "What a stupid choice I made!" That choice—whatever its outcome—festers in the psyche as an unresolved trauma.

The art of life repair enables us to heal our psychic bruises by recontextualizing our perceived failures into successes. We do not return to previously incompleted places to dismiss them or explain them away intellectually. We return to relive and reinterpret them as we reassure, bless, hold, and forgive ourselves. By finding the hidden meanings or lessons within our more difficult experiences, we can drop our huge baggage of complaints, the ceaseless whining and fault finding that weigh us down, so we can live with more serenity of spirit.

Before launching into life review, let's clarify an essential point that can help us avoid sabotaging our efforts from the very beginning. In harvesting, we need to focus not only on *etiology*, the causes or origins of our problems, but on *teleology*, the overall purpose or design of our lives. To grow into elderhood, we cannot continue thinking of ourselves as victims of early-life trauma or parental conflicts. We cannot in good faith take refuge in the thought, "I'm solely conditioned by my origins, and everybody else is responsible for what I've become." The time for playing the blame game has long since past. As Abraham Lincoln is reputed to have said, "The face you have up to age thirty-five is the one you are born with; after thirty-five, it's the face you have made."

When you focus on etiology, you remain stuck in the blame game by marshaling evidence of childhood deprivations. But when you focus on teleology, you adopt a more objective, panoramic perspective that asks the question, "What does the acorn have in mind to help it become the oak tree?" In other words, beneath the limited goals that we strive for on the surface of life, what deeper intention or purpose is laboring to be fulfilled through the unfolding pattern of our destiny?

According to Carl Jung, as we individuate and come increasingly in contact with the inner Self, we discover that our ego is not the sole master in the house of personality. Another power, operating sometimes independently of our conscious intentions, may be steering us to a destination of its choice. Obviously, the surface and deep selves don't always operate adversarily. But if you admit that your life has a goal toward which it's moving inexorably, you might judge differently the outcome of events that once seemed tragic, disillusioning, or painful. Perhaps an invisible force was orchestrating events at life's momentous turning points called *synchronicities*, those intersections when inner necessity and destiny conspired to produce results that reverberate four or five decades later.

In harvesting, therefore, try to suspend the normal ways in which you evaluate success or failure. Search for the deeper, sometimes more elusive patterns that may be operating beneath the surface of everyday events. This panoramic perspective makes it easier to reframe sorrowful, disappointing experiences into occasions for deep learning.

To recontextualize the past, consider your memory to be a filing cabinet marked "plus" and "minus" for the pleasant and not so pleasant incidents. Because the minus ones repel us with their reinforced phobias, most of us don't want to reopen the negative files. Even though we realize intellectually that the aches and pains of a lifetime can be converted into unforeseen good, we tremble with anxiety and hold ourselves back. But what is anxiety? It's the pain that we give ourselves whenever we trespass into emotionally dangerous territory. When we feel anxious, we often take refuge in distracting activities to protect ourselves from painful memories. When we have the determination to overcome the anxiety by remaining present to the pain of past experiences, we discover to our surprise that the pain is eminently workable. By befriending it, we can transform our pain into an ally whose energy can be used for our continued growth.

When we engage in life repair, therefore, we open old files, relive them, recontextualize them for deeper meaning, and then refile them in the "plus" files, free from their negative emotional valences. In our spiritual eldering workshops, we use many techniques to open old files. We prime the pump of memory by making lifetime maps to chart the ups and downs of our relationships and careers. We do journal writing to confront broken beliefs and to mend and replace them with more mature ones. We do forgiveness exercises, a form of moral housecleaning that enables us to harvest the unexpected benefits from the woundings and betrayals enacted by friends, spouses, lovers, children, and colleagues.

In the previous chapter, I mentioned a powerful reframing exercise, called "A Testimonial Dinner to the Severe Teachers." Using the broad perspective of time, you can use this exercise to heal hurtful situations of the past. Divide a piece of paper into three columns. In the first column, make a list of the people who have wronged you; in the second column, describe the apparent injustice that was inflicted on you; and in the last column, explore how it has benefited you in unforeseen ways. To each of the offending parties, say, "I understand now that you did me a great deal of good by your actions when you did ______ for which I want to thank you. I understand now that it was difficult for you, and it was difficult for me, too. But now I forgive you and I am grateful for your contribution to my life." Though deceptively simple, this practice can help release old debts and create a surplus of positive feelings to propel you toward a desirable future.

I don't want to give the impression that forgiving people who have wounded us is easy work, however. It takes up the lion's share of time and energy in life repair. Forgiveness work challenges us with the evolutionary task of ennobling our sufferings, transmuting tragedy and sorrow into understanding and the capacity to love. Because this doesn't come easily, we need to train ourselves in the dynamics of forgiveness. I recommend starting with less challenging situations, then gradually moving up to more demanding ones. Don't begin with Lex Luthor, Superman's archenemy. First, disentangle yourself from smaller resentments. Then, with practice, you will be prepared to handle those intractable relationships that fester like sores beneath the surface of consciousness.

Say, for example, that you carry a grudge against a colleague at work for an offhanded comment he made about you years ago. To release this slight ripple of resentment, sit quietly and take a few deep breaths to center yourself. Place yourself in the other person's shoes for a moment and check out whether there was a misunderstanding in communication. Then ask yourself, "What good will it do to continue being angry with this person?"

As you move your awareness back and forth between the two parties, almost like a dance, the difference between "you" and "me" configures into a third creation, a "you-me." Now a flip in consciousness can take place in which the "you" becomes "me," and vice versa. From this enlarged perspective, real forgiveness can occur. As in the biblical story of Jacob wrestling with the angel, your adversary is in reality a sparring partner with whom you come to clarity about unknown aspects of your nature. In the encounter, as you transform anger into understanding and compassion, you and your adversary can step freely into the future, unencumbered by the baggage of the past.

Martha Kate Miller, who participated in another of our spiritual eldering workshops, learned how a modest, undramatic act of forgiveness has the power to transform an adversary into a friend. Martha is a seventy-year-old faculty member at the Guild for Spiritual Guidance, a training center in Rye, New York, that provides the theological background and counseling skills for people to become spiritual directors. Unlike gurus who lay down a set of undisputed truths and practices, spiritual directors function as trusted teachers, guides, and friends who through long-term, one-on-one relationships patiently midwife their students in discovering their own authentic religious paths and vocations. Working from her home in Rowayton, Connecticut, Martha, who has a background in theology, music, and drama, brings a wealth of practical experience and contemplative expertise to her work.

In considering a relationship that needed mending, Martha remembered an intimidating woman she had known forty years ago when her husband served as a hospital administrator in the Southwest. The woman, who was on the hospital's board of directors, so unnerved her that she adopted a policy of being "scrupulously polite" but emotionally distant to protect herself from her antagonist's disapproving demeanor. After five years of keeping this woman at arm's length, Martha and her family moved to another region of the country. As the years rolled by, however, for some strange reason she kept up the habit of exchanging Christmas cards with her every year.

"I worked on forgiving this woman at the workshop, and several months later, when I was happily filling out Christmas cards, I came to her name on the list," Martha recalled. "I felt this tightening in my stomach, as though I were in the eighth grade with the principal frowning at me. I was about to write my usual 'Hope you have a pleasant year' when I remembered the forgiveness exercises and decided to risk writing her a warm, heartfelt greeting. When her card arrived sometime later, this former 'cold fish' was effusive in expressing her gratitude. Her husband was terminally ill, and my good wishes had given her an emotional boost when it was sincerely needed.

"This is the most human contact we've had in forty years!" Martha exclaimed. "Forgiving her required so little effort on my part, just a slight shift of consciousness and the willingness to risk opening my heart to her. If we practiced such small acts of forgiveness on a daily basis, we would avoid accumulating the huge backlog of resentment that requires us to do remedial work to clear and balance our emotional accounts. In this way, forgiveness would become a natural part of our lifestyle, rather than the unnatural, self-conscious activity it now seems to be because of its relative rarity in our lives."

Many people in our spiritual eldering workshops make forgiveness an integral part of their daily lives through journal work. (We also use journaling for a number of other tasks, including tracking our life history, befriending unknown parts of the personality, and exploring dreams.) Because it's an excellent tool for self-awareness, we use journal work when seeking reconciliation with people who have hurt us or whom we have hurt. Writing helps dismantle the heart's stubborn fortifications so that we can forgive ourselves, others—and in some cases even God. As Rabbi Harold Kushner asks in *When Bad Things Happen to Good People*, "Are you capable of forgiving and loving God even when you have found out that He is not perfect, even when He has let you down and disappointed you by permitting bad luck and sickness and cruelty in His world, and permitting some of those things to happen to you?" As this statement suggests, sometimes we need to do theological as well as interpersonal forgiveness in healing our personal woundedness.

A marvelous tool for practicing forgiveness is the journal technique called "unsent letters." To deal with a grievance, we write a letter in which we vent our deepest feelings, without sending the letter to the offending party. According to psychologist Kathleen Adams, author of *Journal to the Self*, this strategy gives us permission to write without censorship, risk, or fear of hurting others. "Unsent letters are wonderful for expressing deep emotion, such as anger or grief," she writes. "They are also tools of choice for gaining closure and insight. And they are an effective way of communicating your opinions, deepest feelings, hostilities, resentments, affections, or controversial points of view in a safe, nonthreatening atmosphere."

The forgiveness exercises that I have just described are nothing new. We have scriptural precedent for them in Jesus' words: "And forgive us our trespasses as we forgive those who have trespassed against us." All the world's spiritual traditions provide psychotechnologies for melting hardness of heart into compassion. But if you are uncomfortable with traditional spiritual paths, you can use the techniques of humanistic psychology. You can write out affirmations like the following: "I completely release ______ from all grudges of the past. We are both free to have a happier relationship."

## HEALING A PAINFUL MEMORY

Besides forgiveness work, life review involves returning to the "ouch" spots in our memory files and mending our personal history. Taking advantage of the plastic, stretchable nature of time, we return in full consciousness to the scene of actions we now consider unwise from the vantage point of our greater maturity. Still, we thank and applaud our younger self for the unexpected growth that resulted from the seemingly unenlightened decisions we made at the time.

In one exercise, for example, after getting quiet and relaxed, you return to a time of emotional crisis in which you felt alone, misunderstood, unconsoled, and in pain. Reaching back with warmth and assurance from the present, you let your elder self hold your unhealed younger self, trembling with anxiety. Then your elder self says with great compassion, "I bring you a message from your future. You're going to make it. The pain didn't last forever. You took care of things; you managed. You acted nobly and with courage. In God's economy, everything worked out well. There were great lessons involved in your choice, and you learned them with elegance." As the elder self embraces his younger counterpart, the cramp around the pain relaxes. Now you can reach into the pain, hugging, consoling, and finally blessing it. In this way, you move a painful memory from the "minus" to the "plus" side of your memory files.

While work like this can be done alone, we can facilitate the process by being in the company of spiritual intimates who love and accept us in our totality. Because repairing our lives is not public relations work, we need to be around people who accept us with our warts, as well as our beauty marks. Essentially, we are getting rid of the calluses that have formed around the heart. This means releasing the fears, anxieties, and defenses that we have constructed around the vulnerable inner core that spiritual traditions call the Real Self. By removing these calluses, a process the Bible calls "the circumcision of the heart," we become sensitive and innocent again. But the process of recontextualization does not preclude feeling grief over our failures. Life repair doesn't eliminate our pain; it helps us come to terms with it. Entering and owning our pain eventually frees us of it.

When we cut ourselves off from the pain of the past, it takes root in the unconscious where it saps life energy and causes depression. The pain lodges itself in the musculature; it affects memory and perception; and it reduces our ability to respond to people and events in the present with spontaneity and aliveness. We mistakenly think that by keeping our aches and pains at a distance, we will minimize our suffering in old age. But such an attitude actually increases the likelihood of our suffering because whatever we resist increases its power over us.

Gestalt psychologists talk about the paradoxical law of change, which states that we cannot alter a condition, no matter how distressing, until we first totally accept it. We get the same notion in fairy tales when the beautiful princess resists the ugly toad, then finally kisses him, whereupon he changes into a handsome prince. What we run from clings to us like a second skin. But when we stop running and turn around to face our adversary, it transforms itself into an ally that ennobles us. In the same way, if we meet our pains with courage and faith, we will emerge on the other side, with a renewed commitment to life. No longer suppressing our unlived life, we will find creative ways of expressing it.

To illustrate my point, let's look at how a workshop participant, Ephraim Miller, not only recontextualized his life, but made a radical breakthrough into spiritual elderhood. Ephraim is currently a financial consultant living in Evanston, Illinois. When this gentle, multitalented man came to the workshop, he was not only contemplating retirement, but trying to make sense of the tortuous twisting and turnings of his destiny.

In his varied career, Ephraim has served as a chemist, technical writer, editor, and stockbroker. Yet since his youth, he has felt "called" to pursue his deeper spiritual interests. As a young man, he responded to that call by studying Vedanta for ten years with Swami Akhilananda, eventually editing a posthumous collection of his Indian teacher's essays. Years later, after marrying and having three children, the Spirit suddenly seized him. Ephraim left his technical writing job of fifteen years to study comparative religion at a Quaker liberal arts college in the Midwest, then at the University of Chicago where he received academic grants to pursue his studies. Later, when his children had reached college age, he went to work with Merrill Lynch as a money manager. During this period, he and his wife were divorced, and he remarried a number of years later.

"In the workshop, I've been feeling the pain of my incomplete spiritual vocation clamoring for expression," Ephraim explained to me over lunch one day. "I've experienced so much in my life. I've had multiple careers; I've cared for parents in a nursing home; I've experienced parenthood, deaths, divorce, as well as different religious paths. When I view the larger pattern of my life, I see that all this experience was necessary to bring to fruition seeds of wisdom that were planted decades ago.

"Before coming here," he said tearfully, "I planned to retire in five years, pursue my musical and scholarly interests, then move into a retirement home when I grew more infirm. But in the past few days, I've been reborn and initiated into elderhood through reconnecting with the pain of my unlived life. Eldering work feels like a homecoming, a chance to resume the spiritual vocation that got interrupted when I was younger because of the practical necessities of family and career. Now I can go boldly into the future, not with small dreams, but with great ones. I may become a minister in some denomination or a therapist, but whatever I do, I know that spiritual eldering will figure prominently in my plans."

## THE PHILOSOPHIC HOMEWORK

Once we have taken steps to heal our emotional "ouch" spots, we can proceed with greater clarity in doing our philosophic homework. Part of an elder's work, according to gerontologist Barry Barkan, is "to synthesize wisdom from long life experience." Having journeyed up the mountain of advanced age, elders have experienced successes and failures, moments of triumph and exaltation, as well as times of despair and disillusionment. Contemplating the immense distance we have covered and the mysterious unknown that looms before us, we naturally ask ourselves, "What has it all meant? Where did I come from and what is my next destination?"

Elders are equipped to deal with these questions, because the long perspective of time gives them an objectivity and calm curiosity that are unavailable in youth, says Robert de Ropp in *Man Against Aging*.

"The contemplation of an individual life against the background of time brings inevitably deeper insights into the nature of being and becoming," he writes. "How vast a time passed by before I existed and how vast a time will be after I cease to exist! But what is I? What is this self whose days and adventures are drawing to a close? An isolated spark briefly lit, destined to fade forever into darkness? A fragment of a greater consciousness that will return again to the place from which it came? A spirit temporarily imprisoned in flesh? A traveler far from his true home and now about to return?"

As you can infer from this passage, contemplating life's transcendent issues involves asking questions, rather than taking refuge in conclusions. It is not a shallow, academic exercise, but a passionate inquiry, having an urgency born of our encounter with life and our proximity to death. Even if we have addressed some of these questions when we were younger, we can still re-vision our lives from a higher perspective and formulate a living philosophy stamped with the mark of our individuality.

Do you remember studying Philosophy 101 in college? Most likely, your teacher introduced you to the answers that various philosophers came up with, rather than the questions that prompted their inquiries. I think that's pedagogically backward. Far more than answers, we need questions to open the floodgates of our own creative intelligence. They enable us to breathe fresh life into the perennial issues humanity has wrestled with since time immemorial. The Torah may be the answer for Jews, just as the New Testament may be the answer for Christians, but as Abraham Joshua Heschel points out, most people have forgotten what the original questions were.

In our spiritual eldering workshops, therefore, I ask people to raise a number of major philosophical questions. Why are we here? What is our purpose? What is our place in the universe? What do we believe about God, the soul, the afterlife, and reincarnation? Through journal writing, discussions, and contemplative work, people wrestle with these transcendent questions.

For some people, death releases the soul to eternal life in the world to come. For others, the soul reincarnates lifetime after lifetime until it attains moral and spiritual perfection and need not incarnate again. Those unhappy with these otherworldly religious doctrines may view themselves as brain cells of Gaia, the living planet Earth. As integral parts of the greater planetary body, they release their consciousness at death into the global brain and in this way achieve a form of self-transcendence. Others of a more materialistic nature may view death as the cessation of consciousness brought about by the dissolution of the body and brain.

Because there is such a broad range of possible answers to these philosophical questions, we must not impose upon others our specific answers. Each of us must wrestle with these issues and formulate our own positions. The practice of *discursive meditation* can greatly help us in this endeavor. Unlike the more well-known forms of meditation such as chanting mantras and watching the breath, discursive meditation involves directing the mind along a definite conceptual track, enabling us to reflect on and deeply explore a subject in all its depth.

"The working of our minds normally proceeds spontaneously under the action of stimuli and interests of various kinds, and in a disorganized way," writes psychiatrist Roberto Assagioli in *The Act of Will*. "The mind operates independently of the will, and often in opposition to it. . . . Much of our ordinary mental activity, then, does not merit the term 'thought.' It is only when a dominating interest backed by a firm and decided will is able to hold the mind concentrated on an idea or task that it really 'thinks' and we can say that it reflects, it meditates."

To practice discursive meditation, says Assagioli, we must concentrate the mind on a chosen topic, become aware when the mind wanders away, then gently but firmly draw it back to the subject at hand. This task requires persistence, a kind of mental tenacity that probes deeply into a subject. For example, students of spiritual eldering might address the question, "By what definitions of morality have I lived?" By holding discourse with their own soul, they can examine whether they expressed their higher values (such as honesty, justice, compassion, and forgiveness) in the circumstances of their everyday lives. Have they applied their higher values selectively—when it was convenient, for example—or have they maintained them even in the face of public censure? What happened when they consulted their higher values and acted on them, and what happened when they didn't? Which course of action has brought them greater satisfaction and inner peace?

As Assagioli points out, discursive meditation is not simply a passive process of observation, like making an inventory of facts. "It aims at *understanding*, *interpretation*, and *evaluation* of what we discover in ourselves," he writes. We can use this method for dealing with the principal philosophic issues, such as discovering our purpose and clarifying our belief about the continuity of life. Clearly, this kind of inner work requires commitment on our part. Clarifying the ultimate values of our life calls for moral and ethical honesty, a willingness to acknowledge our shortcomings, and a degree of concentration that keeps us from being derailed by mental distractions. Though by no means easy, this kind of disciplined effort is so worthwhile. Many people tell me that grappling with the philosophic homework leads to a growing sense of inner peace and increased harmony in their relationships. Some speak glowingly of the inner freedom they experience when identity and self-worth are unhooked from the obsessive need to be economically productive.

"In elderhood, we can derive our identity more from the level of being, rather than doing," says workshop participant David Mayer, Pam's husband and a retired engineer and city planner.

"As we become more contemplative, we rely less on finding self-worth through our performance in the work world. Gradually, we find another dimension opening up in which our identity comes not from what we do, but from what we are.

"I think that the shift from doing to being is the heart of eldering," he continues. "It means minimizing the pull of the personal ego and becoming more transparent to the workings of Spirit. It's a constant learning experience, and I'm devoting my time in elderhood to moving in this direction. I'm not sure that we ever arrive at the goal, but living a contemplative life helps me move toward it day by day."

## THE VARIETY OF MEDITATIVE EXPERIENCE

Besides wrestling with the philosophic homework, we must proceed to the spiritual level of work and the practice of what we traditionally think of as meditation. In general, meditation refers to the variety of contemplative techniques for accessing, controlling, and directing deeper levels of consciousness. Whichever of the many forms we practice, meditation provides the field for new consciousness to emerge. With this added energy and intelligence, we enhance the work of the preceding three levels and facilitate our progress in life harvesting.

Because there is no one generic form of meditation, you probably are familiar with its many brand names. To a Hindu, for example, meditation might refer to mantra chanting. To a Christian of the contemplative tradition, it might mean concentrating on the sacred heart of Jesus. To a Jew, it might involve chanting the prayer "Shema Yisrael" ("Hear, O Israel") and entering into the stillness pointed to by these sacred words. To a Buddhist, meditation might refer to breath control and the impartial observation of thoughts. To others, it might mean quieting the mind and receiving guidance from the Higher Self. As you can see, meditation is a big basket in which you will find many delicious fruits.

No matter what brand of meditation you use, make sure that it engenders a grateful mentality in you. Regular practice can help break the bad habit of ruminating over the hurtful memories and resentments of the past, which I call mental abscesses. Imagine what holding on to a steady stream of resentment and criticism does to the physical body. It's like circulating old, corrosive oil in the crankcase of your automobile. Eventually, as the engine functions less and less efficiently, you have to take the car in for a major repair. When you drive into a spiritual eldering garage, the mechanic on duty will probably recommend an oil change, a complete flushing out of your old consciousness and an infusion of fresh, clear fluids. Meditation circulates streams of forgiveness, compassion, and intuitive insight throughout the system, making for a smoother ride and fewer repairs.

Like the rudder of a ship, meditation also keeps us on track as we ply our way through the waters of life. We may be tempted to veer to the right in depression or to the left in self-condemnation over missed opportunities when we were younger. But through developing contemplative skills and a grateful mentality, we keep to the middle path as we work patiently and persistently on the ongoing work of self-actualization.

Besides facilitating inner growth, the practice of meditation can help mitigate our dread of aging, according to Zen meditator Claire Myers Owens. "In lives dedicated to internal development, physical appearance painlessly ceases to be of prime importance," she writes in the essay "Meditation as a Solution to the Problems of Aging" in *Old Age on the New Scene*. "A new hierarchy of values gradually emerges, based not on youth and beauty; not on social status, wealth, or intellect; but on inner development, selflessness, readiness to serve others, joy, purity, and moral radiance."

To become an elder who embodies these beautiful qualities, we must take control of our consciousness. Normally, we react to stimuli that impinge on us from the outside, manipulated like marionettes by the various forces that pull at our strings. We react habitually to other people's judgments of us, to changes in the stock market, and to the vicissitudes of daily life. The contemplative arts help us break this prison-bound mentality by enabling us to place our consciousness—if only for a moment at the beginning—on positive states of mind, such as forgiveness, compassion, and wisdom. With practice, as we direct our minds away from their normally rudderless condition, we take hold of the steering wheel of our consciousness and attract these higher qualities into our personalities, making for a richer, more enjoyable harvest.

While there are many forms of meditation that we use in our

spiritual eldering workshops, let me share one powerful technique with you, called "Journey to Our Future Self." As we pointed out in the last chapter, because time is stretchable, we can reach back into the past to repair events and relationships. By the same token, we can turn the clock ahead and make an appointment with our more enlightened self in the future. In meditation, we can contact our Inner Elder, who has already completed the journey to self-knowledge and whose presence inspires us with wisdom and compassion as we struggle to become individuated.

Because your future self is self-realized, you can trust him or her as your teacher. The most enlightened outer teacher may give you directions in getting from New York City to Boston, but only you can unlock the door to your house and enter it. The best guru cannot lead you to the ultimate step of enlightenment. Only the "you" who has arrived can provide that kind of guidance. I submit to you that this enlightened self is accessible to your consciousness at this very moment.

To visit your future self, sit quietly, take a few deep, calming breaths, and then count slowly from your actual physiological age to 120, the biblical age of completion and accomplished wisdom. At the same time, visualize walking up a path that leads to the door of your realized self. At the end of your ascent, when you reach 120, enter his or her abode and look into your Inner Elder's compassionate eyes, feeling reassured about your progress so far. As a pilgrim confronting your highest potential for growth, ask for a word of guidance or a blessing for proceeding on your path. Then, after resting in the silence for a while, take leave of your future self and return to normal consciousness, knowing that you can return again for continued guidance.

"You can't imagine how reassuring it is having a permanent relationship with elder consciousness in the form of my Wise Old Woman," exclaims Meryl Nadell, the social worker who came to the workshop in the doldrums of middle age. "It's like having a coach or guru who nurtures and strengthens me whenever I feel overwhelmed at work or worried about personal relationships. At these times, my inner coach encourages me by saying, 'Come on, you can do it. Stay with it. You'll learn from this experience and take one more step in becoming a wise elder yourself.' This inner contact makes me feel less alone, more protected, and definitely more encouraged in facing life's ups and downs."

Besides giving us guidance for dailing living, the contemplative arts can help us mobilize inner powers to minimize the physical diminishments of old age. Let me tell you about Arnold Buchheimer, a retired psychologist from Pittsfield, Massachussetts, whom I met in another of my spiritual eldering workshops.

In 1988, when "Bucky" had coronary bypass surgery, he developed a staph infection that became life-threatening. His doctors urged him to go on kidney dialysis, but Bucky decided to mobilize his body's healing powers by visualizing his kidneys functioning more efficiently. To strengthen his intention to recover, he also recited an affirmation, a positive statement implanted in the unconscious mind through frequent repetition. Working with his medical team, Bucky brought his 103 degree temperature back to normal within two days, without recourse to kidney dialysis, and completely recovered. Three years later, when he had a severe stroke that paralyzed the left side of his body, Bucky again used imagery techniques, along with physiotherapy, to recover his mobility. He now walks practically without a cane, a feat that has surprised his neurologists.

"As we grow older and survive our various physical debilities, we can use contemplative techniques to enhance the quality of our eldering," he says. "For example, we can use visualization to improve the body's strength, mobility, and energy levels. We also can use it to heal our relationships and to strengthen memory and other cognitive skills that sometimes decline with age."

## SOCIALIZED MEDITATION

So far in our discussion we have been talking about meditation that one does in solitude. When we think of practitioners, we picture them sitting in a conventional meditative pose, with eyes closed, back straight, and attention focused inward. Solo meditators put out a sign, "I am not to be disturbed." But there is a more gregarious form of inner work that we practice in our workshops called "socialized meditation." It involves partners sitting together in spiritual intimacy, a state of openness and trust that inducts them into meditative states of awareness.

Normally, when we are busy "looking out for number one," we relate to people in what philosopher Martin Buber calls an "I/It" relationship. We treat others as objects to be manipulated, controlled, or exploited for personal gain. When we overcome this dualistic way of perceiving, we can enter into what Buber called an "I/Thou" relationship. Psychologist Abraham Maslow calls this a state of "being cognition" in which we cherish the other in his or her uniqueness without any utilitarian considerations.

When we practice socialized meditation, we create the conditions for an I/Thou relationship to emerge. In this sacred form of shared discovery, we speak to our partner from the heart in an emotionally safe environment that is free from the often critical, judgmental nature of normal communication. In socialized meditation, we induct each other into deepened awareness through the medium of a caring partner who acts as a mirror, a reflector of consciousness. Because of our partner's nonjudging presence and genuine interest, we feel safe enough to drop our habitual defenses and to explore our thoughts and feelings without fear of shame or censure. In this interactive partnership, sometimes we are the receiver, listening in silence as our partner speaks from the heart. Other times, when the roles are reversed, we become the sender while our partner listens attentively.

In socialized meditation, we share the unvarnished truth about our fears and difficulties, our aspirations and successes, our most tender feelings and radiant moments of spiritual exaltation. Because we are sitting with a spiritual intimate, someone with whom we can share our deepest experiences and intuitions, we don't have to censor our thoughts and feelings as part of the normal public relations campaign we run to convince ourselves and others that we are lovable and worthwhile human beings. Speaking with disarming candor, we can confront blind spots in our personalities, welcome back emotions and perceptions deemed unacceptable to significant others, and unearth and heal painful memories that have dogged us for decades.

When we practice socialized meditation, insights emerge effortlessly from the field of shared attention as we experience ourselves and our partner with freshness of perception and a spontaneity that bypasses our normally controlled, circumscribed way of relating. At the same time, we enter the mystery and grace of the present moment. In this form of sacred homecoming, insights come tumbling into our minds and out of our mouths with a childlike openness that delights and surprises us. Never has the other appeared to us in such precious humanness, such radiant splendor. And as we see ourselves reflected back in our partner's eyes, seldom have we encountered ourselves with such gentleness and love.

Over the years, I have observed that when people enter this state, they attain a similar level of clarity and objectivity as do accomplished meditators after years of disciplined practice. By socializing meditation, we reduce the time and technical skills normally required to mine our depths, a process that effectively democratizes the benefits of contemplation. (Note, however, that this doesn't replace the need for a disciplined solo practice.)

Let me give you an example of how we can use socialized meditation to explore and deepen our relationship to the Spirit. Suppose that two partners, Vernon and Jeanette, are responding to the question, "How have you experienced the presence of the divine in daily life?" As Jeanette listens with undistracted attention, Vernon feels safe enough to reveal one of his most private and cherished experiences.

"I was one of three final candidates for a position as the public relations director of a large hospital. Because of my background and experience, I fully expected to get the position, but much to my dismay, I was turned down for the job. Distraught and unemployed, with a family to support, I felt empty and worthless, as if my life had come to nothing. Sitting in a restaurant, as I watched the steam rising from my coffee cup, suddenly my mind was lifted into a state of serenity and boundless joy in which I felt affirmed and loved in my core. In that liberating moment, I knew that I wasn't an accident of the universe. This insight was so extraordinary that I walked in the park for several hours, treasuring the awareness that my self-worth comes from within and can't be lost by the vagaries of chance. While in this elevated state, I realized that if I just relaxed, things would improve. Several weeks later, I found a job in a publishing house that has been very fulfilling."

When Vernon finishes speaking, Jeanette tells of a similar experience that she had in childbirth. "There was one moment during the delivery of my first child when the doctor was monitoring my vital signs, the nurse was measuring how much I had dilated, my husband was making a phone call, and the contractions were coming hard and fast. Suddenly, feeling alone and terrified, abandoned by everyone in the universe, I cried out, 'Dear God, please be with me!' In the next instant, I was filled with a deep sense of inner peace and a calm assurance that everything was going to be all right. Instead of feeling abandoned, I felt loved and protected throughout the remainder of the delivery. Vernon, I feel that our experiences were so meaningful that I'd like to sit for a moment in silence and reflect on them. Would that be all right with you?"

What has happened in this exchange? Jeanette and Vernon have created an interpersonal bridge to contemplative awareness. They have used the agency of a mirroring "other" to induct them into a state of meditative stillness. They also can employ this technique to heal emotional bruises from the past. For example, Jeanette might use socialized meditation to process a painful memory of betrayal in her first marriage. As Vernon creates a field of caring attention, he enables his partner to go deeper into her memory banks, just as focused attention in solo meditation enables practitioners to penetrate more deeply into the object of their inquiries. When Jeanette gets stuck in an emotional impasse, Vernon can facilitate the process with an empathic, nondirective response. For example, he might say, "I know this is hard for you but please continue" or "This memory brings up a lot of anxiety. I think you're close to something important." As he witnesses rather than steers his partner's process, eventually she can work through her resistance and come to terms with her painful memory.

In our workshops we use socialized meditation to work on issues of mortality, forgiveness, and the recontextualization of difficult experiences. We even use it to do our philosophic homework as we explore beliefs about God, the soul, and the afterlife. While meditation *à deux* can be practiced at home with trusted friends, I recommend learning it firsthand from a spiritual elder or some other knowledgeable person who knows the inner terrain. If you decide to try it on your own, remember that we cannot create an I/Thou relationship by wishing for it. It takes a courageous willingness to explore our inner landscape with a good friend who accepts us nonjudgmentally, warts and all. Such a trusted intimate stands by us steadfastly as we move from the darkness of restricted consciousness into the sunlight of greater freedom.

## TAKE THE FIRST STEP

So now we have stocked our spiritual eldering tool chest with a number of techniques to help us become sages. These are by no means the only techniques available. Since spiritual eldering derives from many sources, I urge you to be eclectic in assembling the tools that you need from psychotherapists, spiritual teachers, books, tapes, and even television talk shows. What's important is taking the first step in moving from aging to sage-ing.

Whether you do your eldering work alone or in socialized settings, at workshops and meditation retreats, or through solo meditation and journal writing, remember that the work of integrating body, mind, and soul requires time and commitment. By reverencing your body, healing the "ouch" spots in your consciousness, forging a workable philosophy, and practicing the contemplative arts, you can begin shaping your life into a noble masterpiece. Using the tools like the ones presented in this chapter, you can conquer fear and inertia, and begin developing a promising future as a spiritual elder. With just a little practice, you will find new dignity and pride as you repair your past, turn pain into joy, and school yourself in the high art of enjoying the achievements of a lifetime.

# CHAPTER 6

# *The Eternity Factor*

By now, you have taken a number of significant steps in becoming a spiritual elder. You have begun healing and recontextualizing your past, along with formatting new areas of consciousness using practices from the contemplative arts. However, success in eldering depends not only on having the necessary psychological and spiritual understanding; it also hinges on reorienting yourself in time.

To elder successfully, we need to broaden our horizon beyond the transitory events of the day. When we leap beyond the human time scale, which mandates that all our purposes be fulfilled within the biblical life span of seventy years, we acquire a long-term vision of our place in the cosmos. Transcending our normally shortsighted perspective, we root ourselves in something vast, immeasurable—something so transpersonally grand and enduring, that I call it the "eternity factor."

When we are anchored in eternity, we seed action in the present with the benefit of our panoramic vision. We no longer focus on short-term, bottom-line decisions that compromise the Earth's ecological integrity. Instead, we expand our thinking to include vast geological eons of time that affect the future of our descendants and the survival of the planet itself.

Elders are eminently suited for this endeavor. With their greater historical perspective, they stretch the minds of young people beyond the immediate present. Elders understand the folly of living out shortsighted, profit-driven goals that ignore the welfare of the whole. By their very presence, they give testimony to more enduring values that call into question our wasteful consumption of the world's resources, our overreliance on material possessions, and our continued assault on the environment. Having witnessed the futility of short-term goals that prove unfulfilling, elders think in multigenerational spans of time that encourage Earth stewardship.

Obviously, this deepened relationship to time is precisely what's missing in our youth-oriented "now" society. We live by the slogan, *Carpe diem*, which is Latin for "Seize the day." Advertisers exhort us to throw caution and sensible planning to the wind in our ceaseless search for instant gratification. "Buy now!" advertisers shout. "Don't plan for the future, but be young and have fun!" Broadcasting the "carpe diem" theme in a multitude of forms each day, commercials imply that sensory gratification is preferable to moderation, that the "new, improved model" is superior to the older one, whether we need the purchase or not. Our love affair with the new and momentary fuels the conspicuous consumption that forms the foundation of our throwaway society.

A similar obsession with the momentary pervades the news media. Today's newspaper and the six o'clock news are relevant; yesterday's news has already become obsolete. We pay attention to the *figure*—the momentary event—but ignore the *ground*, the historical matrix from which it emerges. Our short attention stems in part because technology speeds up the rate at which change takes place. Before the Industrial Revolution, change in the agricultural era often took centuries to unfold. Now, with the frantic, accelerated pace of modern life, what we learn in school often becomes obsolete within a generation or less. Our restless, electronic society aids and abets the process of foreshortening time by slicing it up into increasingly smaller increments according to the "time is money" philosophy. No wonder our culture suffers from such shortsightedness.

Imagine that you have access to a holodeck on the Starship

*Enterprise.* Through voice command, this magic theater can recreate exact replicas of any historical era that interests you. If you prefer, you can dialogue with Socrates in the Greek agora or enjoy a chariot race in ancient Rome. You can visit the Gothic cathedrals of the Middle Ages or hobnob with artists in Renaissance Florence. You can argue literary theory in the salons of Enlightenment Paris, or take part in the great scientific breakthroughs of the nineteenth and twentieth centuries.

But this broad historical panorama doesn't interest you. Fixated on the immediate and momentary present, you say, "Computer, program only the most current changes in news, entertainment, social trends, and commercial fashion." And so, shunning the larger historical picture, you immerse yourself in the most recent films, the latest MTV music videos, and ephemeral political crises that, like actors, enter and quickly exit the stage of world events. "Our attention span is so short," laments author George Leonard, "that we must convince young people that what happened before the latest Michael Jackson hit has historical relevance and usefulness."

Now contrast our fixation on the merely momentary with the intimations of eternity described by Hermann Hesse at the end of his novel *Siddhartha*. Govinda, the perpetual seeker, has not attained self-realization despite a lifetime of ascetic discipline. He asks his old friend Siddhartha, now a venerable sage, for inspiration and guidance on the path. Siddhartha commands the weary pilgrim to kiss him on the forehead. In a moment of ecstatic revelation, Govinda sees that his friend's core identity has an eternal aspect that lies beneath the temporary mask of personality:

> He no longer saw the face of his friend Siddhartha. Instead, he saw other faces, many faces, a long series, a continuous stream of faces—hundreds, thousands, which all came and disappeared and yet all seemed to be there at the same time, which all continually changed and renewed themselves and which were yet all Siddhartha.... No longer knowing whether time existed, whether this display had lasted a second or a hundred years, whether there was a Siddhartha, or a Gotoma [the Buddha], a Self and others, ... Govinda stood yet a while

> bending over Siddhartha's peaceful face which he had just kissed, which had just been the stage of all present and future forms. His countenance was unchanged after the mirror of the thousand-fold forms had disappeared from the surface. He smiled peacefully and gently... exactly as the Illustrious One [the Buddha] had smiled.

Siddhartha lives *sub specie aeternitatis*, "under the aspect of eternity." As an elder, he has outgrown being captive to *punctive* time, which consists of fleeting events disconnected from a broader historical matrix. He lives in *durative* time, which orients his life against a background of transcendent meaning and purpose. From this perspective, all the passionate strivings of his lifetime blossom into an unshakable serenity that the longer vision of time bestows as its gift and blessing.

## THE ARCHETYPE OF THE ELDER

Like Siddhartha, we, too, have a need to live "under the aspect of eternity." Like him, we crave contact with something timeless that endures beyond the brief flicker of our human consciousness. But how do we contact the vastness of eternity, which seems so abstract and beyond our comprehension? Fortunately, an archetypal image that relates us to eternity is stirring in the depths of the collective unconscious. This image, which I call the Inner Elder, is calling forth the wisdom of our elders at a time when our culture so desperately needs it. Let me explain how this divine image can mobilize our resources for continued growth in elderhood.

In his study of dreams, mythology, art, and world religion, Carl Jung found that "primordial images" in the unconscious shape our behavior, values, and creative capacities. These images, called *archetypes*, influence how we experience the timeless constants of human nature, such as birth, death, love, marriage, parenthood, and the predictable changes of the life cycle. Archetypes "are the pre-existing 'first patterns' that form the basic blueprint for the major dynamic components of the human personality," writes Jungian analyst Robert Johnson in *Inner Work*. "They are inborn within us as part of our inheritance as members of the human race."

We can recognize the influence of an archetype when the unique events of our lives fall into general patterns shared by people worldwide, regardless of cultural or religious differences. For example, if we find ourselves struggling against overwhelming odds and prevailing over opponents with courage and perseverance, we have triggered the archetype of the *hero* or *heroine*. Luke Skywalker battling Darth Vader, David battling Goliath, Joan of Arc struggling against the English for French independence, and a woman officer fighting sexual harassment in the military all share in the heroic archetype. In the same way, we can recognize other archetypes, such as the good mother or father, the *femme fatale*, the Don Juan, the courageous warrior, or the eternal youth (the man or woman who rebels against adult authority by behaving like a young person).

We should not underestimate the power of archetypes to shape our behavior and shift the foundations of our culture. Within the past several decades, we have witnessed the return of the *Goddess*, an archetypal image of the feminine that was worshipped by the ancients as the divine source of life. This image, which affects our capacity for love and our connectedness to the Earth, has played a powerful role in empowering the women's movement and the ecology movement. In an attempt to reconnect men to their masculine depths, the men's movement rallies around the archetype of the *Wild Man*. This image, which comes from a Grimms' fairy tale called "Iron John," helps men contact their instinctual life energy, deepening their capacity for love and generativity. Similarly, the recovery movement takes its impetus from the *Inner Child*, an archetypal image representing renewal, a sense of wonder, hope, spontaneity, and immortality. The recovery movement devotes great time and energy in healing the wounded inner child, whose painful abandonment in childhood leads to the addictive, co-dependent behavior that plagues our society.

Just as these archetypes are seeding our culture with change, so the archetype of the Inner Elder is stirring in the collective psyche. This divine image, which appears in dreams, in films, and in world mythology and religion, represents the wisdom of the ages. The elder activates our developmental potential in later life for the state of self-realization that spiritual traditions call enlightenment. As an alternative to society's youthful ideals of strength and beauty, says psychiatrist Allan Chinen, the elder holds up an image of maturity, based on self-knowledge, transcendence of the personal ego, and the willingness to serve society as a mentor and teacher to the young.

Unlike the hero, whose task is to construct a self, the elder must break free of the personal ambitions and dreams that dominate youth, Chinen points out in *In the Ever After*. As the Higher Self, God, or society replaces the personal self as the guiding force in life, he or she turns away from a preoccupation with status and wealth and learns to heed the dictates of the soul. While the hero struggles to change the world, the elder seeks self-transformation through painful insight and authentic reformation. Where the hero seeks victory in the outer world, the elder seeks emancipation from it, based on freedom from social convention. Finally, while the hero moves "from obscurity into prominence, from present to future," the elder moves in the opposite direction: "back home, into the past, and toward the deeper and more fundamental strata of human experience." By rediscovering and living the eternal verities, he or she counsels and inspires youth, helping them balance their idealistic aspirations with the practical needs of society.

Because the hero and elder extend the boundaries of human consciousness, we need to awaken and balance both archetypes to become complete human beings, Chinen suggests. "The hero conquers the power of the unconscious, personified by dragons and monsters, and his triumph is a victory for reason," he writes. "The hero raises consciousness to its apex. The elder deepens it, illuminating the foundations of human experience. Indeed, if youth is the flower of humanity, the elder is the root, pressed against the darkness of the human heart—and the most sublime potential of man's spirit."

## A PANORAMIC VIEW OF TIME

Besides balancing our culture's one-sided heroism with a moderating wisdom, the archetype of the elder also expands our notion of time beyond our current sound-bite and quarterly-report mentality. It relates us to the vast evolutionary drama that spans eons of time from the Big Bang, through the billions of years it took to create life on Earth, to evolution's end, a point of unimaginable splendor billions of years in the future.

Living at the intersection between time and eternity in this way, the elder asks, "What is the meaning of my life? What have I contributed to the world that makes a difference?" Seen from one perspective, our lives appear as mere blips in an eternal process that dwarfs our sense of self-importance. We appear to be fleeting players in a cosmic drama that takes unimaginable eons of time to unfold. Yet even though we live only a nanosecond in the life of the cosmos, we can choose to say, "No matter how vast evolution is, its purposes cannot be attained without the contribution of my blip of human consciousness. I am the link in the chain through which evolution is connected to the past and through which it continues into the future."

With this shift in awareness, we can more easily grasp in our guts that plundering the Earth of its precious resources and mortgaging our children's futures for short-term profit are clearly devolutionary. Taking the long view redirects our values away from our current shortsighted and mistaken materialism. It also gives us the wisdom and inspiration to begin the reclamation of our endangered planet.

Because elders have "graduated" from the concerns of family and career, they are eminently qualified to serve as caretakers of the environment, according to Brooke Medicine Eagle, a healer and teacher of Crow-Lakota descent. In assuming their special vocation, seniors in the dominant society can draw upon the example of Native American tribal elders, known as wisdomkeepers because of their connectedness to Spirit and the natural world. Tribal elders consider the deeper consequences of their behavior, taking at least seven generations into account before committing themselves to action. In this way, they serve as sacred ecologists who protect all their "relatives"—including human, animal, plant, and mineral life.

For example, before cutting down trees to house their children, tribal elders might say, "If we cut down too much forestland, we'll cause an erosion of topsoil that will affect agriculture. Therefore, we must cut down only enough timber to serve our needs, at the same time respecting the needs of the land, the farmers who will harvest its fruits, and the generations who follow them." In this case, what I call the eternity factor—the felt perception of one's relatedness to time in its cosmic dimensions—can provide ethical guidance for our action in the present moment.

"In Native American society, elders dedicate themselves to providing a beautiful experience of life and a healthful environment to the children who come after them," Brooke Medicine Eagle says. "Elders serve the larger world not from mystic sentimentalism, but from a felt experience, matured through contemplation, that the world is one family that they feel connected to through bonds of love. Their deepened sense of time, and the sense of responsibility it calls forth, heighten the intimate care they extend to all of creation."

Elders naturally serve as environmental caretakers, observes Jungian analyst June Singer, because they know that while human life is transitory, the life of the planet endures.

"Because elders are no longer worried about sending their kids to college or saving for old age, they don't need to prepare for their personal futures; they need to prepare for their transpersonal futures," she says. "This means working for the evolution of life on this planet through activities such as preserving the wilderness, cleaning up the oceans and waterways, or building libraries for our children. Elders express their hope in the future by the contributions they make for the generations that come after them."

Because the archetype of the elder is conspicuously missing from our cultural diet, we rarely think in multigenerational completion curves, as Singer suggests. That's why I say that we need the elder to heal the Earth. Without it, we place the future in the hands of political, economic, and religious leaders who cannot distinguish between elders, who hold the long-term vision for the benefit of society, and the elderly, who frequently hold on to what they have for personal survival.

"The elder differs significantly from the rather rigid, authoritarian picture that many of us have of the elderly," says Singer. "The conventional older person, whom Jungians call the *senex*, generally resists change, holds on to power tightfistedly, and frequently imposes his knowledge on others unsolicited. The elder, on the other hand, is flexible, unattached to outcomes, tolerant and patient, and willing to teach when asked. Unlike the king who wields temporal power, the elder need not impose wisdom on others. Possessing an inner authority, he or she doesn't need to bolster personal power through self-assertion. Yet just because personal coercion is absent, such a person radiates an enormously beneficial influence by evoking the questing spirit in younger people."

Because elders are in touch with the traditions and stories of the past, they can transmit a spark, a living flame of wisdom, to help young people meet the challenges of the present and the unfolding future. Without the continuity of tradition, young people fall prey to the excessive preoccupation with "nowness" that we discussed earlier, an attitude that invites a complete rupture with the past. Such a rootless attitude deprives young people of the accumulated wisdom of our forebears. We see farther than our predecessors only because we stand on the shoulders of giants. We owe a debt of gratitude to scientists such as Einstein and Newton, to composers such as Stravinsky and Mozart, and to the great masters of spirituality, such as Moses, Jesus, the Buddha, and Mohammed. Without their contributions to human civilization, we would still be huddled in a dimly lit hovel yearning for the light, rather than contemplating vast, illumined vistas of the mind and spirit from the elevated balcony of a castle.

When elders hand down a tradition, they transmit something timeless in its truth or universal in its beauty, according to Robert Augros and George Stanciu, authors of *The New Story of Science*. "Tradition is the ballast of civilization," they write. "Without it we are tossed about by the arbitrary winds of fashion." But the heirs of a tradition—whether in art, science, or religion—must make the legacy bear new fruit, otherwise the tradition grows desiccated and eventually dies.

The old-timer, the senex, wants to pass on the tradition uncorrupted by change, for fear of losing "the one true way" of revealed truth or social consensus. Such a person vehemently rejects the innovations needed to regenerate tradition and carry it forward into the future. Elders, on the other hand, recognize that traditions constantly must evolve to avoid stagnation and the excessive veneration of the past that destroys creativity and intellectual curiosity. They know that to be effective in dealing with today's problems, traditions must flower into higher levels of development that build on but do not negate or destroy the achievements of the past.

With their understanding of history as an evolutionary give-and-take between the generations, elders do not impose solutions to problems on young people. Instead, they remind them of the consequences of their actions, trusting in their ability to listen, make wise choices, and work for a more peaceful world. In this way, they allow young people to choose their own courses of action without inciting rebellion against the old guard.

Being in the presence of someone who has awakened the elder archetype is like taking an elevator to the top floor of a skyscraper where there is a revolving restaurant. Sipping a cup of tea as the restaurant makes an unhurried revolution every hour, we contemplate the landscape for miles in each direction because of our enlarged perspective. When we return to the hustle and bustle of life below, we carry this wider vision into our daily transactions.

The elder archetype is like a missing vitamin in our diets, but several factors are conspiring to remedy this nutritional deficiency. For one thing, the increasing visibility of long-lived people in our families, in the media, and in public life is arousing the archetype in the collective psyche. Second, just as dreams often compensate for a lack of balance in our lives, so the elder archetype is stirring in our depths to rebalance our culture's conspicuous absence of elder wisdom. Depth psychologists point out that a man with an inflated ego may dream of being a vagrant or a woman suffering from low self-esteem may dream of being the Queen of England. In the same way, our youth-oriented culture is redreaming the elder to compensate for its lack of guiding wisdom. I believe that the emergence of the elder archetype points to a rebirth of spiritual values that could restore our culture to psychological health and equilibrium.

## THE ELDER IN WORLD TRADITIONS

The archetype of the elder assumes a multitude of forms in world mythology and religion. To the ancient Greeks, for example, Kronos (called Saturn by the Romans) represents the senex who upholds the "old ways" against encroachment by the new. Hindus consider Brahma, the creator of the universe, as the eldest and most respected manifestation of God. Because of his wisdom, this all-wise patriarch mediates the problems that affect both the gods and humanity. Native Americans use the metaphor of Grandfather Heaven and Grandmother Earth to link the wisdom of tribal elders with the indwelling wisdom of the cosmos. In relating to the "grandfather," or timeless, transcendent aspect of deity, and the "grandmother," or temporal, changing aspect of embodied life, Native Americans project a loving, compassionate face on the universe.

As depth psychology reveals, every culture has different archetypal images that serve as access codes to elder wisdom. Often these images take the form of a Wise Old Man or Woman, a personification of the psyche that has panoramic knowledge that is unavailable to normal consciousness. When the elder appears in our dreams as a male figure, he may take the form of a guru, shaman, or magician such as Merlin, who guided King Arthur through the labyrinth of kingship. When the elder appears as a Wise Old Woman, she may be a priestess, sorceress, earth mother, or goddess. Frequently she appears as the *crone*, the wise woman past childbearing age honored in prepatriarchal societies for her serenity and spiritual power.

"As a spokesperson for the Self, the Wise Old Man or Woman grasps the total pattern of our unfoldment and provides guidance that transforms our habit-bound lives into creative inner adventures," observes retired Jungian analyst John Weir Perry, author of *Lord of the Four Quarters*. "We contact the Wise Old Man or Woman in dreams, in meditation, and in altered states of consciousness, those moments of poetic inspiration when we have profound insight into the nature of the world. Suddenly we find ourselves entertaining new thoughts and spontaneously seeing things in new, revelatory ways."

The form of the elder archetype that I am most familiar with is the biblical *Ancient of Days*. Here is how the Book of Daniel describes it: "I beheld till the thrones were cast down, and the Ancient of Days did sit, whose garment was white as snow, and the hair of His head like the pure wool; His throne was like the fiery flame, and its wheels as burning fire. A fiery stream issued and came forth from before Him; thousand thousands ministered unto Him, and ten thousand times ten thousand stood before Him: the judgment was set, and the books were opened."

This awesome, divine figure, the Ancient of Days, represents that aspect of God that is beyond time but which gives birth to it. It transcends everything in the manifest universe and will survive its eventual dissolution. Established in objective truth and transcendental justice, the Ancient of Days witnesses everything that takes place in the universe with boundless compassion. Although this presence transcends space and time, it dwells within the core of our personality, bearing the message, "You are loved as a child of the universe."

When I dilate my identity sufficiently to contact this archetype, I realize that I am a reflection of the whole, a chip off the old block, or stated with more theological precision, "made in the image and likeness of God." Entering into the Ancient of Days, I come in contact with that which is indestructible and truly permanent. When this archetype (or another equivalent form of the Wise Old Man or Woman) is activated in the elder's psyche, it overrides society's "carpe diem" program and provides the time stretching necessary for life review, harvesting, and mentoring to occur.

(In passing, while the Ancient of Days may strike you as a patriarchal potentate, the Kabbalah considers this archetype roomy enough to contain both the Wise Old Man and Woman. Kabbalists say that the Ancient of Days precedes the split of the unified self into its masculine and feminine aspects and actually lies beyond both. So let's not take the patriarchal imagery too literally, or else we will argue about the garments that clothe the figure while missing the essence within.)

I like to think of archetypes like the Ancient of Days as masks of God, interfaces between the infinite invisible and embodied life. What we mean by the Ancient of Days transcends all notions of the human mind and imagination. In effect, we only can grasp what is finite. So how does the finite connect with the infinite? According to the Kabbalah, God wears a multitude of masks, clothing itself in divine images that we can apprehend with our finite minds. When we think of God as a father or mother, for example, these root metaphors create an interactivity between the divine and our human consciousness. The interface creates a vessel in which the transcendent can pour itself. Actually, it works a bit like a modem. A modem takes computer bits and translates them into sound, modulates them, sends them down into the telephone, and then demodulates them at the other end.

("Modem" means *mod*ulate, then *dem*odulate.) My interface with God serves as a modem, creating the possibility of communication between the timeless and time.

The contemplative exercises that we do in our spiritual eldering seminars help strengthen that communication. They act as mind-stretchers, making us more available to the interplay between eternity and the everyday world. Do you remember the exercise, "Journey to the Future Self," that we introduced in chapter 5? In this exercise, we visualize being in the presence of our enlightened self, the realized One who dwells beyond space and time. In the normal way of accessing time, that One is unavailable to me, because he dwells in eternity. But contemplative time stretching enables me to take advantage of the plastic nature of time by leaping into the future. *In eternity, I can reach the future now.* Do you see how important the eternity factor is to eldering work? By entering into the consciousness that I call the Ancient of Days, I can access an inner source of wisdom, which witnesses events from an expanded time horizon, and align myself with my highest and best intentions for growth.

Every once in a while, when I feel confused about the options that confront me, I seek an audience with that One. Having encountered him imaginally once, I have access to him again. In my meditation, I enter his marvelous chamber and bask in his wisdom and love. When I share my confusion with him and ask for suggestions, they come less as action directives than as perspectives on the situation. "Come, let me show you where you are," the Inner Elder says. Suddenly I view my life, with all its confusion and its opportunities, from a platform in eternity. When I see clearly what lies before me and what is required of me, my confusion lifts and I move on to the next stage of my journey.

Besides contacting the eternity factor through meditation, we can evoke it by being in the presence of an awakened elder. Around such a person we receive a nonverbal transmission that can bless and benefit our lives in untold ways. In the Indian tradition, spiritual seekers cherish the presence of the realized elder so highly that they often travel hundreds of miles to receive *darshan*, the benefit of the teacher's radiance. Why? Because the elder, as a witness to your potential unfolding, provides a field of unconditional love and spiritual power that triggers your latent abilities into active expression. Jean Houston had this kind of relationship with Pierre Teilhard de Chardin, the Jesuit paleontologist and visionary. As she once said, "Unconditional love just pours out of people like him, and they look at you as if you were God in hiding. And you are charged, your evolutionary circuits are primed in their presence."

Because the archetype of the Ancient One is embodied in the wise elder, we get inducted into a similar field in his or her presence. Anthropologist Joan Halifax recalls listening to shamanic stories narrated by Guadalupe de la Cruz Ríos, a Huichol medicine woman in her late seventies who lives in the Sierra Madre Occidental of northern Mexico. One story concerned Nakawe, Great Grandmother Growth, the divine being who understands the nature of impermanence that rules the physical world. Transfixed by this wise woman's storytelling ability, Halifax soon began regarding the medicine woman not only as a physical elder, but as a representative of the elder state of consciousness that she was describing. She was listening to Great Grandmother Growth herself discoursing on the nature of transitoriness!

"When an elder embodies the archetype of impermanence, we see the whole cycle of life—birth, growth, flowering, decay, death, and transformation—in her presence," Halifax explains. "We don't receive an abstract discourse on change. We actually participate in the mystery of space and time itself. Because a realized elder evokes the qualities of the Ancient Ones, we get a little taste of it by osmosis. Being around someone who's larger than his or her personality gives us a foretaste of what awaits us in elderhood."

## THE ETERNITY FACTOR IN DAILY LIFE

We don't have to wait for elderhood to have intimations of eternity. As poet William Wordsworth writes in "Tintern Abbey," most of us have felt

*A presence that disturbs me with the joy*
*Of elevated thoughts; a sense sublime*
*Of something far more deeply interfused,*
*Whose dwelling is the light of setting suns,*

*And the round ocean and the living air,*
*And the blue sky, and in the mind of man . . .*

Gazing at the stars on a cloudless night, walking by the seashore at sunset, witnessing the birth of a child, or looking deeply into the eyes of our beloved: Any of these rapturous moments can momentarily push back the partitions separating us from eternity. Listening to a Schubert symphony with rapt attention or painting a landscape with complete absorption also can serve as openings into the timeless dimension. These peak experiences enable us to step off the merry-go-round of habitual perception and to live temporarily with open-eyed wonder.

The timeless moments that we experience in youth and middle age are harbingers of perceptual faculties that unfold in elderhood. We awaken to a timeless aesthetic sense that delights in the mystery and wonder that fill the world. Chinen calls this "the return of wonder," because it restores us to a perceptual innocence that we sacrificed in becoming adults.

In youth, we emerge from a state of oneness with the world to build a separate identity and to pursue our private ambitions. We are like cameras with a wide-angle lens that can encompass both the timeless, changeless ground that supports life and the ever-changing figure in the foreground that compels our momentary interest. To pursue our dreams of success, we replace the wide-angle lens with a close-up lens, in effect splitting the figure from the ground, so we can concentrate on what's immediately before us. By ignoring the larger field, we narrow our sights considerably to succeed in the practical affairs of life. But in elderhood, we again can use the wide-angle lens to take the larger world back in. Overcoming the split between world and self, timelessness and time, we harmonize ourselves with the larger source from which we initially separated and return to a state of wholeness. This homecoming is the call, the potential, and the glory of elderhood.

"In our later years, we feel connected to the world through bonds of tenderness and empathy," says John Weir Perry. "Life becomes more poetic. The ordinary objects that surround us—trees, houses, clouds, animals—shimmer with metaphoric insight, revealing depths of meaning that normally elude our practical minds. We may relate to a tree in the backyard as the Tree of Life that is rooted in eternal life or truth. The blossoming of crocus and forsythia in spring may remind us of renewal taking place in our psyches. When we look at the world under the aspect of eternity, life is animated in ways that constantly astound us."

Polly Francis, a fashion illustrator who wrote a series of essays on old age in her nineties, confirms this observation. "A new set of faculties seems to be coming into operation," she writes in an essay in the anthology *Songs of Experience*. "I seem to be awakening to a larger world of wonderment—to catch little glimpses of the immensity and diversity of creation. More than at any other time in my life, I seem to be aware of the beauties of our spinning planet and the sky above. And now I have the time to enjoy them. I feel that old age sharpens our awareness."

Holding a wider vision does more than just enrich our personal lives. It can help guide our behavior through the tangle of ethical and financial dilemmas that we face as workers and consumers on an environmentally compromised planet. Imagine that Joe McCormack, who works in an automobile assembly plant in Detroit, Michigan, takes a spiritual eldering workshop as part of his preretirement planning. When he returns home, Joe decides to devote a few minutes before work each day invoking the presence of the Wise Old Man through meditation and prayer. He sits in a comfortable chair, closes his eyes, takes a few long, deep breaths, and then visualizes journeying to his completed self, who embodies Joe's ideal of wisdom and compassion. Besides giving him insight into his day-to-day problems, this daily contact begins to sensitize him to the long-term consequences of his actions.

One day at work, when making an inventory of parts, he discovers that the catalytic converter installed in the exhaust system of a certain model will wear out within two years of installation. He further discovers that by spending an extra ten dollars, the company can extend the life of the part for five years. He suggests to his supervisor that the longer-lived catalytic converter be installed. But the supervisor informs Joe, "I'm sorry, but in building this car, we're planning for obsolescence."

Joe disagrees. He says, "The company may endorse planned obsolescence, but I'm building products that last. Look, we both know that economic conditions are difficult, and people probably won't be able to afford new cars every two or three years. Besides, how good is it for the environment to produce cars that fall apart in several years? Let's build for the future."

Despite economic and social pressures to knuckle under, Joe voices his concerns at the plant through letter writing, organizing activities, and meetings with high-level supervisors. Will he succeed? It's hard to imagine that one auto worker can have an impact on the global environment. Yet however small our personal actions may appear, we must never underestimate their importance. "The character of a whole society is the cumulative result of countless small actions, day in and day out, of millions of persons," writes social scientist Duane Elgin in *Voluntary Simplicity*. "Who we are, as a society, is the synergistic accumulation of who we are as individuals.... Small changes that seem insignificant in isolation can be great contributions when they are simultaneously undertaken by many others."

Before long, Joe begins making small but significant changes in his lifestyle. To avoid bequeathing a polluted wasteland to future generations, he begins practicing "conspicuous conservation." He lowers his overall level of personal consumption, buying products that are durable, easy to repair, and nonpolluting in their manufacture and use. He takes seriously the exhortation to recycle paper, glass, and aluminum cans. To fight global warming and acid rain, he cuts down on nonessential driving and supports community tree-planting projects. Joe undertakes these changes not to win merit badges from his family and friends, but to strengthen the bonds of solidarity that he feels with the next seven generations and beyond.

This deepened awareness even extends to Joe's personal relationships. In the past, when he was angry or impatient, Joe would lash out at people in anger. But when he began contemplating the long-term results of his behavior, he saw with incontrovertible clarity that he was creating a legacy of pain that added to the world's growing store of suffering. Now, when someone cuts him off in traffic or when a bank teller takes an unusually long time to complete a transaction, instead of unleashing his fury, he takes several deep breaths and asks himself, "What kind of lessons am I teaching people by snapping at them? Is this the legacy that I want people to remember me for?"

Although the case of Joe McCormack is fictitious, still it demonstrates how activating the eternity factor has the potential of changing our lives. We might think of eternity as a vague, abstract concept that bears little relationship to our busy, practical lives. In truth, however, when elders activate the archetype of eternity, they become conduits of blessing who bridge the spiritual and material worlds with acts of everyday kindness that benefit individuals, the community, and the planetary milieu.

## INITIATION INTO ELDER CONSCIOUSNESS

There are a number of ways to cultivate the elder archetype in daily life. Besides practicing meditation, we can record our dreams in a journal, paying particular attention to figures who personify elder wisdom. We can practice *active imagination*, a technique developed by Carl Jung in which we hold dialogues with images from the unconscious. We can invoke the Wise Old Man or Woman, for example, pose a question, enter into a dialogue with this inner image, and record the exchange on paper. Rather than direct the flow of imagery as in guided meditation, we receive it in a quiet, meditative way. What makes this form of imagination *active*, says Jungian analyst Robert Johnson, is that we consciously go into the inner world, engage figures in conversation, exchange viewpoints, and learn something by listening to the wisdom of the unconscious. By treating the unconscious as an equal partner with its own voice, we can consciously work on issues without waiting for clarification from dreams.

Creative activities such as music, dance, painting, and poetry also help evoke the Inner Elder. Taking long walks in nature often connects us with the deeper, more meditative aspects of consciousness. Cultivating a garden helps deepen our awareness of time by acquainting us with nature's slow, unhurried rhythms of organic growth. Much like time-lapse photography, gardening shows us how the sudden, dramatic blossoming of a rose stems from insignificant, almost imperceptible changes that take great stretches of time to unfold.

One of the most indelible ways of stamping consciousness with the elder archetype is through *rites of initiation*. Throughout history, men and women have undergone ritualized public ceremonies to help them make the transition from one stage of life to another. These ceremonies enable us to leave an outworn stage of life behind and to invest ourselves with a new identity, new roles, and a new way of being in the world. We normally associate initiation ceremonies with puberty, when young people endure trials of strength and courage in leaving adolescence and entering adulthood. But initiation rites also exist to guide people in becoming responsible householders and later in making the transition from middle to old age.

Elder initiation rites formally sever our ties to midlife goals and aspirations, replacing them with the freedom and wider concerns of elderhood. For example, in a ceremony attended by family and friends, Japanese people celebrate their sixtieth birthday by donning special red garments that announce their new elder status. The clothing indicates liberation from social obligations and a return to the innocence and freedom of childhood. In the Jewish tradition, there's a ceremony to celebrate the marriage of the last child. The celebrants form a circle around the mother, who sits in the center on a throne-like chair. They then place a golden paper crown on her head and dance around her, singing triumphantly, "Play, musicians, play, and make a joyful sound! Dance, aunts and uncles, dance around Mom, who has completed her job. The youngest one is married, yes, the youngest one is married!" This joyous ceremony recognizes that a woman's childbearing and parenting years have successfully been completed and that she is entitled to respect for this achievement and for the onset of her wisdom years.

When we ritualize life passages as in these two examples, we publicly reinforce our commitment to grow in new ways. At the same time, we irreversibly seal our psyches, closing the gates to the past and opening up new vistas to the future.

"Through breath, words, and song, public ceremonies remind members of our community to support us in our commitment to elderhood," observes Brooke Medicine Eagle. "So often we just stagger along from one stage of life to another, without assessing our gains, grieving our losses, and integrating both into a new structure. Public ceremonies help us express and release our sadness as we grow beyond a certain identity that we once found precious and meaningful. Ceremonies also acknowledge that we have 'graduated' from one level and are ready for the rights and responsibilities of the next one."

One such ceremony in Native American society, she said, initiates postmenopausal women into the Grandmother Lodge, a tribal support group for those who wish to explore and develop crone or elder wisdom. Meeting on a regular basis, these women turn their attention to the inner, contemplative life that was sacrificed on the altar of parental necessity. They support each other's commitment to work not just for their own well-being, but for the welfare of all living beings in creation. For women in Grandmother Lodges, this pledge to nurture the world might take the form of volunteering in schools, espousing environmental causes, deepening spiritual contact through studying shamanism, or dedicating themselves to teaching their grandchildren on an individual basis.

Brooke Medicine Eagle performs initiation ceremonies for women seeking entry into Grandmother Lodges at Eagle Song Wilderness Camps in Ovando, Montana. During the ceremony (held either indoors or outside when possible), a woman typically removes her old clothing, symbolic of her youth and childrearing days. Escorted by her sponsors, she enters a ritual bath where she is ceremonially cleansed. As she is bathed, the elder women encourage the initiate to grieve—and shed tears if necessary—for the end of her menses and of motherhood. After the ritual bath, they dry and anoint the woman with fragrant perfumes and oils, after which she dons new clothing symbolic of her new station in life. She might put on a white dress to represent wisdom or a black one to represent the onset of cronehood. During the ceremony, she also might receive a special shawl and a new name that is charged with ritual significance.

Wearing a garland of fresh flowers, the woman then steps forward into the circle of older sisters and states publicly her commitment to become a wisdom person. She might say something as simple as, "I commit my energy, love, and passion to nurturing and serving all of life. I will carry out my larger purpose by modeling compassion in all my relationships and actions." After the witnesses pledge to support the woman in her task, they share with the initiate words of wisdom for her journey. The ceremony concludes with a celebration of food, song, dance, and sharing.

In a similar vein, Jean Bolen, a Jungian analyst and author of *Goddesses in Everywoman*, has devised a simple yet powerful ritual to help postmenopausal women reclaim the wise woman archetype. The women gather on a private ranch in Montana where they develop bonds of friendship and trust by sharing stories about their lives. After laughing and crying together, delighting in their triumphs and mourning their losses, Bolen leads them into an underground ritual cave where they seek rebirth through the wisdom that comes from the "nourishing dark." Sitting in a sacred circle, the women light a candle to illuminate the darkness. Then, one by one, they hold up the candle and speak about the wisdom they have learned in surviving to a grand age. In this way, each participant claims the wise woman as her own.

Women must consciously revive the wise woman archetype, Bolen explained, because it has been assaulted and devalued over the centuries. From prepatriarchal times through much of the Christian era, the crone or wise woman commanded respect as a priestess, healer, midwife, teacher, and psychopomp, a spiritual guide who escorted the soul through the portals of death into the next world. But during the Middle Ages, the Inquisition launched a systematic campaign to suppress women's direct spiritual knowledge. Declaring wise women to be witches, the Church persecuted them for a period of three hundred years, denigrating older women as ugly, obnoxious, foul, wrinkled, and useless to society.

Memories of this persecution live on in the collective psyches of modern women, invalidating their inherent wisdom and inhibiting the expression of their autonomy. When they invoke the life-affirming image of the crone, women declare war on misogynistic stereotypes that keep them weak and powerless. The crone invests a woman with a sense of inner wholeness and power, freeing her from the expectations of others and giving her an ability to act decisively in the world based on a commitment to higher values.

Bolen believes that the current generation of women is helping restore the wise woman archetype to an honored place in our culture. The return of this archetype signals an end to the old woman as an over-the-hill, devalued, and discardable nonentity who has little or no contribution to make in politics, economics, and education. As this nurturing, liberating power awakens within older women, it brings forth the spiritual wisdom and experience needed to help heal our technologically ravaged world.

"Many of today's postmenopausal women, who were active in the women's movement during the past three decades, are defining for themselves what a wise woman is and does in the 1990s," Bolen says. "Besides being autonomous and creative, the new wise woman has the courage and conviction to speak up in defense of the planet, the world's children, and the downtrodden in society, including women, oppressed races, and elders. The return of the wise woman archetype might help infuse our institutions with more compassion, so that we treat people humanely while operating in the long-term interest of the Earth and the next generation of children."

Like women, when men activate the elder archetype, they, too, enter into a renewed relationship with the feminine. In becoming elders, men typically turn away from their hard-driving absorption in work, career, and financial security to focus on inner development. This means welcoming back the capacity for feeling and intuition that they sacrificed in their pursuit of success. In later years, men are more at ease with their tender feelings, responding to beauty and the suffering of others with a deepened sense of empathy. But besides enjoying a friendlier relationship with the feminine, men also acquire the ability to speak with authority and wisdom. In tribal societies, for example, older men serve as peace chiefs, political advisors, sacred ecologists, and spiritual leaders whose wisdom is considered crucial for the well-being of society. I believe that once men in our society claim the elder archetype as their own, they will express the same capacity for wisdom as elders do in tribal societies.

Like women's rituals, men's ceremonies have some of the same core elements that sever people from their former identities while investing them with the responsibilities of elderhood. For example, a man approaching retirement might take a weekend retreat with members of his community who already have passed the threshold into elderhood. He might undertake a modified Vision Quest, spending quiet, contemplative time in nature, reviewing his life and and seeking a vision of his new path. Later, he might share his discoveries in a sweat lodge, an enclosed structure made from saplings with heated rocks in the center pit. Sitting in a council of elders, with steam billowing in the darkness, the initiate might say, "When I was younger, I sacrificed a good deal of my intuitive awareness and sense of oneness with life to build my personality, career, and family. Now I'm ready to reconnect with the larger world and to establish my relationship with God on a deeper level." At this point, his older brothers might speak about his strengths and his contribution to the community; point out the challenges that await him as an elder; and give him a special article of clothing signifying his entry into his new estate.

## CREATING PERSONALIZED CEREMONIES

Now that you understand how ceremonies serve as vehicles for deepening the experience of elderhood, you may want to participate in one yourself or orchestrate one for someone you know. In planning a ceremony, whether you hold it outdoors or in a meeting room, whether you invite members of a large community or a small group of friends, remember that you can personalize the event to fit your own requirements.

"We can create rituals to honor elder family members, friends, and co-workers in the context of our everyday lives," counsels Brooke Medicine Eagle. "We certainly don't have to emulate Native American rituals. Nor do we have to use traditional religious forms and language to express our appreciation of older people. A ritual might involve something as simple as organizing a dinner in the park to honor an elder for his or her contribution to the community. When someone in the family retires, we can launch the person into elderhood through a ceremony in which people express their appreciation through little speeches, poems, songs, dance, and artwork.

"We shouldn't disown our own ability to create meaningful rituals, believing that religions have an exclusive monopoly on this function. Each of us has a direct connection to the Great Spirit. That means that each of us can create beautiful ceremonies to make elders feel special, loved, and valuable."

We need to create meaningful ceremonies for elders because the glue that connects them to the community has come undone in the modern era. Our culture provides few ritual forms to help people adjust to the transitions common in later life. Essentially, they are on their own. Creating personalized rituals to commemorate menopause, retirement, relocation, change in health status, and death can help elders move through these transitions in growthful rather than dysfunctional ways.

There's another reason why elder ceremonies are especially

important nowadays. In the last few years, our culture has focused singlemindedly on the hero's journey to self-development and personal achievement. But no matter how passionately we pursue the hero's journey, it only takes us to the portals of old age, where we eventually must surrender our role in society and continue into the uncharted territory of spiritual eldering. We need elder ceremonies to help make the transition into menopause or retirement an occasion for victory that we celebrate among friends, rather than an ignominious defeat that we bear in solitude. By invoking the archetypal Elder during times of transition, we receive encouragement to continue our journey into the unknown as we reach toward the state of fulfillment symbolized by our completed self. Awakened to the vast continuum of time, we take our stand in eternity, seeding the present moment with the perennial wisdom that the world so desperately needs.

# Chapter 7

# *The Conscious Transit at Death*

When lived consciously, old age is marked by two crucial rites of passage: the entry into elderhood, which we can celebrate through initiation ceremonies, and the final exit from the physical body, the transition at death that ends our earthly pilgrimage. Living as we do in a secular culture that represses both death and transcendental experience, we generally do not regard dying as a growth stage and an initiation in consciousness. Yet despite the prevailing materialistic view that death is an unmitigated catastrophe, a growing number of people are beginning to treat the process of dying as a unique opportunity for spiritual awakening.

With the help of loving counselors, they work through their fear and anger, dissolve resentment, heal relationships, and make peace with their destiny. By "finishing business," they remove the calluses that obstruct the heart, the spontaneous, loving core that connects them with their essential nature. Without the need to hide behind inauthentic masks, they become sensitive and innocent again, awakened to the piercing beauty and preciousness of life.

A case in point is a sixty-eight-year-old businesswoman named Miss Martin, who transformed from a repugnant caterpillar into a graceful butterfly by meeting her death consciously. In *Death: The Final Stage of Growth*, Mwalimu Imara, a colleague of Dr. Elisabeth Kübler-Ross, describes how this terminal cancer patient changed from a lonely, intimidating woman into a more open, loving person who valued human friendship above all else.

Imara and Kübler-Ross, the psychiatrist renowned for bringing death out of the closet, befriended this cantankerous woman at a time when she was abandoned by her own family. Possessed by her work but having few friends, Miss Martin lived an isolated existence, having made few deposits in the bank of human affection. To break through her isolation, the hospital staff became her family, providing the loving support that enabled her to release her old identity and to become a new person.

Over the course of several months, as human friendship and the presence of death melted her rigid defenses, Miss Martin received a splendid education—an intensive, if you will—in giving and receiving love. As a result, she worked through her grief, accepted her approaching death, and stopped her verbal assaults of the staff. She also released her persona of the rich but bitter old lady by embracing the full spectrum of her human emotions, including joy and sorrow, love and hate, confusion and clarity. Near the end of her life, she had removed so many calluses from her heart that she could say in all honesty, "I have lived more in the past three months than I have during my whole life. . . . I wish I knew forty years ago what I know now about living. I have friends."

The experience of conscious dying that transformed Miss Martin, which once might have seemed unusual, has become more available in recent decades, thanks to the growing influence of the death awareness movement in the United States. This movement draws heavily on the work of hospice, the compassionate health care approach that provides a safe, warm, and technologically nonintrusive environment for the dying. Proponents of conscious dying vehemently oppose sterile hospital settings that separate the patient from his family and friends. Nor do they believe in taking heroic measures to prolong life when the natural, organic end to physical existence is at hand. Advocates of conscious dying, therefore, make the patient as comfortable as possible, without unduly protracting the dying process through technological wizardry.

While some in hospice tend to treat death as an unfortunate ordeal, many in the death awareness movement do not accept physical cessation as the tragic end of existence. They regard it as a transcendental birthing process, the culminating moment of a lifetime that serves as a transition to other states of consciousness. Viewing death not as their mortal enemy but as their birthright into continued growth, they teach death preparation techniques that make the transition as serene and fearless as possible. By providing the patient with unconditional love and treating death in a more enlightened manner, they help make dying into a peaceful, potentially transformative experience.

While preparing for death might strike many people as morbid, only our modern culture, with its materialistic bias, has lost touch with the spiritual technologies that for centuries guided the dying through this transcendent process. In the West, for example, the Catholic Church traditionally has performed the last rites to help the dying make the transition to the afterdeath state. In Judaism, members of the Chevrah Kaddisha, a sacred society of men and women functioning as helpers to the dying, have guided people through the death process and later prepared their bodies for burial. In the East, *The Tibetan Book of the Dead* has guided yogic adepts and laypeople through the profound experiences of physical death, journeys through the afterdeath state, and eventual rebirth. Only now, as we explore the hidden treasures within our spiritual traditions, are we rediscovering the psychotechnologies for a conscious departure from physical life.

"All the greatest spiritual traditions of the world, including of course Christianity, have told us clearly that death is not the end," writes Sogyal Rinpoche in *The Tibetan Book of Living and Dying*. "They have all handed down a vision of some sort of life to come, which infuses this life that we are leading now with sacred meaning. But despite the teachings, modern society is largely a spiritual desert where the majority imagine that *this life* is all that there is. Without any real or authentic faith in an afterlife, most people live lives deprived of any ultimate meaning."

According to Sogyal Rinpoche, the modern denial of death affects not only the individual, but the whole planet. Without a long-term vision to guide their behavior, nothing restrains people from selfishly exploiting the planet for their own immediate profit. Fear of death and ignorance of the afterlife are fueling the destruction of the environment through an unrestrained materialism. Death education, he asserts, holds the key not only to the meaning of life, but to our very survival.

"Peaceful death is really an essential human right," he writes, "more essential perhaps even than the right to vote or the right to justice; it is a right on which, all religious traditions tell us, a great deal depends for the well-being and spiritual future of the dying person.... There is no greater gift of charity you can give than helping a person to die well."

## THE SCIENTIFIC MANAGEMENT OF DEATH

In a culture that worships scientific knowledge and professional expertise as the path to salvation, Sogyal Rinpoche's compassionate views go against the grain of common wisdom. Most of us abdicate the management of our dying and delegate it to doctors, scientists, and gerontologists. As the end of life approaches, we put our faith in the intensive care unit, presided over by the priest/doctor who prolongs our lives as long as possible through medical technology. Having demystified the transcendent nature of dying and having reduced it to a pathological physical process that is managed by doctors, we surrender the right to die our own deaths. When, despite all medical interventions, we succumb to death, we usually sleep through the event, drugged, sedated, and unconscious of this great transformative moment. Many of us would rather die this way because our unavoidable appointment with mortality calls forth anxiety that paralyzes us emotionally, rendering us incapable of entering the experience with awareness.

Until recently, women's experience of childbirth had much in common with medically supervised dying. The process of childbirth was hidden and shunned, just as death is today, explains Anya Foos-Graber, author of *Deathing*, a how-to manual for conscious dying. Because doctors considered childbirth a pathological problem rather than a natural process, they anesthetized women in labor and took control of their deliveries through surgical intervention. During the past few decades, women radically have altered how children are born by practicing conscious childbirth techniques such as the Lamaze method. Using relaxation, breathing, and mental-focusing techniques, practitioners of

Lamaze have taken back much of the control that previously was usurped by physicians. Working with fathers-to-be as support persons, women receive skillful preparation in recognizing the various stages of childbirth and cooperating with these organic processes in the most conscious, comfortable way possible.

Just as Lamaze has changed childbirth, argues Foos-Graber, so must we provide people with the methodology to transform death from a terrifying experience into an occasion for spiritual awakening. To leave the world consciously, a process she calls *deathing*, Foos-Graber teaches somewhat the same techniques used for consciously birthing people into the world. Drawn from the teachings of yoga and Tibetan Buddhism, her method includes relaxation, breathing techniques, and mental-focusing exercises that keep the person as undistracted as possible amidst the myriad impressions that clamor for attention at physical death. To keep awareness on track, she recommends having a trusted support person available to guide and coach the dying person—whether awake or in a coma—through this dramatic phase shift. By learning to recognize and cooperate with the predictable stages of the dying process, she says, we make our transition into death "aware, awake, responsible, and joyous.

"Let me assure you: The benefits of prepared, voluntary actions at the death moment exceed the claims of the best savings plans or life-insurance policy," Foos-Graber writes in *Deathing*. "By allowing yourself to think about the unthinkable, you can make it less forbidding. By facing up to your mortality, you will be able to fulfill your life in deeper, richer ways. By taking responsibility for your death, you will be doing the most practical thing you could do for yourself, and the most selfless, giving thing you could do for your loved ones."

This advice takes on added meaning to the spiritual elder who is devoting the last quarter of life to harvesting, passing on a legacy, and preparing for death. Those elders who prepare consciously through meditation, reading, and death rehearsals take out "life/death insurance" for a more comfortable journey. They make incremental payments in conscious awareness that can be cashed in for a sizable premium when the end approaches. Those who encounter death unaware make one lump-sum payment with resources that might not be adequate to the challenge. How can we acclimate ourselves in this strange new country when its sights, sounds, and natural phenomena arouse terror in us rather than curiosity?

Life gives us ample warning to prepare for our appointment with death. Throughout our middle years, despite the best diet and exercise regime, the body reminds us of our mortality through its gradually diminishing energy level, slower metabolism, and changes in skin tone and hair color. When a close friend dies of a heart attack or a sibling of cancer, the magical notion of our immunity from death grows less and less tenable. When handled consciously, however, the death of a beloved friend or family member can serve as a wake-up call, urging us to deepen our relationship with thanatos and to proceed with all due haste in the work of life completion. Such a reminder needn't paralyze us; rather, it can strengthen our resolve to become spiritual elders.

In the East, where aging and death are more openly befriended, many people take up spiritual disciplines to prepare for the moment of departure. Tibetans claim that because death represents the culmination of the life cycle and its most intense concentration of energy, whatever thoughts and feelings we hold accompany us and to a large extent determine the quality of our afterdeath experience. They therefore train the dying to attain a clear meditative state of awareness, devoid of fear and distraction. This clarity enables them to recognize the enlightened state of mind that appears at death, merge with it, and attain spiritual liberation.

Hindus regard a dying person's state of mind as the principal guarantor of his destiny. In the Bhagavad Gita, the Gospel of Hinduism, Krishna gives the following instructions on dying: "Whatever a man remembers at the last, when he is leaving the body, will be realized by him in the hereafter; because that will be what his mind has most constantly dwelt on, during this life." Gandhi spent so many years on inner work that when he was assassinated, his dying words were "Ram" (a Hindu name of God). In that brutal instant, a lifetime's work flowered into wisdom because, to put it simply, Gandhi had packed his bags and was ready. As Shakespeare says in *King Lear*, "Ripeness is all."

# CONSCIOUS DEATH IN THE WORLD'S SPIRITUAL TRADITIONS

There are many exemplary tales of spiritual elders who died in such a state of conscious readiness and acceptance. When Sri Ramana Marharshi, the renowned Indian sage, was dying in 1951, his grief-stricken disciples pleaded with him not to leave them bereft of his physical presence. "They say I am dying," he replied, "but I am not going away. Where could I go? I am here." At the moment of his physical death, when he heard disciples singing hymns to God, one eyewitness wrote that "Ramana's eyes opened and shone. He gave a brief smile of indescribable tenderness. From the outer edges of his eyes tears of bliss rolled down. One more deep breath, and no more. There was no struggle, no spasm, no other signs of death: only that the next breath did not come."

Now also consider the inspirational death of Rabbi Israel ben Eliezer, known as the Baal Shem Tov (Master of the Good Name), who founded the Hasidic movement in the eighteenth century. When death was imminent, he summoned several close disciples to his bedside and demonstrated to them how limb by limb life was receding from his body as the soul prepared to return to its supernal home. He then instructed his students to apply this spiritual knowledge to others who were on the verge of death. Just before he died, the Baal Shem Tov said to a larger group of disciples, "I have no worries with regard to myself. For I know quite clearly: I am going out at one door and I shall go in at another." After the disciples prayed for him, he whispered, "My God, Lord of all worlds!" and then recited a verse of the psalm: "Let not the foot of pride come upon me." With that, he peacefully expired.

In *The Wheel of Death*, Zen Buddhist teacher Philip Kapleau tells the deathbed story of the contemporary Zen master Roshi Taji. As death neared, one of the roshi's senior disciples scoured the pastry shops of Tokyo for a certain confection that the master loved. The disciple presented the pastry to the roshi, who despite his weakened condition munched on the cake with enjoyment. As the roshi's energy waned, the disciples leaned closer and inquired whether he had any final words of instruction.

"Yes," the roshi replied.

The disciples leaned forward with great eagerness. "Please tell us!"

"My, but this cake is delicious!" the master said. And with that he died.

What a delightful teaching not only about facing death with equanimity, but about living each moment with relish. Normally, with our tunnel vision, we fear that thinking about death and preparing for it will infect us with spiritual cooties that will hasten our inevitable end. But as these spiritual elders so clearly demonstrate, when we come to terms with our mortality, we enter the present moment with fearlessness, increased intensity, and a sense of gratitude that makes everyone and everything seem almost unbearably precious. After suffering a heart attack and surviving, psychologist Abraham Maslow spoke of the gratitude he felt for his "postmortem life." The confrontation with death, he wrote, "makes everything look so precious, so sacred, so beautiful that I feel more strongly than ever the impulse to love it, to embrace it, and to let myself be overwhelmed by it."

Does facing death with openhearted acceptance seem beyond your ken? Do you think that only Zen roshis, Hasidic masters, and yogis can face death with serenity? Then consider Maurine Holbert-Hogaboom, a psychotherapist from St. Marys City, Maryland, who attended the spiritual eldering seminar at Omega Institute. An actress most of her life, she received a master's degree in psychology and theater at age sixty-five. As a therapist, she employs Psychosynthesis, a holistic approach developed by Italian psychiatrist Roberto Assagioli, to train actors in their craft.

In her youth, driven by an irrepressible drive to become an actress, Maurine left her native Texas during the Depression and joined a traveling burlesque show that went to New York City, where she landed a role in a Lillian Hellman play that launched her career. At eighty years of age, full of vitality, an unquenchable curiosity, and metaphysical *chutzpah*, she hopes to experience death with the same adventurous spirit that propelled her into acting more than five decades ago.

"Because I regard death as an integral part of life, I intend to die consciously, in full possession of my wits," Maurine says with characteristic vigor. "I've always lived with the assumption that if you weren't afraid of life, you wouldn't be afraid of death. I approach death with a curiosity and sense of wonder that surprise me. In fact, I suspect that death may be the greatest adventure of all. I don't want to die at this point, simply because I have unfinished business to attend to. But when I've completed the last step of my journey, I want to experience death just as I've experienced life—with a joyous capacity to wholeheartedly embrace whatever lies on my path."

Ephraim Miller, the financial consultant from Evanston, Illinois, shares Maurine's expectation of death as an adventure of the spirit. "Death is a natural process by which the limited sense of self that we identify with throughout our lifetime opens up and becomes permeable to larger realms of consciousness," he states. "If that isn't an adventure, I don't know what is! I look forward to everything in my life—intimate moments shared with my wife, Ann, pleasureful moments listening to music or reading a good book, and the transcendent moment of death, which is a transition to another state of existence. I sense in some irrefutable way that the universe is not a collection of random particles and sensations. Ultimately, there is a greater consciousness that gives it meaning, and I am an integral part of that deathless being."

## THE MODERN DENIAL OF DEATH

While Maurine and Ephraim intend to open their doors to death at the appropriate time, most people by contrast plan to bolt them shut and struggle valiantly against the Grim Reaper, their implacable enemy. Dylan Thomas expresses this attitude in a well-known poem addressed to his dying father:

> *Do not go gentle into that good night,*
> *Old age should burn and rave at close of day;*
> *Rage, rage, against the dying of the light.*

Many preindustrial societies would take exception with the poet's vehement denial of death. The Egyptians, for example, were intensely preoccupied with death, in large part because they expected to be judged in the afterlife before a tribunal presided over by the god Osiris. The pyramids, the rites of mummification, and *The Egyptian Book of the Dead*, a guide to the soul's moral judgment in the afterlife, all attest to the significance of death preparation in ancient Egypt.

In the Middle Ages, Christians practiced the *ars moriendi*, the craft of dying, which consisted of contemplative exercises, such as meditating on a skull or on the crucified Christ, as a preparation for death at any instant. People in medieval society suffered from a short life expectancy and constant exposure to death through epidemics and plagues. By meditating on death and the brevity of their earthly pilgrimage, they hoped to mitigate the terrors of physical life and secure for themselves a blissful existence in the next world. Works of popular literature emphasized the theme *memento mori* ("remember death"), reinforcing the Church's mission of preparing people for the afterlife.

Today, in our largely rootless, secularized culture, we think of *memento mori* as the slogan of life-hating Puritans who try to encroach on our inalienable right to fun and pleasure. Our new motto, reinforced by the youth-worshipping media, might well be, "Forget death." We insulate ourselves from physical death by shunting the dying to modern hospitals, where they are banished from the realm of the living. We further distance ourselves from the benediction of natural death by entrusting our well-being to medical technology. Because technology has increased our control over the physical world, we expect to transfer this same mastery to the organic processes that support the body—often with disastrous results.

According to Jungian analyst Clarissa Pinkola Estes, "God as machine makes monstrous things occur, such as stroke victims lying like fallen flowers beside a dead vine, kept in some facsimile of dead bloom for years on end, with tubes and chemical fertilizers." We endure this travesty of life, she explains, because in our obsession with tricking death through technology, we have forgotten that true healing involves soul making, the conscious passage from this life to the next. Since, however, death has been uprooted from its traditional spiritual context, modern people do not welcome it as a nurturing midwife. Instead, we encounter death only with the greatest doubt, anxiety, and fear.

Fortunately, the climate surrounding death has changed within the past several decades due to the emergence of the death awareness movement. In her groundbreaking book published in 1969, *On Death and Dying*, Dr. Elisabeth Kübler-Ross outlined five stages experienced by the dying: denial, anger, bargaining, depression, and acceptance. This predeath psychology has now become so commonplace that people frequently inquire of a dying patient, "Which stage is she passing through?" Later in the 1970s, Kübler-Ross, along with Drs. Raymond Moody and Kenneth Ring, popularized the *near-death experience* (NDE). This phenomenon occurs when a person who is pronounced clinically dead typically rises out of the body, travels down a dark tunnel, encounters a brilliant white light, reviews his or her life, and then returns to ordinary reality with a transformed spiritual attitude. During this period, Robert Monroe, a former New York broadcasting executive, brought out-of-body experiences (OOBEs) to public attention through his books *Journeys Out of the Body* and *Far Journeys*. In these books, he chronicles his travels outside the physical body to locales far removed from ordinary reality, unbounded by space, time, and death. I'll explore NDEs and OOBEs a little later, but for now let me point out that these phenomena have strengthened the case for the continuity of life after death.

Hollywood has responded to this resurgence in afterdeath studies with films that reveal our abiding curiosity about the end of physical life. *Resurrection*, for example, shows a housewife whose near-death experience following an automobile crash transforms her into a spiritual healer. The highly popular film *Ghost* depicts the continuity of life after death, along with communication between the living and the dead. *Defending Your Life* depicts a comedic vision of the afterlife in which the deceased must appear before a celestial tribunal in Judgment City and defend their lives on the basis of whether they lived courageously on Earth. If candidates are successful, they graduate to other realms of existence. If they fail, they must return to Earth for further education. One can sense in this film a lighthearted but sincere attempt to deal with the themes of the soul's judgment in the afterlife and reincarnation, twin pillars of religious thought in the East and the West.

So far in our discussion of modern attitudes about death, we have been speaking of the afterlife as if it were one country united by a monolithic culture. But because the world's spiritual traditions envision it according to their own unique cultural and theological premises, the afterlife may be more like a confederation of states, in which each member shares common concerns with its partners but retains its own language, customs, and heritage.

In the following sections, I will present various concepts of the afterlife and evidence in support of life after death. As you consider this information, please remember that there's no one "correct" view, but rather an open, limitless field of possibilities. In fact, you may completely reject the notion of an afterlife as spiritual consolation and nothing more. While I have no vested interests in imposing the afterlife on you, I do urge you to consider the spectrum of ideas and the anecdotal evidence from modern consciousness research as part of your philosophic homework in spiritual eldering.

## THE AFTERLIFE IN THE WORLD'S SPIRITUAL TRADITIONS

From the beginning of time, humankind has wrestled with the question posed by Job in the Bible, "If a man die, shall he live again?" Down through the ages, the world's spiritual traditions have proposed answers that span a broad spectrum of possibilities. According to the ancient Greeks, the soul descends to a murky netherworld called Hades, where it spends eternity in unceasing gloom. The Jewish patriarchs had a similar notion of the netherworld, called Sheol in the biblical tradition. When Saul seeks counsel with the deceased Samuel about an upcoming battle with the Philistines, the witch of Endor, functioning as a medium, tells the king that he will soon join his mentor in the underworld. Clearly, the notion of a glorious afterlife had not yet sprouted in the Hebraic tradition.

After the destruction of the Temple in A.D. 70, the belief in the resurrection of the body and the afterdeath existence of the soul became part of the rabbinic Jewish worldview. By this time, the Apostle Paul was combing the Mediterranean world, broadcasting the message of eternal life through the resurrection of Jesus Christ. Soon Church fathers were depicting heaven as the eternally blissful abode of those who lived just and pious lives on Earth. To enter Paradise, according to medieval Christian theologians, the soul at death must balance its earthly accounts in Purgatory, a postmortem way station where it cleanses itself of earthly misdeeds through acts of spiritual purification.

"In purgatory the soul suffers for sins committed on earth, whether gluttony, avarice, pride or lust, or any of the other numerous offenses against God and humanity," writes Kenneth Kramer in *The Sacred Art of Dying*. "Prayers assist and support souls through this difficult journey. It is not until Christ's second coming that the Final Judgment is consummated when bodies are resurrected and rejoin their souls."

By the time of the Talmud, Jews, too, held that the experience of purgatory prepared the soul for an ascension to the heavenly spheres. Let me briefly outline the soul's journey in purgatory and the celestial worlds as conceived by the Kabbalah and then compare this view with the Tibetan teaching, which it resembles in some respects.

According to the Jewish sacred teachings, after death the soul passes through seven levels of purgatory, after which it bathes in the River of Light (called the Great White Light in the Tibetan tradition). It then ascends to the Lower Paradise, where it joins departed relatives in beatific fellowship and enjoys the rewards of all the virtuous deeds that it performed on Earth. Once these experiences are exhausted, the soul, yearning to rise to a higher level, again immerses itself in the River of Light and enters the Upper Paradise, the world of celestial knowledge. On this level, the sojourner's mind enters into communion with learning so vast and ecstatic that all of eternity cannot exhaust its riches. One can ascend to a still higher level, which the Zohar, the principal text of Jewish mysticism, calls "being drawn into the body of the King." Absorbed into the godhead, one merges with the source in an act of surrender also described by the Hindu tradition as the drop flowing into the ocean.

Most people don't choose this highest path, because its utter unfamiliarity causes them to recoil from the unknown. Instead, they choose to dwell with their loved ones in more familiar territories, enjoying the landscape of Paradise. Fortified by the *mitzvot* (the good deeds or "good karma") that they performed on Earth, they digest the meaning of their experience, seeking a deeper, richer understanding of it. Once the soul has absorbed all that these heavens have to offer, it applies for reincarnation and the promise of further perfection gleaned in the school of terrestrial life.

The soul's journey as described by *The Tibetan Book of the*

*Dead* has much in common with the Jewish sacred teachings. At the moment of death, explains Sogyal Rinpoche, the body dies, the senses dissolve, and the ordinary mind drops away. Consciousness then merges with the "Clear Light," "the primordial ground of our absolute nature, which is like a pure and cloudless sky." When the clouds that obscure the Ground Luminosity disperse, our innermost essence shines in its splendor, with an awareness that is at once pure, radiant, intelligent, and eternally awake. Christians and Jews call this state of realization God, Hindus call it Brahman, while Buddhists call it Buddha nature. The dawning of the Clear Light, which offers the greatest opportunity of a lifetime for liberation, is similar to the Jewish doctrine of "being drawn into the body of the King."

"Even though the Ground Luminosity presents itself naturally to us all, most of us are totally unprepared for its sheer immensity, the vast and subtle depth of its naked simplicity," writes Sogyal Rinpoche in *The Tibetan Book of Living and Dying*. "The majority of us will simply have no means of recognizing it, because we have not made ourselves familiar with ways of recognizing it in life." For most people, therefore, the dawning of the Clear Light lasts no more than a snap of the fingers, after which they recede from the overwhelming effulgence and flee into a state of *avidya* (unconsciousness).

When we awaken, we confront the natural radiance of the enlightened mind in the form of deities manifesting as a transcendental display of sound, light, and color. If we recognize these manifestations as the projections of our minds, we can merge with them and attain liberation. However, if we fail in this task, we fall into the "karmic bardo of becoming," an intermediate state between death and a new rebirth. In this confusing, dream-like dimension, we may return home and have the disconcerting experience of being unable to communicate with our loved ones. Until we realize that we cast no shadow or make no reflection in a mirror, we may not even suspect that we have died. (It's for this reason that Jewish people cover the mirrors during the week of grief and mourning following someone's death. We do this to spare the departed one the shock of looking in the mirror without seeing a physical reflection.)

Once we realize that we no longer have a physical existence, we relive the experiences of our past life. We also may undergo a form of life review similar to the postmortem judgment we find in the world's spiritual traditions. Finally, after wandering restlessly through the phantasmagoric landscapes of the bardo, the urge for rebirth becomes increasingly urgent, and we return to the Earth through the force of our unfulfilled desires.

As you can see, there exist many beliefs about the afterlife. In generalizing about them, we could say that the traditional Western monotheistic religions—Judaism, Christianity, and Islam—believe that the human soul is independent of the physical body and continues in another form after death. Eastern religions, such as Buddhism and Hinduism, along with Kabbalah and some forms of Sufism, the mystical school of Islam, hold that the soul undergoes successive reincarnations until enlightenment is attained. These beliefs exist side by side with today's scientific materialism, which holds that nothing survives the death of the body, because consciousness is extinguished when the brain dies. Such a totally materialistic philosophy, says consciousness researcher Charles Tart, reduces hope, love, joy, and intellect to nothing but "electrochemical impulses in a biocomputer that originated by chance in a universe of dead, randomly moving material particles." This view, he says, "invalidates vital aspects of human nature and creates a dismal outlook on life."

While the afterdeath teachings I have outlined may sound like fantasy in our secularized world, I believe that they make us citizens of a larger perceptual universe, a Common Society of Being that links the physical and nonphysical worlds. When we open-endedly investigate the issue of postmortem surival as part of our philosophic homework, we sense that we are multileveled organisms having physical, emotional, intellectual, and spiritual dimensions. Each time we investigate the contours of our being, they prove much larger than our senses might indicate. As we move beyond the physical body, we expand into larger fields of knowledge and being.

What, then, dies when we die? From the perspective of our multileveled organism, it appears that we slough off only the physical part of our being. Once we are in touch with the entirety of our organism, we find it less threatening and fearful to handle the absence of the physical component. Realizing that we are rooted in a multidimensional universe, we sense that our departed loved ones do not just disappear into some kind of cosmic black hole, but continue on in a different form. We also sense that we are connected with them even though we are physically separated.

According to *The Tibetan Book of the Dead*, the deceased are particularly receptive to the heartfelt thoughts, feelings, and prayers on their behalf. That's why lamas, spiritual friends, and family members recite the *Book of the Dead* to the dying person during and after his transition. (The actual name of the book, *Bardo Thodol*, means "The Great Liberation Through Hearing in the Bardo.") By sending thoughts of love and encouragement to our loved ones, we help them expand into greater luminosity, rather than contract into fear and forgetfulness.

Instead of distracting the departed with our lamentations, we can send them our blessings. For example, to a person who has suffered through a long, debilitating illness, we can say, "Dear friend, I send you loving supportive thoughts for the journey ahead. Do not be afraid: It's a shock to drop the body, but it's not the end of your existence. Now that you've abandoned your old, worn-out body, go forward to your new life in anticipation of a pain-free, comfortable existence. Go in trust and peace, knowing that friends and guides will appear to help you through this transition."

## EVIDENCE OF LIFE AFTER DEATH

For the last 150 years, there has been a growing literature of psychic research on postmortem existence. This research has taken a quantum leap in the last two decades as new developments in consciousness research have strengthened the case for survival after death. By far, the most convincing evidence comes from the numerous documented cases of people who have undergone near-death experiences.

According to Raymond Moody, a pioneer in near-death studies and author of the groundbreaking book *Life After Life*, the NDE is a worldwide phenomenon that transcends cultural bounds. Researchers have observed the same core phenomena among subjects in the United States, Norway, Sweden, Denmark, France, Germany, Italy, Spain, England, and the former Soviet Union. Researchers also have noted that a surprising number of people have undergone the experience. A Gallup poll conducted in 1982, for example, revealed that more than 8 million American adults have had near-death experiences. Moody, who has interviewed more than 2,500 NDErs, is convinced that these people have had glimpses of the beyond.

At the beginning of the core experience, NDErs feel ecstatically peaceful, devoid of pain, fear, or bodily sensations. Hearing a loud ringing or buzzing sound, they separate from their physical bodies, rise above them in an out-of-body experience, and observe events in the immediate environment as detached spectators. NDErs next enter a dark, dimensionless space, then move rapidly through a tunnel, drawn forward by a great white light, often characterized as beautiful and loving. Many people report entering a world of preternatural beauty, a peaceful realm of celestial landscapes and ethereal music where they temporarily may be reunited with deceased loved ones. Some people encounter a luminous being of light in whose compassionate presence they undergo a panoramic life review. At a certain point, they decide or are commanded to return to their worldly commitments, and reluctantly they reenter their bodies.

When they return to life, NDErs undergo a radical shift in their personalities and values. According to near-death researcher Kenneth Ring, author of *Heading Toward Omega*, the NDE serves as a "catalyst for spiritual awakening and development." NDErs, he observes, show a greater appreciation for life and have an increased capacity for loving others. As their interest in personal status and material possessions wanes, they focus on spiritual values, developing an inward closeness to God and an appreciation for the unity of the world's religions. Most telling of all, they almost unanimously report losing their fear of death.

"I *know* there is life after death!" writes one of Ring's respondents in *Heading Toward Omega*. "Nobody can shake my belief. I have no doubt—it's peaceful and nothing to be feared." According to a second subject, "This experience was a blessing to me, because I now know with certainty that there is a separation of body and soul and there is life after death." Another subject with an unassailable conviction about survival after death writes, "As a result of that [experience], I have very little apprehension about dying my natural death . . . because if death is anything,

anything at all like what I experienced, it's [got to] be the most wonderful thing to look forward to, absolutely the most wonderful thing."

Like NDEs, out-of-body experiences (OOBEs) suggest that consciousness can exist independently of the body, supporting the likelihood that the Self can survive after physical death. OOBE literature is replete with accounts of people at the threshold of death who floated above their bodies to watch with amazed detachment as doctors struggled desperately to resuscitate them. Many accounts describe how voyagers separate from their physical bodies and travel to remote locations.

In *What Survives?*, a collection of essays by renowned scholars and spiritual teachers about life after death, consciousness researcher Stanislav Grof gives a remarkable example of an out-of-body experience. Kimberly Clark, a social worker in Seattle, was assigned to a migrant worker named Maria, who had a severe heart attack and was admitted to a coronary care unit. Several days after her admission, Maria had a cardiac arrest, but because the woman was closely monitored, doctors quickly resuscitated her.

Afterward, in a state of extreme agitation, Maria told her social worker about having had an OOBE. "The strangest thing happened when the doctors and nurses were working on me," Maria said. "I found myself looking down from the ceiling at them working on my body." Distracted by something over the emergency room driveway, she "thought herself" outside and traveled up to the third-floor ledge on the north end of the building where she found herself "eyeball to shoelace" with a tennis shoe. Maria wanted someone to validate her experience, so with mixed emotions the skeptical social worker made a thorough search of the patients' rooms on the third floor—and to her amazement discovered the tennis shoe!

OOBEs like Maria's occur more frequently than one might assume. Recent studies demonstrate that as many as 30 percent of the American population may have had at least one OOBE, writes consciousness researcher John White in *A Practical Guide to Death & Dying*. According to Dr. Stanley Krippner, director of the Center for Consciousness Studies at Saybrook Institute in San Francisco, three independent studies show that at least three out of ten people have had OOBEs. Ernest Hemingway—never considered a wide-eyed mystic in literary circles—experienced an OOBE after he had been badly wounded. "I felt my soul or something coming right out of my body," he writes, "like you'd pull a silk handkerchief out of a pocket by one corner. It flew around and then came back and went in again and I wasn't dead anymore."

People who have undergone OOBEs generally have the unshakable conviction that they will survive physical death. They have firsthand evidence that consciousness can continue functioning without a physical body. "Through my experiences," says Robert Monroe, author of *Journeys Out of the Body*, "I have come to one incontrovertible conclusion: We do survive physical death. I believe that the OOBE is the most effective way to demonstrate the unreality of death."

## HELP FROM THE SPIRITUAL TRADITIONS

Obviously, in this short space I only have hinted at the wealth of evidence that points toward life after death. There exists a vast afterdeath literature that includes cases of people who remember past incarnations or who experience spontaneous contact with the dead. Part of your philosophic homework might include familiarizing yourself with this body of evidence. But reading is only the beginning. If you are convinced that death is not a final annihilation but rather a transition to expanded states of being, you might begin preparing for this transcendent moment through exercises that simulate the death experience. As John White says in *A Practical Guide to Death & Dying*, "Learning to do anything well requires sustained practice and varied exercises that deepen your skill and understanding. Dying is no exception—dying well, that is."

Many of the techniques involved in conscious dying come from the world's spiritual traditions, which consider death preparation as integral to our "higher education." We might think of meditation, for example, as the technique *par excellence* to prepare us "to die before we die." Through deep and consistent practice, we learn to transcend the ego, an experience of ego death that temporarily dissolves the personal self into a larger field of consciousness that is beyond space and time. Spiritual practices such as meditation make us better equipped to die consciously, because when it's time for our transition, we have "died" many times during meditation and have lived through it.

As part of their spiritual training, Buddhist monks often meditate on the impermanence of life and the inevitability of death. To increase their familiarity with death and to decondition themselves of their automatic fear responses, they sometimes meditate in graveyards, using a human skull or a thigh bone as an object of meditation. On Yom Kippur, the Day of Atonement, Jews wear their death shrouds as prayer shawls, receiving a foretaste of the inevitability of death and using this awareness as preparation for living a better life. Jews who bathe in a *mikveh*, a ritual bath of purification, or Christians who are baptized by immersion also have profound experiences of death and rebirth, of dying before they die. These spiritual practices put us on good terms with our mortality, so that when it's time for our departure, we can say along with St. Paul, "O Death, where is thy sting? O grave, where is thy victory?"

In the past few decades, counselors schooled in spiritual practice have been helping dying people use their transitions as occasions for inner awakening. Spiritual practitioners such as Ram Dass and Stephen Levine, author of *Who Dies?*, gently encourage the dying to explore their unfinished business, losses, and fears as part of a process of self-inquiry. In this spirit, they confront the question, "Who am I without my name, spouse, home, career, and credit cards—without all the paraphernalia that props up my personal identity?" Inspired by the urgency of approaching death, this investigation often brings people face-to-face with their spiritual essence, which is experienced as deathless, unconditionally loving, and free from the self-protective images that separate them from other people.

To facilitate this process, counselors need to show unconditional love to the dying. After all, as Sogyal Rinpoche points out, "The dying are losing their whole world: their house, their job, their relationships, their body, and their mind—they're losing everything." At the same time, they are facing the deepest fears of a lifetime, including the fear of increasing, uncontrolled pain, the fear of dependence and loss of control, along with fear of the unknown. Given this vulnerable condition, says Sogyal Rinpoche, how could the dying not be panicked, angry, or grief-stricken?

For these reasons, counselors need to be sensitive listeners who encourage people to express their deepest thoughts and feelings about dying without fear of censure or judgment.

"Dying will bring out many repressed emotions: sadness or numbness or guilt, or even jealousy of those who are still well," Sogyal Rinpoche writes in *The Tibetan Book of Living and Dying*. "Help the person not to repress these emotions when they rise. Be with the person as the waves of pain and grief break; with acceptance, time, and patient understanding, the emotions slowly subside and return the dying person to the ground of serenity, calm, and sanity that is most deeply and truly theirs."

## EXERCISES IN DEATH PREPARATION

There are many helpful manuals that can help prepare us for a conscious transition. John White's *A Practical Guide to Death & Dying*, for example, contains instructions for writing a detailed description of our death, visualizing our last hour on Earth, imagining our own funeral, and videotaping our final farewell to family and friends. The book also includes an exercise in which we listen to Richard Strauss's *Death and Transfiguration* and then record in a notebook our thoughts and impressions about death. These exercises, by and large, desensitize us to our largely irrational fears about dying.

Let's look in some detail at *Deathing*, Anya Foos-Graber's approach to conscious dying. Her method includes practical techniques for encountering the actual moment of death with dignity, mental control, and a sense of equipoise that keeps fear to a minimum. As I have already indicated, spiritual teachers urge the dying person to remain calm and undistracted in order to encounter the light of expanded awareness with a serene, focused mind. But disease symptoms, the unfamiliar phenomena that accompany physical cessation, along with the unfinished business and separation anxiety that often attend this moment all make it hard to concentrate. For these reasons, Foos-Graber teaches people to practice deep diaphragmatic breathing to calm the mind and control fear.

How can breath control produce these desired results? According to yoga psychology, there is a direct relationship between breathing and our mental and emotional states. Swift, shallow breaths reflect a distracted mind and emotional disturbances such as anxiety, fear, and anger. Slow, deep breaths, on the other hand, tend to quiet the mind and dispel negative emotions. By breathing in a slow, rhythmic manner, dying people gain a strong measure of mental control, making it easier to remain centered in the midst of pain and imminent separation from the body. As the mind attains a state of meditative clarity, people more easily can release the body and visualize merging with the light of their higher nature.

To aid in this often daunting task, Foos-Graber teaches the "fail-safe" technique of calling on the name of a spiritual preceptor, such as Elijah, Jesus Christ, or the Buddha. She likens this practice to hitchhiking into the afterlife by focusing on and identifying with an enlightened being who represents one's highest spiritual ideal. Dying people also may synchronize their breathing and visualizations by reciting affirmations, positive suggestions repeated often and with conviction that help keep the mind undistracted. Christians, for example, can recite, "Lord Jesus Christ, have mercy on me," while Jews can chant, "Hear, O Israel, the Lord our God, the Lord is one." Both can say, "Into thy hands I commend my soul."

Foos-Graber also teaches people to recognize the often bizarre but predictable bodily sensations that signal that departure is imminent. These include heaviness in the lower limbs, a sinking or floating sensation, alternate feelings of heat or cold, a lightening or softening of the body, shallow breathing, a sense of peacefulness, a disorientation in space and time, or a cacophony of sounds and visions (including images of drought, tidal waves, earthquakes, and multicolored landscapes) that indicate that the body's solid form is dissolving. People with the best of intentions and preparation may be overwhelmed by these phenomena or may simply lapse into unconsciousness. For this reason, a support person repeatedly can remind the dying person to remain calm, to have no fear, to remember the spiritual teacher, and to move upward toward the light, rather than downward toward the body.

At such a crucial time, the support person might say something like the following in a slow, gentle voice, "Dear friend, I want you to know how much I love you and will miss you. Relax, breathe away all feelings of anxiety, and know that the process is unfolding as it should, peacefully, without effort or strain. As your outer vision begins to fade, pay attention to the promptings of your inner vision. You may experience many sensations, or witness emissaries drawing close to guide your passage out of the body. Reject nothing; let everything happen naturally. In the midst of these confusing phenomena, remember your spiritual teacher and the name of God with which you resonate. As you say good-bye to your body, prepare to recognize the unconditional love and wisdom that soon will claim you as its own. We've taken care of all your physical concerns, so your passage can be as effortless, focused, and peaceful as possible. Go in peace, dear one."

Foos-Graber recommends that the dying person and the "coach" practice the breathing and visualization exercises for as long as six weeks to six months. To facilitate their training sessions, she also recommends making an audiotape (either in the dying person's own voice or in the support person's) and using it for a number of trial runs. Part of training also includes encouraging the dying person to resolve all unfinished business and to clarify his or her beliefs about the afterlife. The moment of death is definitely not an ideal time to find out what we believe!

"At the moment of death there is no time for the usual delays and hemmings and hawings of the critical mind," Foos-Graber writes in *Deathing*. "We must be prepared beforehand with conditioned responses that will activate automatically. Right deathing can ensure that we will be ready—rather than unaware and helpless—at the final, definitive moment of consciousness."

Psychologist Gay Luce draws heavily on Foos-Graber's methods in a seminar that she leads entitled "Death: The Opportunity of a Lifetime." During the seminar, after guiding people through a life review and forgiveness exercises, she asks them to imagine their last day on Earth. In preparation for their final leavetaking, participants consciously release attachments to their bodies, senses, relationships, the physical world, along with the hopes and dreams, aspirations and disappointments of a lifetime. Then, in an all-night ceremony, they rehearse the deathing process in dyads, alternately playing the role of the dying person and the guide. During the ceremony, they also read instructions on dying from *The Tibetan Book of the Dead*.

"These practice sessions help people overcome their fear of death while preparing them to go through the death of a parent, spouse, family member, or beloved friend with greater equanimity," Luce says. "By revealing the enduring values that make life meaningful, these sessions also help people set priorities in their careers and personal relationships, based on their desire to live as loving, service-oriented individuals. In a very real sense, death training is life training."

## AN ALTERNATE VIEW OF THE AFTERLIFE

In spite of all the data that I have presented, you may remain unconvinced by notions of the afterlife, preferring instead to trust the evidence of your empirical experience. Or you simply may remain an agnostic, neither believing nor disbelieving in any of the evidence. Can you still count yourself as a spiritual elder? Of course! Even if you oppose the idea of life after death, you can continue on the path to elderhood by coming to terms with your mortality in whatever way is compatible with your belief system and by proceeding with the work of life harvesting.

Similarly, you needn't practice conscious dying to earn a spiritual eldering merit badge. Some people take the attitude, "Death is a unique, once-in-a-lifetime experience, not to be missed under any circumstances." But others prefer to die gently in their sleep, undisturbed by the anxiety of parting with the body. They take the attitude, "Let me sleep through it. If I make it to the other side, good; but if I don't make it, I won't upset myself." Remember, there are no "right" or "wrong" ways of dying. As Ram Dass says, "Death is absolutely safe. Nobody fails at it."

In keeping with this open-ended approach, those who don't accept theological notions about the continuity of life might consider surrendering themselves at death into the greater life of Gaia, feeding their increment of consciousness back into the planetary genetic pool. Regardless of religious orientation, they can say, "Among the millions of life forms that are possible, what a privilege for me to have been a brain cell of planet Earth!"

In *Cat's Cradle*, Kurt Vonnegut depicts this attitude through the Bokononist Death Ritual. In this fanciful science-fiction novel, the Bokononists serve God by lying down on the floor, raising their legs, and massaging each other's feet, sole to sole, while communing with God. When one of the old Bokononists is about to die, he recites the prayer, "God made mud," which describes the miraculous process by which God awakens mud to a world of unsurpassed beauty and wonder. At the end of life, before mud lies down and goes to sleep, it exclaims, "I was some of the mud that got to sit up and look around. What memories for mud to have! I loved everything I saw! Lucky me, lucky mud."

If we assume this attitude, then like the Bokononists, we, too, can say at death, "How fortunate I was to live!" When the time comes to release our consciousness to the greater planetary pool, our death seems less "terminal" when viewed from the perspective of Gaia's transpersonal organism. As we upload our experience into the Global Brain through mentoring, journal work, and meditation, we ensure that it is "saved" for future generations. By contributing our small but important increment of consciousness for the growth and evolution of Gaia, we, too, can exclaim, "Lucky me, lucky mud."

This form of Gaian immortality is in no way inimical to other, more traditional notions of postmortem existence. People with all spectrums of belief about the afterlife can find their place within this worldview. Whether we believe in being recycled as part of Gaia's ongoing existence; whether we subscribe to life after death as taught by the world's spiritual traditions; whether we embrace a synthesis of the two views or hold to neither, as elders we still must close our accounts, finish our business, and prepare for the *mysterium tremendum* that occurs at life's exit point. To improve the quality of our at-death and subsequent experience, we need to begin preparing for it now.

We will reap great rewards for this preparation, not only when pushing off from death's promontory, but throughout the remainder of our days. For by confronting death in life, we come out of hiding and open our hearts to the human community, so that like Miss Martin at the end of her life, we can say, "I have friends." At the same time, we put aside our proud but pathological sense of separateness and give up the deadening, habitual ways of living that the spiritual traditions call sleep. Interdependent with the greater web of life and brimming with sensory vitality, we will no longer postpone our engagement with life. By confronting death, we finally will learn the art of living.

# *Part Three*

# Spiritual Eldering and Social Transformation

CHAPTER 8

# *Mentoring: Seeding the Future with Wisdom*

In the popular movie *The Karate Kid*, Mr. Miyagi, an older Okinawan man who is skilled in the martial arts, takes on a hapless adolescent boy named Daniel as his apprentice. Daniel, a newcomer to the neighborhood, is being terrorized by a group of malicious teenage boys who are studying karate with an aggressive, unscrupulous teacher. Miyagi feels great affection for Daniel and recognizes that the self-deprecating youth has a certain potential that the teenager cannot see in himself.

For Miyagi, karate is not just a pugilistic technique, but a way of life. Therefore, when he teaches Daniel how to defend himself, he not only stresses mastery of technique, but also models the inner, spiritual side of the discpline. With generosity, encouragement, good-natured humor, and patience, the older man transmits the essence of his wisdom to the receptive youth, who becomes a "peaceful warrior" like his mentor.

In the transmission, Daniel learns much more than the technical aspects of karate. Receiving priceless instruction in the art of living, he learns how to meet adversity with valor, how to distinguish between inner strength and mere bravado, and how to develop self-worth. He even receives encouragement in overcoming his problems with the opposite sex. At the end of the movie, as Miyagi proudly shares in Daniel's triumph over his tormentors, we sense the potential for fulfillment that lies in mentoring a young person.

Hermann Hesse's delightful novel *Siddhartha* reveals how a mature man also can benefit from apprenticing himself to a wise elder. As a young man, Siddhartha, the proud son of a Brahman priest, leaves home in search of enlightenment and joins a band of wandering ascetics. When he meets the Buddha, he decides not to follow the enlightened one as a monk, but to follow the master's counsel of becoming a lamp unto himself. Siddhartha then gives up his ascetic ways and gets enmeshed in the worldly pursuit of sensuality and wealth. Many years later, disgusted by his empty existence, he renounces his materialistic lifestyle and apprentices himself to Vasudeva, an old ferryman who lives in a hut by a river.

Like Miyagi, Vasudeva does not immediately begin transmitting verbal wisdom to his mentee. Realizing that the ground must be prepared before seeds can blossom into fragrant flowers, he waits patiently and listens as Siddhartha narrates the particulars of his life. Because his teacher is at home with the full range of human experience—the height of spiritual realization as well as the depth of human folly—Siddhartha does not have to polish his image in relating to his mentor. He enters into spiritual intimacy without the need to censor his faults or promote his virtues:

> He mentioned everything, he could tell him everything, even the most painful things.... Vasudeva listened with great attention; he heard all about his origin and childhood, about his studies, his seekings, his pleasures and needs. It was one of the ferryman's greatest virtues that, like few people, he knew how to listen. Without saying a word, the speaker felt that Vasudeva took in every word, quietly, expectantly, that he missed nothing. He did not await anything with impatience and gave neither praise nor blame—he only listened. Siddhartha felt how wonderful it was to have such a listener who could be absorbed in another person's life, his striving, his sorrows.

Like Miyagi, Vasudeva doesn't teach his apprentice abstract doctrines or esoteric techniques. He teaches Siddhartha life craft, the skillful means to handle the challenges of his daily activities. For Siddhartha, working the rice fields, gathering wood, and making oars with Vasudeva are not merely mundane pastimes. They are the vehicle through which his mentor demonstrates how to bring a sense of the sacred into everyday affairs. Through his relationship with Vasudeva, Siddhartha eventually polishes the rough edges of his personality and learns to accept and bless life as it is. When he becomes self-realized, he transmits the essence of his wisdom, a compassionate sense of the unity of life, to others searching for self-knowledge.

## INTERGENERATIONAL BESTOWAL

Both *The Karate Kid* and *Siddhartha* illustrate the age-old practice of mentoring, the art of intergenerational bestowal by which elders pass on to younger people the living flame of their wisdom. As philosopher Martin Buber points out, in the crucible of this generative relationship, the elder helps forge a center in the younger person. Mentors do not impose doctrines and values on their mentees in an attempt to clone themselves. Rather, they evoke the individuality of their apprentices, applauding them as they struggle to clarify their values and discover their authentic life paths.

To individuate, to become our unique selves rather than secondhand imitations, we need someone standing behind us, saying as it were, "I bless you in the heroic, worthwhile, and difficult task of becoming yourself." Such a person evokes our questing spirit, not by giving answers, but by deepening our ability to question and to search for meaning. As we work through anxiety, doubt, and occasional discouragement in our quest for a genuine life path, our mentor acts as a midwife, helping us breathe more easily as we give birth to ourselves in the world.

In the presence of a wise elder, we can talk about our failures and shortcomings, our indiscretions and foibles, without feeling judged or shamed. We feel respected and appreciated, in large part because the mentor does not treat us like an underling. Even when we speak with confusion and self-reproach, the mentor nods with understanding and says, "It's all right, you made an error but you can start again. And maybe it really wasn't a mistake but an opportunity for deep learning. I did the same thing earlier in life. It's not easy to acquire wisdom, but it's possible and eminently worthwhile. Just keep on in your journey."

What empowers the mentor to act in such a compassionate way? A natural unfoldment takes place in the psyche, which signals at a certain time when the accumulated wisdom of a lifetime reaches the state of overflow. Awakened to elderhood, we pour the distillate of our lives into other vessels, an act that not only seeds the future, but that crowns our lives with worth and nobility.

When we are younger, we transmit our life essence in a more physical way, as libido urges us to preserve our genetic endowment through having children. In elderhood, as it becomes invested in transmitting a pattern of experience larger than the genetic code, libido takes the form of mentoring, a spiritualized form of conceiving and giving birth that transmits our "seed" in nonbiological ways. When, for example, Pablo Casals took on five master students, he "impregnated" his apprentices with musical techniques and insights, part of the legacy of his long career.

Mentoring preserves valuable life experience from disappearing with the inevitable decay of the physical body. If you work on a computer for an hour and there's a power outage, that work simply disappears from the computer's memory. Similarly, if you don't "save" your life experience through mentoring and through leaving legacies, the wisdom that you have synthesized through decades of difficult learning will disappear as your physical medium of storage and expression wears out. How sad! That's why an elder's heart leaps up when a younger person says, "Please take me on as your student or apprentice. There's so much I want to learn from you."

What do elders have to teach? Over and beyond an exchange of verbal information and technical skills, they transmit what can't be acquired from books. When the transfer of sheer data just isn't sufficient, they impart the wisdom of a lifetime (including the personal attitudes, moral and ethical judgments, and aesthetic appreciations that characterized them) through the fire of a unique relationship, the give-and-take of a living dialogue with a younger student or apprentice. When an elder fertilizes a young person's aspiring mind with his knowledge and seasoned judgment, the student receives a living spark, a transmission, that may one day blossom into wisdom.

As recorded in his popular books, anthropologist Carlos Castaneda received such a transmission when he apprenticed himself to Don Juan, a wily old Yaqui sorcerer who guided his young academic charge through the mysterious and perilous process of becoming a shaman. Thomas Merton, the well-known Catholic monk who helped deepen the East-West religious dialogue, served as a mentor to numerous novices seeking spiritual direction. And in his celebrated dialogues with Bill Moyers in *The Power of Myth*, Joseph Campbell mentored a whole generation of people on the relevance of mythology in the modern world.

Today, because of the professionalism of modern life, we generally don't seek out elders for this kind of wisdom. By default, we go to professional licensed therapists and vocational counselors instead. Yet from the dawn of human history until the modern era, elders passed down to succeeding generations the essential knowledge needed to raise children, earn a living, preserve culture, and carry on spiritual traditions.

In the religious sphere, there is a venerable tradition of mentors passing on the living spark of realization from generation to generation. We find such mentoring between Moses and Joshua in the Old Testament and among Jesus and the apostles in the New Testament. We find a similar pattern of mentoring in the family. From the Neolithic age to the dawn of the modern era, for example, young men would learn from their fathers and grandfathers how to wield and fix plows and when and how to sow seed, while young women would learn from their mothers and grandmothers how to care for children, recognize and gather herbs for healing, and set up households. A natural communal support system wove elder wisdom into the fabric of society.

But beginning with the Industrial Revolution, mentoring became institutionalized and bureaucratized as factory-like schools began teaching young people the specialized skills needed in industrial society. It may surprise you to know that until several centuries ago, rabbinical students didn't study in seminaries. Besides what they learned in sacred literature, they received their training through direct apprenticeship to practicing rabbis. The growth of rabbinical seminaries represented an institutionalization of the apprenticeship method. As the transmission of culture in every field became the province of schools, factories, and professional elites, one-on-one or small-group mentoring disappeared from the cultural landscape, depriving us of a source of wisdom that sustained human civilization for thousands of years.

Because of urbanization and industrialization, our world has been deprived of elder wisdom. In our society, we compensate for this loss of wisdom by a professionalism that supplies us with the technocratic information that we need, but it's delivered without the life-giving, caring field once provided by elders. This is not to argue against serious professional training. However, the lack of direct mentoring at home, in education, in the workplace, and in religion has contributed to an alienation in modern life that no amount of professional expertise can compensate for. The restoration of mentoring as a cultural force could go a long way in humanizing our institutions and in providing the intergenerational glue to combat social problems, such as family dysfunction, drug addiction, and sexual abuse.

## AN INTERACTIVE RELATIONSHIP

Having lost touch with the dynamics of mentoring, we need to refamiliarize ourselves with this essential form of loving human communication. We can think of mentoring as an intimate form of communion through which an elder inducts a younger person into a wisdom field. Like a tuning fork vibrating at a certain frequency, the mentor entrains the mentee into a similar resonance. Or to use another analogy: Think of a canal lock that fills and empties, allowing boats to rise or descend to different levels. Because the elder is at a higher level of experience than the younger colleague, mentoring enables the water to move from one level to another through spiritual intimacy.

In this exchange, communication is always a two-way process that mutually benefits both parties. The elder has more life experience and wisdom, so naturally the higher seeks its own level by flowing into the lower. At the same time, the mentee, having more vitality, naturally rejuvenates and invigorates the elder with energy and an influx of fresh ideas. Without this exchange, the elder may remain locked in the past. With their penchant for experimentation and their forward-looking mentality, young people give elders the gift of encountering the present and anticipating the future. What mentees receive, says Maurice Friedman, professor emeritus of religious studies, philosophy, and comparative literature at San Diego State University, is a readiness to bridge the past and the future.

"As elders, we can help young people respond to the challenges of modern life by drawing on our sense of historical continuity and our familiarity with how our forebears dealt with the perennial questions of human existence," he says. "When we tell stories about the Hasidic masters or Sufi teaching tales, for example, it's not to glory in the past, but to find precedents for dealing with the unknown, frequently shattering questions of the present era. The twenty-first century is nothing but questions that we've never heard before. In the fire of a mentoring relationship, young people develop a readiness to meet new, unforeseen situations in ways that carry life forward."

For a relationship to bear fruit as Friedman describes, the mentor must not be in a hurry to impress his knowledge on the mentee. If the communication is only one-way, from transmitter to receiver, the mentee probably won't stick around for further sessions. The best mentoring involves giving an ear to students or apprentices. Young people frequently want to try out new ideas, and elders can best serve them by listening attentively and nonjudgmentally, without forming premature conclusions that could short-circuit youthful initiative and enthusiasm. As the elder listens, clarification takes place in the mind of the younger person. Sometimes the elder needn't say a word for learning to occur. The greatest transmission often comes from wordless, attentive listening.

According to philosopher Sam Keen, author of *Fire in the Belly*, the mentor best serves the mentee as a "permissionary," someone who gives the younger person permission to carry on the work of self-exploration. A permissionary doesn't force a premature conclusion to the mentee's quest for meaning, even if the person is making a dark passage through fear, doubt, and discouragement. Rather than abort the mentee's quest by providing answers, the mentor deepens the person's ability to keep the questions alive while journeying through the nourishing dark.

"The mentor stands by the mentee and encourages him to

continue on without panicking," Keen says. "The mentor says, 'Take it easy. You won't always know where you are, but it doesn't mean that you're lost. By remaining faithful to the darkness, you'll keep right on schedule. Now tell me, is it still dark?' The mentee answers, 'Yes, I can't see a damn thing.' And the mentor responds, 'Good, continue on. Don't try to use your eyes now. Think, feel, use your other senses to chart your course.' In this way, the mentor acclimates the mentee to his unknown depths, from which authentic being emerges."

Maurice Friedman, whose mentor was philosopher Martin Buber, confirms this observation. Throughout their long and fruitful relationship, he translated twelve of his teacher's books and numerous lectures into English. Whenever he spent time with Buber, who had a gentle, penetrating gaze, Friedman felt summoned to be present, accountable, and uniquely himself.

"Once when we were working together at Princeton in 1958, Buber came downstairs and just looked at me, as if posing a wordless but absolutely compelling question to my being," he recalled. "That look will always remain with me. To this day, I can't translate into words the full import of that question. Perhaps I've been answering it all these years through my writing, teaching, and counseling. That gaze called forth my questing spirit, urging me forward into my own unique responses to life's deeper issues."

When a relationship of deep trust has been established with a mentor, sometimes a few words delivered with timely emphasis can dispel clouds of despair and empower the student to new levels of achievement. I had this experience in 1955 at Boston University when I took a course in spiritual disciplines and resources with Howard Thurmon, the Dean of the Chapel. Howard, a mystic and a poet, was a minister, a friendly, thoughtful man who took me under his wing.

Once I came to him feeling victimized by life. "I'll never achieve my heart's desire, because I'm weighed down with so many responsibilities at home and with my congregation," I complained with a despair that felt as bottomless as my momentary lack of faith. Howard paused, took a quiet moment to reflect on my predicament, then looked me straight in the eye with his warm, insistent gaze. "Zalman," he said, "was there ever something that you wholeheartedly desired that you didn't get?"

Suddenly, before my mind's eye and in the depths of my entrails, I felt the willingness of the cosmos to fulfill our heartfelt prayers. I didn't need long-winded sermons or theological tracts to convince me of the gift-giving nature of divinity. Nor did I need intense psychoarchaeological diggings to understand how my feelings of unworthiness were blocking the inflow of life's blessings. Because he knew my depths, Howard simply reached in and set in motion my own ability to trust myself and the beneficence of the divine will. That's how one well-placed sentence, delivered with care and understanding by my mentor, converted despair into hope, feelings of failure into trust. This moment of grace, in which the original goodness of the universe revealed itself through spiritual intimacy, still resonates in my psyche nearly four decades later and serves as a gate-opener for my faith in God.

## MENTORING: A HUMAN-HEARTED RELATIONSHIP

By now, you may be wondering whether you have the necessary qualifications for becoming a mentor. First, realize that you don't have to be a Martin Buber or a Howard Thurmon to be of benefit to young people. A mentor is not some exalted, superhuman being who magically dispenses wisdom to specially qualified apprentices. Stripped of all mystification, mentoring refers to a simple, human-hearted situation in which an older person says to a younger one, "I've learned something about life, my friend. I love you and I am available to share it with you."

Since we all have areas of expertise, mentoring can take place in an almost limitless number of settings. Over the years, we acquire invaluable experience as parents, businesspeople, scientists, teachers, bank tellers, nurses, and a wide array of other professions. If we esteem our experience enough, we need to find the appropriate means to pass it on. For example, an emeritus English professor might take on an adolescent boy and teach him creative writing. A retired piano teacher might mentor a young neighborhood girl who shows an interest and aptitude for the piano. A retired mechanic can teach young people about car repair. A gardener can teach a young housewife how to cultivate an herb garden.

Joseph Smryski mentors staff members and inmates at the

Northwest Regional Correctional Facility in South Burlington, Vermont, where he serves as the assistant superintendent. A former priest who is approaching sixty, he has been mentoring people for a number of years without considering himself an elder. When he took a spiritual eldering workshop with his wife, Teresa Martin, he began to redefine himself as an "elder in training," with the special task of modeling to his younger colleagues and to violent offenders a more human-hearted approach to prison reform.

"In the workshop, I realized that for years I had unconsciously been groping in the direction of elderhood without having a model to guide me," Joe remarks. "Now that I have a model to focus my aspirations and guide my behavior, I can embrace being a mentor with more dignity, confidence, and effectiveness."

Joe has always vehemently opposed the hard-line approach to prison reform that urges society "to lock prisoners up and throw away the key." The caseworkers he mentors, many of whom have been prison guards, consult with him about how to take a more humane approach with the inmates. The prisoners themselves do not regard Joe as an aloof, intimidating authority figure, but as a good father who remains involved in their struggles for dignity and self-respect.

"As a mentor, I share my full humanness with the inmates, always stressing what we have in common rather than what separates us," he says. "Without sounding immodest, I offer them a model of their potential that doesn't overwhelm them by making the attainment seem so out of reach. My presence says to them, 'I've trod the path of overcoming adversity, and if you persist in spite of all your doubts and self-reproaches, you, too, can overcome and make something worthwhile of your lives.' "

Like Joe, Gloria Krasno, a sixty-four-year-old counselor who works as a patient advocate for the Mental Health Association in Milwaukee, Wisconsin, also enjoys sharing her full humanness as a mentor. A former yoga teacher, she regularly invites students and friends to her home where they engage in open-hearted dialogue with her that often brings clarity and a sense of equanimity to their lives.

"Many people come with marital and vocational problems, a sense of general confusion about their life paths, or battered self-esteem," reports Gloria, who has been married for forty-four years and who has six children and four grandchildren. "Through my ability to listen and respond intuitively to their problems, they often leave with a sense of renewed purpose and the courage and perseverance to continue on their chosen paths."

Gloria, who has taken a number of spiritual eldering workshops, approaches her mentoring with a deepened sense of inner authority since she has assumed the stature of an elder. "I no longer feel embarrassed about acknowledging that my special gifts can contribute to the growth and well-being of other people," she says. "We all have special gifts, of course, but I can claim them now unreservedly as an elder of the tribe. Other people sense my inner empowerment and spontaneously seek me out."

Gloria tells the story of a forty-year-old woman who approached her at a spiritual conference and announced with unaffected sincerity, "You have something that I need." The woman, who intuitively sensed that Gloria had achieved a healthy synthesis of spirituality and sexuality in her marriage, needed to befriend an older woman who modeled the development that she was seeking and who gave her permission to grow in that direction. Their ensuing friendship not only helped the younger woman achieve a more satisfying personal relationship, but also helped Gloria heal early-life wounding that devalued her contribution as a strong and competent woman.

"Because there were few women mentors available when I was growing up, I feel especially happy to serve as a spiritual midwife to younger women," Gloria explains. "As a young woman, I was wounded when I knocked on doors and people told me, 'Go away. You're a woman and don't have the proper professional or religious qualifications.' By mentoring younger women, I heal this wound and grow in self-esteem as I watch my mentees enjoy satisfying personal and professional relationships."

## MASTERY IN THE ART OF LIVING

When you become a mentor, you will teach more than technical information about your area of expertise. You will impart lessons in the art of living that can be transferred to your mentees' personal circumstances. In the words of Rebbe Leib Sures, a Hasidic saint, "I did not go to the Maggid [great teacher] of Mezeritch to learn Torah from him, but to watch him tie his shoelaces."

How can the mundane act of tying shoelaces be of benefit to your mentee? In general, 90 percent of our lives consists of practical actions like this. Usually, because our minds are occupied with a thousand and one things, we tie our shoelaces with instrumental proficiency, but we are not entirely present in the activity. As an elder, you can teach younger people how not to hurry through troublesome chores with disgruntled haste, but how to perform them more consciously, with a calm, focused, and patient quality of mind. While mindfully modeling the "how to" of daily life, you will find numerous occasions to discuss substantive issues, such as the search for meaning, career choice, marriage, and family life.

Since we live in a culture that stresses professional certification, you might wonder what formal steps are required to launch your mentoring vocation. The answer is surprisingly simple: Nothing very formal is required at all. No one needs to stand over you with a curriculum vitae, saying, "We see by virtue of your experience in the business world and in raising a family that you're qualified for the position." Life itself, the great equal opportunity employer, enlists you to give back with generosity what you freely received from your teachers.

When you were younger and searching for spiritual guidance, you may have found solace in the axiom, "When the student is ready, the teacher appears." Teachers *did* appear, and you profited from their wisdom. But now that you have matured and crossed the threshold into elderhood, the revised axiom might read, "When the mentor is ready, the mentees will appear." When you embody the nobility of elderhood in your being, you will be so radiant and magnetic that people will be attracted to your wisdom and will actively seek you out. You needn't wear a badge or be a card-carrying graduate of the University of Elderhood to qualify as a mentor. Your being provides all the certification that you need.

How, then, do you make contact with mentees? In the normal course of living, as you walk down the street, have unexpected conversations with people at the supermarket, or spend time with grandchildren at family outings, have your antenna out for potential contacts. Sometimes a look of pained perplexity on the face of a divorced person or the intensity of someone's spiritual seeking triggers the mentoring impulse. You may feel a tugging at the heart, with the implied message, "I'd like to get closer to this person. Maybe I can shed some light on her path."

We also can trigger the mentoring impulse by responding to the question, "What would I grieve for if I failed to transmit it?" An accountant might express his predicament this way: "In helping homeowners prepare their income tax, I can lower their tax burden and help improve the quality of their lives. I haven't seen my techniques written about in any books. Because I would grieve the loss of this special knowledge, which is my personal contribution to the welfare of others, I would like to share it with accountants who are active in the profession."

Similarly, a nutritionist might say, "I've discovered that by eating foods in a certain sequence, people release a certain enzyme that vastly improves their digestion and overall health. It saddens me that this discovery isn't available to many people. Therefore, I would like to share my findings with other nutritionists and with clients."

To ensure that your special legacy is preserved, I suggest that you make an inventory of the skills and knowledge that represent your own treasure trove of life experience. Once you have completed your inventory, ask yourself, "Who are the likely candidates and customers to benefit from this experience?" In the above examples, the accountant's "customers" might include other accountants, neighborhood friends, or people in senior centers who might be puzzled about filling out their income tax. In the case of the nutritionist, customers might include other nutritionists, but also parents enrolled in parenting classes or people at senior centers interested in nutritional guidance.

Once you have discovered a match between your knowledge and your potential customers, find a way of getting acquainted with them. If you were the accountant, you might meet your colleagues at professional gatherings or in their offices and say, "I freely give you the fruits of my knowledge, and I would like you to remember me for it." If you were the nutritionist, you might encounter your colleagues at health fairs, professional conferences, or in their offices. Like the accountant, you might say, "I give you this information freely, and remember me when you help your clients. It's my gift to life and my legacy to the future."

## GUIDELINES FOR GETTING STARTED

Mentoring is a little like dancing. Sometimes the partners move with grace and lightfootedness, while other times they step on each other's toes. Sometimes they move listlessly to the same old tune, while on other occasions they improvise new dance steps as the music inspires them to deeper levels of self-expression. To help you in mentoring, here are a few suggestions for moving more gracefully on the dance floor.

**Listen with great spaciousness of heart and mind to your mentee's genuine concerns before attempting to share your wisdom.** In the famous teaching tale, a Zen master keeps pouring tea into a university professor's cup, even when it is filled to overflowing. "Like this cup," the Zen master says, "you are full of your own opinions and speculations. How can I show you Zen unless you first empty your cup?"

Similarly, a skillful mentor first makes sure what the mentee's cup contains. When offered some empty space, the mentor then proceeds to fill it with wisdom. Through a communion of two hearts attuned to each other in love and respect, the mentor encourages the mentee to empty the cup of Self by speaking about his or her personal concerns, doubts, hopes, and ambitions. Such listening creates the possibility for receiving to take place.

If the mentor insists on dispensing wisdom regardless of the mentee's willingness to receive, the person will be repelled and leave in disgust and frustration, never to return. The mentor should not expect to transfer great realizations unsolicited. For optimal learning to take place, the mentor should dispense wisdom in carefully measured increments in response to the mentee's inquiries and genuine needs. Proceeding this way works much better than the indiscriminate pouring out of information for which no container has been made.

**Don't impose but evoke your mentee's innate knowing.** Let's say that one of my mentees is wrestling with issues of faith and freedom, calling to mind Dostoyevsky's response to the problem. I could say to the young woman, "There's a question that you haven't yet formulated that Dostoyevsky covers in 'The Legend of the Grand Inquisitor' in *The Brothers Karamazov*. Read it and we'll discuss it next time." What have I done? I have aborted this person's learning process. I have shown her a map of the territory and obviated her need to ever go journeying on her own.

Rather than imposing knowledge in a hierarchical flow from "expert" to "unlearned one," I can evoke it using the Socratic method. If I am skillful enough to probe the mentee's mind, I may pull out Dostoyevsky's question so she has the "aha" experience, a moment of intellectual eureka. Now the mentee is on a voyage of discovery, in which the novelist's speculations can be confirmed in her own experience. In successful mentoring, the answers we search for do not come from the mentor's external authority, but from the mentee's ability, mediated by the teacher, to contact a source of inner authority.

**Don't try to impress your mentee by claiming to be perfect; be your searching, tentative, very human self instead.** Mentors often labor under the false assumption that they have to reveal only their virtues, while sweeping their shadow qualities under the rug. That means that the mentor must strive to act like a plaster saint rather than a human being of flesh and blood. Under the strain of such perfectionistic striving, the dank odor of your hidden garbage will not remain hidden for long. Your mentee will learn more about being a complete human being by your willingness to share both the bright and darker aspects of your personality with complete candor. When you insist on modeling balance and wholeness rather than a rigid, unappealing perfection, your mentee will learn to trust you and his own shadow qualities, allowing both of you to work through your human shortcomings.

Remember, mentoring is not public relations, image-building work. Even if all the world is a stage, as a mentor you are not playing the role of sage. You are radiating your authentic being, regardless of whether you receive rave reviews from the critics or hisses and boos. When you are a true sage, you consider your time and energy too precious to be expended in meeting other people's expectations.

**Respect and call forth your mentee's uniqueness.** When you mentor, you do not create a mirror image of yourself as Henry Higgins attempts in *Pygmalion*. So please avoid the temptation of fashioning an ideal follower based on your own failed spiritual hopes and ambitions. If you do not cherish the mentee's uniqueness but burden the person with your hidden agenda, the mentee will rebel, causing pain to both parties. Following Sam Keen's example, be a "permissionary" who honors your mentee's authentic calling.

Mike Kotar, a seventy-year-old retired social service manager living in Denver, Colorado, has a unique way of acknowledging his mentees' talents and accomplishments. He sends them special cards and certificates that celebrate their unique characteristics, especially when they have struggled through difficult life transitions and have grown in the process. For example, he sends "Certificates of Fortitude" to mentees who demonstrate persistence and courage in working through personal problems. He also sends "Certificates of Attainment" to people who achieve career goals, such as graduating from college or receiving promotions at work.

"Whether my mentees succeed at first or need continued encouragement, I stand by them and direct their attention to the wonderful potential that I see within them," Mike says. "No matter how many times they may stumble and fall, I know that by reminding them of their extraordinary qualities, they eventually will manifest them and succeed."

**Recognize that like everything else under the sun, mentoring has its seasons.** Just as being familiar with a child's developmental process helps make you a better parent, so knowing the predictable stages of mentoring makes you a more effective teacher. Let's look briefly, then, at the five stages of the mentoring relationship.

In the first stage, moments of helpfulness and friendship shared between an older and younger person naturally blossom into a covenant of mentoring. Let's say that you are a potential mentee living next door to me. From time to time, you help me carry packages upstairs when I return from shopping at the supermarket. One day, after unloading the groceries, we have a conversation that leads unexpectedly and spontaneously to a state of spiritual intimacy. In this moment of deep encounter, the possibility of a mentoring relationship announces itself.

In the second stage, which I call the "shakeout" or "union negotiations," we test our initial moments of spiritual intimacy. We look at whether the mentoring relationship has the depth and elasticity to fulfill the needs of both parties. During this phase, we negotiate the terms of the relationship, making our mutual expectations and limitations explicit. For example, as a mentor,

I reject having the role of father projected onto me, because it perpetuates unhealthy dependency in the mentee. The young person, too, may react with justifiable rebellion if the role of obedient son is projected onto him. During the shakeout phase, as our expectations and hidden agendas come to light, I might say to the mentee, "Listen, I don't want to be your father." He might respond, "Fine, I'm not looking for a father. I already have one."

During the third phase, as we strip away the impediments to genuine encounter, a deepening trust develops between the mentor and mentee. However long this bridge-building process takes, if successful it leads to stage four, when the deep work of mentoring, the transmission of wisdom, naturally unfolds. By now we have eliminated many of our illusions. We have forged bonds of deep trust in the crucible of a relationship that I call "close encounters of a higher kind." Now the real transmission can occur as I give over my life experience and wisdom to my mentee.

In the final phase, which I call "graduation," the mentor and mentee essentially have finished the urgent work that initially brought them together. The files have been moved from the mentor's hard drive into the mentee's; the uploading is complete. At this point, even if we don't choose to see each other anymore, we still remain good friends. As Sam Keen observes, "A point arrives in which the mentee passes from being exclusively under the mentor's wing to a state of reciprocity in which both harbor each other under their wings. The mentor recognizes the mentee as a friend and equal, not just a young hawk."

## MENTORING IN THE FAMILY

So far we have been discussing mentoring as an activity that takes place outside the family. But mentoring essentially has its roots inside the family in the experience of grandparenthood. An undeniable biological imperative impels grandparents to serve as natural mentors to their grandchildren, whether as storytellers, educators, vocational counselors, or conservators of family traditions. When this same impulse expresses itself as nonbiological grandparenting, elders transmit their knowledge to chosen students and apprentices, rather than to blood relatives.

In either case, the model for mentoring clearly comes from the multigenerational family. Throughout history, a natural transmission of values took place from grandparents to grandchildren when the family lived under one roof. Living in close proximity to grandchildren, elders educated them in essential values, carried on religious traditions, and made history meaningful by preserving a living link to the past. Today, however, because the traditional family has splintered into the nuclear family and in many cases the single-parent family, we are losing the natural transmission that used to take place intergenerationally.

When grandparents and grandchildren live close together, they form a natural alliance that leads to a fruitful and precious form of mentoring. Because most of us receive certain emotional "hot potatoes" in growing up, such as unrealistic expectations or damaged self-esteem, we naturally rebel against our parents as we search for our own identities. Our grandparents, who are once removed from the scene of parental conflict, often provide us with safe refuge. They serve as trusted allies, confidants, mentors, and counselors, whose love and encouragement seem like manna from heaven.

Let me share with you how an alliance between a grandfather and a misunderstood teenage girl helped reunite a mother and daughter in bonds of mutual respect. In this case, the "grandfather" happened to be me, functioning not so much as a rabbinical counselor, but as the girl's trusted champion.

Once when I was in Minneapolis, a distraught mother pleaded with me to counsel her rebellious fourteen-year-old daughter, whom she described as a "complete punk." I consented and soon found myself facing a young woman with luminescent green hair shaved into a Mohawk. She also wore deeply highlighted eye makeup and a black body stocking punctuated with numerous holes.

"I'm glad to see you," I said. "Imagine that there's a computer keyboard in front of you. What file would you like to call up from my memory?" She thought for a moment and said, "I hear that you're a Kabbalist. I'd like to know more about the mystical Tree of Life and how the soul fits into the picture. I don't completely dig what I've read." So we launched into an animated discussion on some of the more subtle aspects of the esoteric doctrines of Judaism. It soon became clear that I was dealing with an intelligent young woman whose unconventional appearance served as an exclamation point to her search for authentic values.

After chatting for a while, I asked whether her mother might join us. "Cool," she replied. To the distraught mother, I said, "You have a very bright young woman here who is already aware of the spiritual material that I teach. What she's wearing and how she's living are identity costumes that she's trying on for size. I want to reassure you that your daughter isn't crazy. She's a good person, and there's no possibility of her falling down a social sewer."

You should have seen the grateful look that I received from this young woman! Grandfather Zalman, part ally and part good-natured trickster, had affirmed her worth and blessed her sincere struggle for self-identity. When mother and daughter left the room, I saw a rebellious, out-of-reach teenager taking her first, tentative steps in emerging as a real person.

This anecdote shows the potential for healing that's available when elders claim their rightful and necessary role as mentors in the family. Under our current family system, however, grandparents rarely play such a role. They provide occasional custodial services, babysitting for their grandchildren when parents need a break from their childrearing responsibilities. Imagine, though, if grandparents weren't marginal but central to children's education. What a blessing for the whole family! For this to happen, psychologist Gay Luce points out, adult children must free themselves from the resentment, disappointment, and unresolved conflict that contaminated their parental relationships. In doing forgiveness work, they can release their parents from limited childhood perceptions and begin appreciating them for the wisdom they have acquired.

"When we're at peace with our parents, we can send them our children knowing that they will receive spiritual nourishment and wisdom," says Luce, who for many years directed the SAGE project, which used holistic techniques to evoke wisdom in older adults. "We can say, 'This time with your grandmother is very precious. She has valuable things to teach you. Even if you can't understand the full import of her wisdom, listen respectfully, because you'll receive priceless insights that will guide you when you're older.' "

With their understanding of the long-term cycles that govern human events, grandparents can help young people cooperate with, rather than resist or fear, the unfolding pattern of their lives. Imagine that a seventeen-year-old girl comes to her grandmother grief-stricken because her boyfriend has just broken up with her. The grandmother, who has endured adolescent infatuation, the full spectrum of mature love, and the ripening of compassion, shares in the young woman's sorrow. But she knows that what seems tragic today may bring good fortune tomorrow.

Perhaps when the dark clouds have lifted, her beloved granddaughter will find a more suitable companion. Perhaps the breakup will spare her the sorrow of an even more agonizing rupture in the future. She doesn't articulate this in so many words, but when asked by her grandchild how to deal with disappointment, the grandmother reveals the momentous turning points in her life when destiny took precedence over personal desire. By sharing the unvarnished truth of her stumblings and eventual triumphs, the grandmother teaches that all the pain and joy that we experience are worthwhile and necessary when viewed in terms of the larger pattern of our lives. As she listens to how her grandmother accepts and blesses the mysterious outworkings of destiny, the young woman feels reassured that if she endures, one day she, too, will be a similar source of inspiration for her own granddaughter.

"Elders have a greater capacity than younger people to see all of life and how it's connected," Luce says. "The wisdom that accompanies this wider vision cannot be acquired by reading books, listening to tapes, or attending seminars. Many young people seek it by studying with Eastern gurus, while their grandparents sit at the kitchen table at home like Zen masters, dispensing wisdom that usually goes unnoticed. If we restored elders to positions of respect within the family, we could profit from their wise counsel and receive valuable lessons in living by more enduring values."

This is not to suggest that the family will magically return to the "good old days" of multigenerational living. According to Julia Braun Kessler, author of *Getting Even with Getting Old*, grandparents and their adult children in the near future will continue to live by the current pattern of "intimacy at a distance." Given this trend, we need to promote the practice of conscious mentoring within the family. This social cement can help patch the cracks in the family structure, says Maggie Kuhn, especially since elders can play the same five roles in the family that they play in the wider social sphere. They can serve as mentors, mediators of conflict, monitors of family relationships, mobilizers of change, and motivators of people's highest potentials. Given back some of their authority to impart wisdom, elders could help the family regain its equilibrium as a support system, rather than a pressure cooker from which most people are trying to escape.

## MENTORING IN THE WORKPLACE AND IN THE SCHOOL SYSTEM

Mentoring not only can help humanize the family, but the workplace as well, says Maggie Kuhn. Through mandatory or early retirement policies, elders are removed from the job market, depriving society of irreplaceable skills and experience. Besides perpetuating negative stereotypes about aging, these policies damage elders' self-esteem and socialize young and middle-age adults to internalize gerontophobic myths about old age. As an alternative to retirement, mentoring enables older workers to remain in the workplace as trainers of younger workers.

"Like tribal elders, mature workers can initiate young people who are starting out in their careers," Kuhn observes. "Mentors can work full- or part-time depending on their interest and commitment. Enlightened companies like this arrangement because of the continuity of leadership it provides. These companies also find mentoring to be cost-effective, since in-house workshops given by seasoned workers who know the ropes cost less and are more successful than out-of-house training programs."

In the near future, an increasing number of companies will sponsor innovative preretirement programs to prepare older workers for their new role as emeritus workers and mentors. "We are witnessing the end of yesterday's retirement, with Grandpa asleep on the porch, the gold watch the company gave him ticking in his vest pocket, and his friends coming over later to go fishing or play cards or checkers," write Ken Dychtwald and Joe Flower in *Age Wave*. "Later life is rapidly becoming a time when you do not stop working completely, but instead shift gears to part-time, seasonal, or occasional work, mixed with productive and involved leisure activities."

As elders assume a more respected place in society, mentoring will radiate outward from the home and workplace, affecting all aspects of contemporary life. In the religious sphere, for example, Maggie Kuhn believes that churches and synagogues can become like extended families, providing emotional support for people based not on kinship, but on common concern. Under this arrangement, lonely older people and children who seldom see their grandparents could form the deep, nurturing alliances that used to take place in extended families.

In education, elders increasingly are giving young people big infusions of love and energy by serving as mentors in our school systems. Across the country, surrogate grandparent programs give elder volunteers a sense of belonging, while children who seldom see their grandparents receive the special nurturance that they crave. At the same time, these programs strengthen community ties in an era when our mobile postindustrial society threatens to further erode our sense of weakening social cohesion.

For example, in 1988, at P.S. 92, an inner-city elementary school in Brooklyn, New York, a group of elder retirees served as volunteers in an afterschool program, called "They're All My Kids," which was designed to enhance kindergartners' academic success. Serving as mentors, role models, and tutors to children from a predominately low-income neighborhood, elders in the local minority community worked with their "adopted grandchildren" once a week. They used extracurricular activities to improve school readiness skills and to raise self-esteem. They also passed on traditional values that strengthen the family and, ultimately, the community.

Besides succeeding in its academic goals, the program enjoyed an unexpected social fallout. In an area in which affluent families send their children to private schools, "They're All My Kids" began changing how local residents viewed the neighborhood school. As the elder volunteers began infusing the neighborhood with a sense of civic pride and social responsibility, educators and parents put forth a greater effort in upgrading the school's academic base, making it more accountable to the entire community. In this respect, elders became the nucleus not only of educational improvement, but of community renewal and the intergenerational transmission of values. Programs like this illustrate that elders' commitment to traditional values could play a vital role in revitalizing our inner cities.

In another much-publicized program in Brookline, Massachusetts, elders proved themselves to be intergenerational allies by supporting a tax increase for local schools. Typically, older people without school-age children are reluctant to approve of such tax hikes. To avoid the possibility of intergenerational conflict, the Brookline school system enlisted older people to work as a special constituency on behalf of children. Elders served as tutors, taught English as a second language, and shared their life experiences with students (one of the best ways to break down age-based stereotypes). At the same time, the public schools served hot lunches to senior citizens, provided facilities for health screening, and offered transportation for shopping during the day and to cultural events in neighborhood schools at night. As a result of the intergenerational bond of friendship and trust created by the program, Brookline's elders voted strongly to support the bond issue, at a time when measures that limited educational tax bases received broad public approval.

Intergenerational programs like this are growing in popularity and influence across the country. They match older mentors with economically disadvantaged youth; break down age segregation by encouraging elders to teach oral history in junior and high schools; or create alliances of elders and young people to work together on projects of neighborhood revitalization, such as planting trees and removing graffiti from public buildings. These projects demonstrate that when elders feel that they have a stake in the community and the future of its young people, they work tirelessly and with great sacrifice for public education, urban renewal, and social justice.

Whatever form mentoring takes, it surely helps combat the sense of alienation that pervades modern life. Indeed, if lack of community is one of the major diseases of modern civilization, then mentoring has the potential of acting as a potent antibiotic to heal the social body. Elders who mentor in inner-city public schools prevent kids from becoming muggers and purse snatchers. Volunteer counselors in drug abuse programs weaken the influence of drug lords over our youngsters. Operating in this way, elders can increase their usefulness to society while producing more intergenerational glue to overcome the social fragmentation that we suffer from.

On reaching elderhood, says Dhyani Ywahoo, a Cherokee teacher and founder of the Sunray Meditation Society in Bristol, Vermont, an intentional community dedicated to planetary peace, members "vow to be an ear for anyone seeking counsel." In a public ceremony, they announce their availability to serve others as mentors, counselors, and friends so that members of the community might grow to their full potential. When such an attitude takes root in our society, younger people will not feel so resentful in supplying elders with Social Security. And elders will feel genuinely valued by providing a higher order of "social security" to the generations that follow them through their cultural, moral, and spiritual contributions to society.

## Chapter 9

# *Elders as Healers of Family, Community, and Gaia*

Now that we have familiarized ourselves with mentoring, let's look a few decades into the future when spiritual elders will have assumed a more dominant role in society. Imagine that we have been transported magically into the twenty-first century where we observe the following scenarios:

- As intergenerational strife gives way to increased harmony, families become natural environments of healing and reconciliation, with children and elders spending time together as natural allies. Although elders continue living apart in separate households, they help ease the burden of the two-career nuclear family by serving as mentors to their grandchildren. In becoming sages, they provide the moral and spiritual foundations to help heal the dysfunctions of the postmodern family.
- In large metropolitan areas and small towns across the country, groups of civic-minded elders, called Guardians of the Community, monitor the proceedings of their local city councils on a regular basis. Serving as upholders of the common good, these public-interest groups carefully study issues and

make recommendations to council members before important laws are promulgated. When lawmakers are tempted to enact legislation that would benefit a powerful interest group to the detriment of other citizens, the Guardians act as whistle-blowers who mobilize public support to oppose the issue.

- Unified in their desire for a healthy planet, groups of elders throughout the country act as ecowardens, protecting the environment from shortsighted business interests. These environmental activists frequently protest the construction of shopping malls and freeways that compromise the integrity of local habitats and that destroy biological diversity in their bioregions. Identifying deeply with the land and its many endangered species, they relate to the natural world as a loving "thou" to be appreciated and defended, rather than a lifeless "it" to be exploited for economic gain.

While some people might call this vision utopian, I believe that a confluence of social, political, and spiritual forces is giving birth to a new wisdom culture. In *The Five Ages of Man*, Gerald Heard posits that the emergence of long-lived elders in second maturity will usher in an era of unprecedented human development. The current demographic picture in the United States and Western Europe underscores how ripe conditions are for such a development. As mentioned earlier, the U.S. Census Bureau predicts that by the year 2000, one seventh of the population will be over sixty-five. By the year 2030, when the baby boomers will be passing through old age, gerontologists predict that at least one in every five Americans will be elderly. Continued improvements in lifestyle and medical technology will support these gains in longevity.

The widespread availability of psychotechnologies from the world's spiritual traditions, as well as recent advances in brain-mind research, have given elders the means to develop extended consciousness to match their extended longevity. While elders can now bring their lives to completion for personal reasons, in this era of ecological devastation, individual transformation has planetary consequences. As social critic Theodore Roszak has observed, "The needs of the person are the needs of the planet; the needs of the planet are the needs of the person." I believe that the emergence of long-lived elders is occurring at this time in Earth's evolutionary history because the accumulated wisdom that comes from personal harvesting has planetary survival value.

On a tiny planet with advanced technology and limited resources, self-actualized elders show us how to outgrow our obsessive concern with status, wealth, and possessions, the hallmarks of materialism. By exploring the spiritual dimension of life, they encourage younger people not to equate standard of living with quality of living. As both older and younger people learn to find fulfillment in nonmaterial ways and consume less of the Earth's resources, they reduce the damage inflicted on the environment and become willing collaborators in healing the planet.

## BEYOND PRODUCTIVE AGING

In their search to lead meaningful lives, many elders are beginning to embrace their newfound spiritual vocation as planetary spokespersons. They feel that the recent emphasis on keeping the elderly in the harness of "productive aging," although an improvement over the traditional pattern of education, work, and retirement, scarcely addresses their deeper spiritual needs. Under the conventional approach, elders who reach retirement age disengage from the work world. Elders who practice productive aging, on the other hand, continue working in an attempt to remain youthful, vigorous, and economically competitive with younger people. While it represents an advance over our culture's current dysfunctional view of aging, like gerontologist Harry Moody, I can only give two (not three) cheers for this approach.

In advanced industrial societies such as our own, elders have become passive recipients of social services, medical care, and government entitlements such as Social Security. Saddled by the staggering national debt and rising health care costs, some young people view elders as "greedy geezers," unproductive parasites motivated by self-interest who devour the lion's share of the federal budget. (More than one half of all federal domestic spending goes to seniors.) As a social policy, productive aging both eases and aggravates intergenerational tensions by encouraging older people to seek employment in the job market. Insofar as this approach combats age discrimination and mandatory retirement, I support it. After all, in today's uncertain economy, many elders will be forced to continue working just to make ends meet. The question is: Will they compete with younger workers, extending their middle-age posture into old age, or will they work as elders?

Because spiritual elders have gone through a transformational process, they no longer work with the same motivation as those who compete for success and status in the workplace. Having released their addiction to the youth culture, they seek to transcend the ego motivations that drive most productive activity. In a society addicted to personal success as life's *summum bonum*, those who attempt to free themselves from self-serving motives become role models of a more mature human development. If elders must remain in the marketplace, then by adopting a service orientation, they can model to their younger colleagues how to transform work from cutthroat competition into a source of inner fulfillment. At the same time, they can reduce generational antagonism by refusing to invoke age, rank, and experience as a means of oppressing younger workers who are eager to climb the social ladder of advancement.

Unfortunately, because few people have gone through training in spiritual eldering, we rarely find such open-hearted behavior in the work world. Many elders feel obliged to maintain the same productive levels as their middle-aged colleagues, inviting their contempt and envy—contempt, because they cannot produce as quickly as their younger counterparts, and envy, because of their seniority and because in areas of wisdom, experience, and competence, they pose a threat to the career-minded who are seeking advancement.

"While productive aging propagates the image of elders as active, engaged, and vital, ultimately it presents a rather weak and incomplete vision of life," says Harry Moody. "By insisting on the productivity of the old, we put the last stage of life on the same level as the other stages. This sets up a power struggle over who can be the most productive, a competition that the old are doomed to lose.

"By celebrating efficiency and productivity, we abandon the moral and spiritual value of life's last stage, stripping old age of meaning. What we need is a wider vision of late-life productivity that includes values such as altruism, citizenship, stewardship, creativity, and the search for faith. In short, we need a spiritual vision that recognizes the value of elders' noneconomic contributions to society."

## ELDERS' INVISIBLE PRODUCTIVITY

Without appreciating what I call elders' "invisible productivity" in our families and neighborhoods, in business and political life, younger workers feel justifiably resentful in having to pay one dollar in every seven they earn to support the Social Security system. In return for their sacrifice, they feel squashed financially by unproductive "old geezers." This form of intergenerational resentment would diminish significantly once young people acknowledged elders' social and cultural productivity.

What do spiritual elders contribute to society? Elders evoke our higher potential by widening our vision of human unfoldment. They contribute wisdom, balanced judgment, and enduring values to a society whose moral and spiritual foundations have eroded over the past several centuries. They serve as models for our own aging Self, enabling us to embrace the movements of our own life cycle with deepening hope and faith, rather than paralyzing fear. They affirm our basic worthiness, strengthening our will to live, our aspirations, and our devotion to ideals. In this way, they act as representatives of Earth's long-term investment in evolution and as guardians of the commonwealth of species fighting for survival in the natural world.

Elders contribute to our personal and collective well-being through a process that I call "holding the field." In the last chapter, I described how when we enter an elder's field of unconditional love and spiritual power, we receive a nonverbal transmission of energy and goodwill that aids us in our growth. The elder, commissioned as it were by life to carry forward evolution's higher intentions, stands beside us and blesses us as we struggle to grow beyond our current level of understanding into new light. Such a person has the dispassionate vision to recognize the fully developed oak tree in our current acorn consciousness. By holding the field—by recognizing our inherent potential, by desiring the fullest expression of our unique gifts, and by empowering us to act through an infusion of loving wisdom—we receive a spark, comparable to a spiritual battery jump, that enables us to embrace our destiny and to move courageously into the future.

I had a shimmering moment of insight into the dynamics of this process several years ago when I attended a Native American Sun Dance ceremony in Oregon. During this religious ceremony, braves abstained from food and drink for four days. Pierced at the chest by metal hooks and connected by threads to a central pole, the braves danced rhythmically around the column in the hot sun. An old man wearing a cowboy hat sat at the periphery of the circle, silently watching the ceremony. Whenever spiritual guidance was needed for certain stages of the ceremony, one of the braves walked over to the elder, whispered in his ear, received instructions, and then returned to his dancing brothers. I was greatly touched at one point when the elder motioned in my direction and invited me to be a pipe bearer in the ceremony. It was akin to one elder acknowledging another, a special and holy moment in my life.

In the interchange between the old man and the braves, I saw a viable model of the spiritual elder that's totally missing in our modern youth culture. Without wielding outward political power, the elder commanded the respect of the younger men because of his wisdom and experience. Without moving, he dwelled at the center of all movement, holding the field for his tribe. And without speaking much, the elder awakened the innate wisdom that usually lies dormant and unacknowledged within the hearts and minds of his younger charges.

Because elders can hold the field for individuals as well as the greater community, they help weld disparate elements of society together in wisdom and understanding. Elders can hold the field for a young man or woman seeking a career, for a husband and wife having marital problems, or for various factions of a community gridlocked over racial issues. To illustrate my point, let's jump several decades into the future when a group of elders holds the field as neighborhood ombudsmen in a suburb of Denver, Colorado. Serving as arbitrators, they help neighbors settle property disputes, resolve minor contractual disagreements, and clarify personal misunderstandings. Now imagine that Mary Holmes, the receptionist of a prominent orthopedic surgeon, Dr. Victor Gray, complains of being sexually harassed by her boss. Mary feels intimidated by the overcrowded, expensive, and slow-moving legal system. So she consults with Simon Fischer, a retired high school history teacher, who has gone through training in spiritual eldering and who serves his community as an ombudsman.

After discussing Mary's legal alternatives, they mutually decide that the surgeon should make an appointment to visit Simon in his home. When he and the ombudsman meet, the doctor confesses to loving Mary, who continually rejects his advances. Simon listens dispassionately, then responds more as a mediator than a judge: "Do you think that your present behavior will get you what you want? Do you think it's right? After all, Mary is a married woman who is absolutely devoted to her husband. At the same time, she loves her work and wants to do it without the threat of sexual harassment. The consequences of your present course of action can only lead to legal and professional embarrassment. Can we work out a solution that respects the needs of both people?"

While such problems rarely admit of easy solutions, do you see the potential of mediating disputes in this manner? Because the ombudsman-elder is not coming from a power position, the encounter does not have the built-in resistance of labor-management confrontations. To mediate the conflict, the witnessing elder speaks with the authority of inner experience, rather than using the intimidation of law to force results.

As Gerald Heard points out, spiritual elders do not express their influence primarily through political or economic fiat. Functioning essentially as an advisor, the elder "is consulted only because he can give the inspiration of true seership," he writes in *The Five Ages of Man*. "He can give a true picture of the process as a whole, in which frame of reference all the executive functions must operate or they must in the end miscarry. Yet his influence is all the more authoritative precisely because he exercises no personal coercion. He must be obeyed because instead of having to enforce his rulings, the nature of things carries out the enforcement. The authority of those who really know the laws of life and nature is self-sanctioning."

To function as Heard suggests, elders must change their orientation from the predominately "doing" mode to the more contemplative "being" mode. For example, after a powerful inner experience initiated her into elderhood, Anne Dosher, the community psychologist from San Diego, realized that she could no longer operate in the workplace as before. "Even though I was experienced at organizing agencies and political advocacy groups on the local and national levels, I knew intuitively that I must never again initiate another formal organization," Dosher recalls. "Now, as a consultant and resident elder to San Diego County's Executive Team, I find that the 'elder field' that I create in management meetings draws forth the competencies of others who do the necessary organizational work. As a result of this shift from doing to being, I've learned that my presence as an elder produces the optimal environment for community-building."

## ELDERS' NEED FOR TRUE "SOCIAL SECURITY"

Anne Dosher's invisible productivity in the workplace underscores our need to rethink the meaning of "social security." This term refers to far more than the financial entitlements that people receive for their physical support. It suggests that although elders may figure only marginally as productive members in the workplace, they still have a secure social role to play in society.

According to psychologists such as Erik Erikson, elders' higher-order needs for altruistic community service and environmental activism supersede their lower-order needs for food, shelter, and personal comfort. Yet they remain fixated on their basic needs, rather than on their higher impulses, because the "social security" that comes from having an integral role to play is generally absent. Without an acknowledged role to play in the world, elders are robbed of their dignity and self-worth and suffer from a gnawing anxiety that comes from feeling socially useless. When as a culture we recognize the value of elders' invisible productivity (through mentoring, for example), our limited understanding of social security will broaden from the merely financial to include its cultural, moral, and spiritual dimensions.

Social security on the financial plane is bound to erode in the next few decades unless elders find ways to contribute to their communities. They can no longer say in good faith, "I've put in my time in the workplace. Now I'll just sit back and let younger people carry me." It's easy to see why young people might view elders who espouse this attitude as burdens to society. If old folks gobble up nutrients in the form of entitlements and medical care without giving back anything of value in return, we can understand young people's desire to withdraw support from these parasitical members of the social body. How, then, can we ensure that elders' longer life spans don't weaken society's immune system, making it susceptible to systemic breakdown?

"In order to welcome the elderly back into the moral community, we need more than a renewed appreciation for the gifts of age," says gerontologist Thomas Cole. "We need to understand the obligations and responsibilities, as well as the rights and opportunities of old age." In other words, when the children leave home and the pressures of making a living have receded, elders should assume the mantle of responsible citizenship, working for the common good of society.

To mobilize the altruistic energies of older volunteers, Cole, Ken Dychtwald, and other prominent gerontologists have proposed the creation of a national Elder Corps. Funded by federal and state government and administered on the local level, such a program would enable elders to serve as volunteers in schools, hospitals, universities, hospices, rehabilitation programs, daycare centers, and nursing homes. Elders would be paid in the coin of social recognition or with a nominal salary if they are not financially self-sufficient.

Actually, elders have a precedent for this form of public service in the Civilian Conservation Corps, the Depression-era program designed to rebuild America's infrastructure through community-based projects. Imagine the great infusion of love our fragmented communities would receive if elders unleashed their untapped energy and experience through a contemporary equivalent of this program. Elders would take part in urban and rural reforestation projects, help repair our decaying cities, and work with drug- and alcohol-addicted youngsters in healing their lives. I even can foresee a coalition of elders and young people working together to rebuild our cities. Not only would this partnership regenerate our fragmented communities, but restore intergenerational solidarity between old and young.

As part of the new emphasis on responsible citizenship, I also can foresee recruiting retirees into programs of elder duty. Just as jury duty is citizenship in action, so can elders express their civic spirit as mediators in neighborhood senior centers, as para-clerical aids in synagogues and churches, as tutors in local schools, or as volunteers in social service agencies. Under the program, local communities would require elders to serve a specified length of time once a year; anything beyond that would be strictly voluntary. In exchange for their efforts, participants would receive community credits that could be cashed in for medical benefits, social services, or discounts from local merchants. By rendering public service in this way, elders could help earn some of the respect they so desperately need. Younger people would revere them not because of obligation ("I'm an elder, so respect me"), but because they embody the attitude, "Through giving, helping, and growing beyond personal self-interest, I express my ongoing commitment to the greater community."

In the following sections, we will look at three areas in which elders can contribute to our greater well-being: in family life, in the political sphere, and as ecowardens for Gaia. But remember: In making their contributions, elders should *not* exhaust themselves by working at an activity level consonant with earlier stages of life. Shunning mere busyness, they should work with mindfulness and equanimity, holding the field as sages motivated by the well-being of the whole.

## SPIRITUAL WISDOM IN THE FAMILY

It's hard to predict the future of the family, because the forces arrayed against it are imposing. Because our personal values stress individualism, personal autonomy, and social mobility, we have shattered the extended clan and ensconced ourselves in nuclear families. Currently, however, the already assaulted nuclear family is splintering into single-parent and blended families, further weakening the ties that bind the generations.

"As modern social history shows, the unsupported nuclear family, no matter how affluent, if it lacks an extended network of kinsmen, servants, and elders, is too often unequal to the task of raising emotionally healthy children," writes David Gutmann in *Reclaimed Powers*. "The unbuffered nuclear family does appear to be increasingly incapable of raising children who can avoid addictions, who do not need cults or charismatic totalitarian leaders, who can grow up parental in their own right."

I'm not claiming that a revived elderhood will serve as a social panacea. But as empowered elders return from the periphery to the center of the modern family, they can model for their children and grandchildren how to meet life's challenges with spiritual wisdom, grace, and courage. As mentors to younger people, whether in their immediate families or in the larger community, spiritual elders encourage the inner side of human development. By example as well as by instruction, they can help family life become a training ground for contentment and inner satisfaction. They can model how to slow down our feverish pursuit of material possessions by embracing inner-directed values that stress unconditional love, self-acceptance, and service to others.

Franne Alter, a clinical social worker from Fort Lauderdale, Florida, receives this kind of modeling from her mother, Charlotte, an artist with an irrepressible spirit for living. In her early eighties, Charlotte exudes an aura of playfulness and intellectual curiosity that instantly separates her from the ranks of the morose elderly. A deeply spiritual person who draws on a wellspring of intuitive knowledge, Charlotte has made peace with her mortality. "An awareness of the presence of death liberates me," she says, "making me fearless in my relationships and appreciative of our amazing world."

Franne brought her mother to the Omega seminar on spiritual eldering ostensibly to strengthen their mother-daughter relationship. What this loving daughter received as an extra bonus was preparation for her own eldering. "My mother models for me that life is a spiritual quest for wisdom that continues unabated into and throughout elderhood," she says. "By her example, she demonstrates that elderhood is the supreme summit of life, an attitude that I now try to communicate with all my clients."

As Franne has learned, by reintegrating elders into the family, we receive a deeper education into the meaning of the life cycle. Under our current arrangement, which banishes older people to nursing homes and retirement villages, we perpetuate the illusion that old age and death are not a part of life. In this regard, we are miseducating our children, cutting them off from organic processes that are fundamental to the human condition. We rarely see firsthand how elders mobilize their inner resources to deal with the losses and fears that accompany the inevitable diminishments of the physical body. Nor do we witness the inner alchemy by which they triumph over physical decline by converting despair and emptiness into faith, hope, good humor, selfless love, and a transpersonal commitment to the universal concerns of humanity. But this is precisely the modeling we need in order to become fully human ourselves. Without this creative contact with our own aging, we will resist the inevitable encounter with mortality, which deepens our ability to feel compassion for all human suffering.

"To receive the elderly into our inner self . . . is far from easy," write Henri Nouwen and Walter Gaffney in *Aging: The Fulfillment of Life.* "Old age is hidden not just from our eyes, but much more from our feelings. . . . We not only tend to deny the real existence of old men and women living in their closed rooms and nursing homes, but also the old man or woman who is slowly awakening in our own center. They are strangers, and strangers are fearful."

When we activate and accept the elder within us, we will more easily embrace the aged as our future selves and welcome them back into the family. The family will become a support system and a source of spiritual nourishment, rather than a seedbed of dissatisfaction and dysfunction. Our sense of social rootlessness will diminish as neighbors and neighborhoods join together in a widening net of true community.

## NEW FORMS OF INTERGENERATIONAL SOLIDARITY

So far we have been discussing the reintegration of the elder into the traditional family. But given the relentless pressures on the nuclear family, elders' unprecedented longevity, and the uncertainties of our postindustrial economy, new forms are evolving to meet the needs of an aging society. In *Age Wave*, for example, Ken Dychtwald and Joe Flower discuss the emergence of the "matrix family," which is bound together not by bloodline, genetics, and economic obligation, but by friendship, conscious choice, and shared values.

Searching for a sense of community, a multigenerational group of biologically unrelated people who are committed to certain core values can "make relatives" with one another and live together in a shared housing arrangement. While some elders gravitate toward small-group living in private homes or apartment buildings, others opt for co-housing. In this arrangement people buy their own units in a housing complex but share meals and other activities together in a common building. Still others with a common spiritual outlook form intentional communities. Today, older people who refuse to live in retirement communities and who don't want to live alone can choose from a wide variety of collaborative living arrangements in an attempt to create new forms of family.

Whether living in traditional or alternative families, elders can transmit energy, love, and wisdom to the next generation without restricting the field of activity to their biological grandchildren. As one of my mentors once said, "We grow up in a family linked by ties of blood, but as adults we are free to create a family of choice based on bonds of affinity and shared spiritual outlook." As an elder, I personally know young men and women whom I would love to adopt as my spiritual grandchildren. Perhaps you do, too. There are so many young people today who need to be adopted and encouraged. If left unsponsored, these children can be "adopted" by the drug lords and crack-house operators of the inner cities or by video games in large shopping centers or video arcades. On the other hand, with just a few hours of contact a week, we can "adopt" a young person from a broken family who needs the encouragement, understanding, and guidance that only we can provide.

Maggie Kuhn knows from firsthand experience how elders can enrich the lives of young people. She lives in an intergenerational housing arrangement in Philadelphia with three young women between the ages of twenty-five and thirty who are studying to be rabbis. Because she is extremely frail, with a severe case of arthritis, osteoporosis, and macular degeneration in both eyes, the young women care for her physical needs. In exchange, they receive wisdom from a role model of realized elderhood, a feisty, spirited woman who despite her infirmities can declare, "I'm having a glorious old age. It's been a great event in my life to get old, and I thoroughly enjoy and recommend it to everyone."

A Presbyterian who has taught theology in seminaries, Kuhn finds the exchanges with the rabbinic students intellectually and spiritually stimulating. "What riches we share with each other!" she exclaims. "The energy, interest, and perspectives that they bring to my life expand my spiritual horizons. Older people rarely have the opportunity for this kind of religious and cultural cross-pollination unless they're involved in intergenerational living."

As a counterforce to the modern indignity of institutionalization, multigenerational housing enables Kuhn and countless other elders to live in homelike settings with their privacy intact. This arrangement not only eliminates loneliness, but keeps elders in their neighborhoods, where they can preserve the integrity of their local communities while carrying on a sense of continuity with the past. But more than anything else, shared multigenerational housing exposes young people to exemplars of spiritual eldering who model what David Gutmann calls "the strong face of aging."

"I tell young people, 'Being an elder of the tribe is awesome, demanding, and exhilarating,'" Kuhn states. "Elders have a purpose for living that's stronger than any physical disabilities that might slow us down. As the mind and spirit triumph over the body's infirmities, we work passionately to achieve our goals of social justice, environmental safety, and cross-cultural understanding."

## SPIRITUAL ELDERING AND THE RENEWAL OF OUR COMMUNITIES

As elders reclaim an honored position in the family, they also play an increasingly crucial role in rebuilding our strife-torn communities. By serving as tribal elders in the public sphere, they infuse political life with a broad vision guided by a concern for global ecological health and social justice. As stewards of the community and the environment, elders also serve as guides on our journey beyond individualism into a more planetary sense of identity.

Beginning in ancient Greece and continuing through the Renaissance into the modern world, we have extended the rights of the individual to women, children, slaves, minorities, the handicapped, the disenfranchised, and the disempowered. Since the Enlightenment in Europe, as Western culture embraced liberal political theories that emphasized personal liberty and as the Industrial Revolution fueled our desires for endless material progress, a pathological sense of individualism began to dominate all aspects of life. We gradually lost our sense of connectedness to our communities, to nature, and to the Earth itself. I believe that our obsessive concern with individualism has peaked in the West. Now, as the pendulum begins to swing toward the opposite pole, we are awakening to a transpersonal, transnational sense of identity that makes us planetary citizens.

Neither the Star of David nor the Cross do as much to awaken our highest aspirations and deepest allegiance as the photograph of planet Earth taken by the astronauts from outer space. When viewed from the moon, our radiant blue-and-white planet reveals no artificial divisions of nations or states, but an undivided wholeness that arouses our deepest yearnings for peace and harmony. As an evocateur of our continued species growth, the Earth calls to us, "Children, you must grow up. Enter into loving relationships with each other, other cultures, other species, and me. Learn to live with connectedness, rather than an isolating individualism."

To take the leap into planetary consciousness does not negate our religious, cultural, and ethnic identities. It means putting these aspects of our being in the service of our greater identity as earthlings.

"Over the past few thousand years, we've gone from living in families and clans into villages and small townships, to states, countries, and transnational organisms like the European Economic Community," says Peter Russell, author of *The Global Brain*. "As we continue developing, perhaps by transcending all national boundaries, we'll begin to function as a single human species, with the awareness of being one humanity on the planet. To do this, we must develop a new form of consciousness that balances self-interest with altruism. Thus the paradox is that self-interested consciousness is no longer in our long-term self-interest. What truly serves us in the long term is holistic awareness, which allows us to feel as one with everyone else. What the mystics have taught us has now become an evolutionary imperative."

As we take tentative first steps in creating a global society, elders who have assumed positions of leadership can reassure those who control the reins of society that the journey beyond self-interest and excessive individualism will not result in social chaos or diminishment of the Self. In fact, quite the contrary, it makes for greater social cohesion and enhancement of the Self. As the head of a family or tribe, the elder keeps the community together. Now, as an agent of planetary unity, the new elder urges us to extend our notion of community to embrace all nations, cultures, and religions.

"Children," the elder says, "there's no need to fight over scarce resources. There's enough for all of us if we learn to share. As Gandhi said, 'The world has enough for everyone's need, but not enough for everyone's greed.' "

## THE COUNCIL OF ELDERS

Now let's leap several decades into the future when society takes seriously the advice of Leon Shenandoah, a Native American spiritual elder, who observed that wise elders in every nation should be appointed as advisors who work for the welfare of all people. "Spiritual consciousness is the highest form of politics," he once said in an address to the United Nations General Assembly. "Every human being has a sacred duty to protect the welfare of our Mother Earth."

With this understanding, people in second maturity across the country have reactivated the ancient form of tribal government known as the council of elders. Functioning in an advisory capacity to governmental bodies, religious congregations, and educational institutions, elders meet in council, weigh and consider issues from the larger perspective, then make recommendations to aid legislators, spiritual leaders, and educators in making decisions. "In these settings, elders don't have the last word, but the deep word," says Jean Houston. "Given back the power to impart wisdom, they exert their influence not through legislative or economic power, but through the force of moral and spiritual persuasion."

Let's see how the council of elders might work on issues of national and global importance. Imagine that in the year 2044 elders participate in global town meetings linked by an electronic communications network. Every morning ETV—the Elder Television Network—broadcasts sessions called the Senators of the Earth. On the screen today, the following notice appears: "The subjects for discussion are 'Resolving Border Disputes in Central Asia' and 'Solving the Food Shortage Crisis in South America.' Please read the files on your home computers to familiarize yourself with the issues involved."

To guide viewers in their search for social justice and world peace, informed elders in ETV stations in New York, Chicago, Los Angeles, London, Paris, Tokyo, and other cities around the world discuss and debate these issues throughout the day. In the afternoon, after study and contemplation, members of the global network cast their votes on proposed courses of action. After the votes are tabulated and a collective consensus is reached, elders then link up with members of their local social action networks to coordinate efforts in influencing their elected officials on national, state, and local levels.

Linked by electronic communications, the seers of the planet "hold the field" for social and political action based on the contemplative insight of its wisest citizens. Like Native American peace chiefs whose wisdom ensured tribal survival, elders provide the moral, spiritual, and visionary leadership needed for planetary survival. Obviously, they can use electronic town meetings to deal with problems closer to home, such as national energy policy, state educational reform, and local environmental action. But they don't have to wait for all this sophisticated electronic equipment to be in place before acting. Following the advice of Marty Knowlton, founder of Gatekeepers to the Future, they can organize themselves into study groups (councils of elders) whose commitment to the future leads to community-based activism.

Imagine, for example, that a group of elders suspects that a local landfill is exposing residents to hazardous waste. Through researching the issue of garbage overload, they learn that American industry produces 250 million tons of hazardous material each year, with as much as 90 percent of it improperly disposed. They further learn that according to the Environmental Protection Agency (EPA), there are more than thirty thousand hazardous waste sites in the country.

Alerted to the problem, several of the elders visit the nearby toxic waste dump to find out whether any hazardous waste is contaminating local drinking water. They inquire into the history of the dump, checking whether the site is lined to prevent toxic runoff into the groundwater and whether any testing has been conducted by the EPA. After researching these issues further at the local planning board, city hall, and the county health department, they conclude that in all probability the dump is leaking hazardous materials into the groundwater, exposing residents to the threat of cancer, leukemia, metabolic disorders, and other health problems.

Meeting in council, they decide to form a "Hazardous Waste Task Force" and to present their findings to local lawmakers. With members of the news media attending a special meeting of the city council, the elders propose enlisting the help of the EPA to investigate the site and to clean it up if their suspicions are confirmed. When council members approve their proposal, they continue monitoring the legislative process, making sure that the appropriate agencies follow through on the action plan.

Now imagine if other elders in the community met every afternoon in local senior centers not to play cards and kibitz, but to serve as members of neighborhood tribunals. Functioning like small-claims courts, they would settle minor disputes in other than judicial settings. As I envision it, the neighborhood tribunal might operate under a system borrowed from Jewish law, which requires three people to form a court. The plaintiff chooses a person (in this case, an elder) to represent his or her side of the case, while the defendant chooses another elder to represent the opposing viewpoint. The two representatives meet together and select a third party to serve as the master of the tribunal. They then hold court, as it were, interrogate the parties, and render their decision.

(Imagine setting up such a tribunal in Israel to resolve differences among Christians, Jews, and Muslims. If a Jew and Muslim have a dispute, they would select Jewish and Muslim court members, who would be presided over by a Christian. If a Jew and

Christian have a case, then a Muslim would be the presiding aribtrator. Such a system could work in many cultures worldwide, promoting conflict resolution on the neighborhood level.)

If we converted senior centers into neighborhood tribunals, imagine how much litigation in small-claims court we could avoid. At the same time, consider the social and spiritual benefits when senior centers function not only as gathering places for recreation, but as the hub of spiritual elder training. With a shift of emphasis, we could use already existing facilities to help people in their contemplative homework and in preparation for elder duty.

While these visionary possibilities percolate in our collective imaginations, let's not forget that elders can do much today to create a better world. We can act as enlightened elders in our communities *now*, forming broad-based coalitions with people of all ages and political persuasions on issues that transcend personal self-interest. Whether we live at home or in retirement centers, we can express our passionate interest in social justice by writing letters to our elected officials and to newspapers. We also can join organizations such as Greenpeace, Friends of the Earth, or the Sierra Club.

"As we age, our responsibilities should not lessen but increase," Marty Knowlton says. "In many ways, elders are the dominant force in society. We control 75 percent of the wealth, and because we typically vote in greater numbers than younger people, we wield enormous political clout. Elders have the potential of influencing the political, economic, and cultural agendas of the future."

## CARING FOR OUR DEVASTATED PLANET

As an integral part of their mission to build the future, elders need to foster a renewed relationship with our devastated planet Earth. They can help us relate to the natural world not as an economic resource to exploit, but as the life-giving source of our physical and spiritual well-being. Without sensing the presence of the divine within nature, we risk transforming our beautiful planet into what ecotheologian Thomas Berry calls "wasteworld." Unless we become planetary stewards, we will bequeath a technologically ravaged, desacralized world to our children and to future generations.

Our Mother Earth is like a sick person suffering from a life-threatening illness. Consider her symptoms: The chemical soup that we have created on the surface of the planet and in the atmosphere has seriously damaged the ozone layer, leading to a drastic increase in the incidence of skin cancer. Each year we destroy 27 million acres of rain forest, an area the size of Pennsylvania. This wanton destruction of forestland, which contributes to the global greenhouse effect, compromises the planet's climatic stability.

We dump 80 billion pounds of toxic waste into our waters each year, seriously threatening the health of our aquifers. At the same time, agricultural practices in North America lead to the erosion of 6 billion tons of topsoil each year. Soil depletion of this magnitude here and around the world may turn fertile farmland into deserts, reducing our food-producing capacity in an era of increasing world hunger. If all this weren't enough, our lifestyles of wasteful consumption have so filled our landfills in many metropolitan areas that we may soon run out of space to dispose of our ever-increasing waste products.

According to Thomas Berry, elders carry within themselves both the blessings and the burdens of the twentieth century's love affair with technology that unwittingly created this ecological horror. Seduced by the lure of endless material progress, elders unthinkingly jumped on the scientific bandwagon that promised a superabundance of automobiles, highways, shopping malls, and the labor-saving gadgetry that we find indispensable. So entranced did people become with the industrial world of concrete and steel that they became autistic in their relationship with nature. They felt estranged from a sense of communion with the natural world of wind and rain, meadow flowers and pineland forests. In this autistic state, people reduced the natural world from a communion of subjects with an inherent right to exist into a collection of objects whose role was to fulfill human needs. This separation from nature has led to the unprecedented destruction of species and habitats, loss of intimacy with the Earth community, alienation, and spiritual impoverishment.

"The current generation of elders—my generation—needs to reflect on how our unconscious attitudes and behavior have contributed to the ecological crisis," Berry says. "But we musn't limit ourselves to soul searching alone. A transformation of momentous proportions is now taking place that eventually will establish a new ecological balance between the human community and the Earth. Because elders have lived through the momentous changes of the twentieth century, they can serve as bridges between the old and new paradigms. With their professional expertise, economic power, and moral responsibility, they can help us make the transition from our technologically based culture into the emerging ecological age."

According to Berry, during the past 65 million years that geologists call the Cenozoic era, the Earth brought forth a multitude of species, including flowers, birds, and mammals. This creative effusion continued relatively unchecked until the eighteenth and nineteenth centuries, when we used our Promethean scientific knowledge to gain increasing control over the natural world. In our enchantment with technological growth, we attacked the Earth with such savagery that we irreversibly disrupted the planet's evolutionary processes. Now, with the death of innumerable species and ecosystems worldwide in a state of regression, the Cenozoic age essentially has ended and humanity stands poised between two paths. The first, the Technozoic, leads to a future of increased exploitation of Earth's resources and continued consumerism. The second, the Ecozoic, calls for a new mode of human-Earth relations in which we acknowledge our interdependence with the community of life species. By choosing this path, which means committing ourselves to lifestyles of sane consumption and practicing an Earth-cherishing spirituality, we can begin the process of nursing our ailing planet back to health.

"The well-being of the planet is a condition for the well-being of any of the component members of the planetary community," write Berry and Brian Swimme in *The Universe Story*. "To preserve the economic viability of the planet must be the first law of economics. To preserve the health of the planet must be the first commitment of the medical profession. To preserve the natural world as the primary revelation of the divine must be the basic concern of religion.... The well-being of the Earth is primary. Human well-being is derivative."

How does an elder with this planetary sensibility live? In his late seventies, Berry himself serves as a wonderful model of the spiritual elder who feels responsible for future generations. To avoid bequeathing a completely toxified world to the next generation, over the past fifteen years he has summoned people to environmental activism through his impassioned writings and frequent public speaking. As an ally of the future and a spokesperson for the new paradigm, he urges people to make concern for the environment the central organizing principle of civilization.

"I sense in a quite real way that my life is integral with the life of the planet," he explains. "That means that my sense of survival is linked to the planet's survival, as well. If my outer world is degraded, then my inner world is degraded, too. If I lose the trees, birds, and various plants that make up the natural world, then my imagination is impoverished. We have a good sense of the divine because we live on a beautiful planet. If the planet is degraded, then our sense of the divine is correspondingly degraded.

"It's unbelievable to me that people would be cruel enough to bequeath a sick, degraded world to our young people. I act on behalf of the Earth because I don't want to be cruel. I simply want to be a decent human being."

## EARTH AS A LIVING ORGANISM

Since few of us were raised with this kind of ecological sensitivity, you may be wondering how we can acquire Berry's sense of "Earth decency." One way is to take seriously the revolutionary view shared by many biologists, geologists, and physicists that the Earth is a living organism, a single, self-regulating entity that coordinates all the activities of the biosphere. First postulated in 1975 by English scientist James Lovelock in his book *Gaia—A New Look at Life on Earth*, this startling theory, called the Gaia Hypothesis, rejects the notion that the Earth is a hunk of dead matter hurtling through space around the sun. Lovelock proposed that "the entire range of living matter on Earth, from whales to bacteria from oaks to algae, could be regarded as constituting a single living entity... endowed with faculties and powers far beyond those of its constituent parts." He named this living organism Gaia, after the Greek earth goddess who was worshipped as the mother of all living beings.

In studying the conditions that make life on Earth possible, Lovelock observed that some mechanism appeared to be regulating the distribution of atmospheric gases, creating the perfect chemical conditions for life to flourish. He concluded that a "complex entity" had been maintaining the oceans' level of salinity, surface temperatures, and constant levels of atmospheric oxygen and nitrogen, all of which were optimal for the survival of life. This complex entity is none other than Gaia, the living Earth, an organism possessing a type of transcendent consciousness that enables it to interact with the various lifeforms in the biosphere. Take this thought and dwell on it for a moment: Earth, our Mother, is alive! As the mother of all living beings, the Earth has not only brought forth our beautiful living environment, but also has birthed our particular mode of human consciousness, with which we can enter into communion with her.

If the Earth is indeed an organism, then how is she breathing? Through the rain forests, which are her lungs. This insight helps explain why on some deep, inchoate level we feel so grief-stricken about the destruction of the rain forests. We intuitively sense that Earth, our Mother, is suffering from emphysema, a life-threatening illness. We feel saddened and depressed by the toxic poisons that clog her bloodstream, the planet's lakes, rivers, and oceans. Global water tables—which we can think of as the electrolytes of Gaia's body—are so out of balance that they threaten the physical health and vitality of millions of people. Like thoughtless, immature children, intent on fulfilling our own needs, we have assaulted the planet and taken advantage of Gaia's generosity, unaware of the adverse consequences to our mother's health. Now, as adult children with a sense of gratitude for Gaia's lovingkindness, we need to become planetary caregivers, undertaking the admittedly long-term project of restoring her to health.

In this work of environmental reclamation, we do not act as a consciousness *on* the Earth, but as a consciousness *of* the Earth. Over billions of years of evolutionary history, the Earth has labored to bring forth the self-reflecting species that we call humanity. We have emerged from the planetary milieu as an offspring and integral expression of the planet's creative efflorescence. Lovelock has gone so far as to propose that taken as a species, humanity makes up Gaia's nervous system and brain. Because we are linked electronically through worldwide information systems, humanity has become like a huge "global brain," in which each of us is an individual nerve cell.

In a profound sense, then, the planet becomes aware of itself through us. We are the eyes and ears of the world. When there is a hole in the ozone layer, for example, the Earth becomes aware of it through our intelligence, our perception, and our reaction to the problem. And when we experience a heartfelt hallelujah for the beauty of a sunrise or the playful majesty of dolphins splashing in the ocean, the Earth looks at a reflection of itself through us and says, "Ah, I look so beautiful!" When Gaian consciousness is activated within us, we don't need angels singing to us in divine chorus in the afterlife to convince us of the wonder and privilege of being offspring of planet Earth.

The awakening of Gaian consciousness not only ends our alienation from nature, but connects us in bonds of sympathy with our neighbors. In this regard, Pierre Teilhard de Chardin, the Jesuit priest, paleontologist, and philosopher, believed that evolution on the Earth was leading inexorably to the "planetization of mankind" into a "single, major organic unity."

In Teilhard's view, life first developed on the biosphere through a process he called *biogenesis*. Eventually this process leads to *noogenesis*, the emergence of human consciousness and the proliferation of knowledge through education, scientific research, and global communications. In effect, the biosphere gives birth to the "noosphere," the planetary sphere of mind, which Teilhard called the "spirit of the Earth" and a "brain of brains" (what Peter Russell called the Global Brain). During this epoch, humanity begins moving in the direction of unifying as a single species. Teilhard also refers to a transcendent goal in the far distant future toward which humanity is heading, which he called the "Omega Point," the culmination of human evolution. Since point Omega lies eons of cosmic time in the future, Teilhard viewed the planetization of humanity as the next evolutionary goal toward which we should strive.

As a state of universal love, the planetization of humanity "does not enslave, nor does it neutralize the individuals which it brings together," he writes in *The Future of Man*. "It *superpersonalizes* them.... Imagine men awakening at last, under the influence of the ever-tightening planetary embrace, to a sense of universal solidarity based on their profound community, evolutionary in its nature and purpose.... [It is] a new kind of love, not yet experienced by man, which we must learn to look for as it is borne to us on the rising tide of planetization."

To take part in this "new kind of love," Buddhist scholar Joanna Macy, author of *World as Lover, World as Self*, urges people to awaken the *ecological self*, the transpersonal mode of being that shifts our identity beyond the human family to include the non-human world. To realize our larger biospiritual identity, we must transcend what philosopher Alan Watts called the "skin-encapsulated ego," the notion that our personal self is separate from the web of life. We do this by broadening our sense of identity to include other animals, mountains, rivers, clouds, and minerals—the whole interdependent web of terrestrial life. This process, which Macy calls the "greening of the self," ends our separation from nature and creates the basis for effective environmental action.

What blocks our sense of compassion for the Earth and its species, Macy says, is our fear of being overwhelmed and shattered by opening ourselves to the magnitude of world suffering. In defense of the skin-encapsulated self, we anesthetize ourselves through denial, manic consumerism, and an obsessive concern with our personal welfare. To escape from this isolating activity, she counsels people to grieve for the plight of the Earth by releasing unacknowledged feelings of sadness, anger, and powerlessness.

"We are capable of suffering with our world, and that is the true meaning of compassion," she asserts. "By uncovering our feelings of inner distress and not putting Band-Aids on them, we experience a sense of solidarity with the world from which a growing conviction of responsibility for its well-being and a path of social action begin to emerge."

## AWAKENING GAIAN CONSCIOUSNESS IN ELDERHOOD

When elders do their contemplative homework, paying attention to what I call the Eternity Factor, they grasp in their gut with incontrovertible clarity that they are integral to planetary evolution and environmental defense. Elders view the emergence of their individual lives—from childhood, through adolescence, maturity, and then second maturity—as part of the evolution of the planet, a process spanning vast epochs of geological and cosmological time. When the Ancient of Days springs to life in the elder's psyche, intellectual ideas, such as the Gaia Hypothesis and the Global Brain, drop down from the head to the heart. They take root in the soul as felt experience and direct perception that arouse our deepest allegiances on behalf of humanity and the Earth.

Elders can deepen their sense of Earth stewardship by practicing meditations that stimulate those areas of the brain associated with intuition. Most of us in growing up learned to develop the analytical mode of consciousness that severed our sense of connectivity to the environment and our communities. By developing our intuitional capacities through meditation, we step beyond the prison of our skinbound self and return to the bosom of nature, feeling as one with the greater environment.

By deepening their Gaian connection, elders feel a deep sense of purpose and usefulness, rather than the sense of alienation and self-rejection induced by the youth culture. Because elders are no longer productive in the economic sense, they generally feel devalued and marginalized by society. But the older person who has become a guardian of Gaia affirms with justifiable pride, "I am integral to the Earth. I am a beloved brain cell in the greater organism of Gaia. Through me evolution seeks its greater expression and fulfillment."

Let's look at several ways that elders can develop and express Gaian consciousness.

**Participate as elders in intergenerational support groups united by a common environmental concern, such as recycling, planting trees, protecting the local water supply, or combating world hunger.** To clarify where you can best serve, spend some time writing in your journal, meditating, and consulting with like-minded friends and colleagues. When you commit to a course of action, be sure to approach your work joyously. "When you become an environmental activist," says Joanna Macy, "make your contribution as a gift to the Earth, not as a long-faced, self-righteous duty."

**Practice a lifestyle that puts the well-being of the Earth first.** Elders can become planetary healers through a number of practical strategies: by supporting candidates with "green" sensibilities; by reducing fuel consumption and nonessential driving; by choosing investment funds that screen companies according to ecological criteria; by cutting down on meat consumption and buying more organic food; and by speaking out on environmental issues in religious congregations and educational organizations. These lifestyle choices contribute to what social scientist Duane Elgin calls "voluntary simplicity," a way of living that is "outwardly more simple and inwardly more rich." People who adopt this lifestyle reduce their levels of consumption to keep our world more ecologically viable. At the same time, they liberate themselves from overreliance on material possessions as a means of finding security and self-esteem. By choosing nonwasteful lifestyles, they tend to find greater satisfaction from within.

Practitioners of voluntary simplicity ask themselves, "How much do I need for optimal health and well-being?" And in her maternal solicitude, Gaia answers, "You can have the resources that fulfill your genuine needs. But beyond this level of sustainable, appropriate consumption, you exceed the limits of health, both for me and for yourself." When elders model voluntary simplicity to their peers, family members, and younger friends, they help break our addiction to the glamorous temptations of consumer culture. In this way, they demonstrate their commitment to the health and survival of life on Earth.

**Acquaint yourself with the mystics of the Western tradition.** How can exposure to Meister Eckhart and Hildegard of Bingen in the Christian tradition and to Kabbalah, the Jewish mystical tradition, help heal the Earth? In untold ways, says Dominican priest Matthew Fox, a visionary theologian who believes that our problems with the environment, family stability, and social injustice stem from an impoverished spiritual life that cuts us off from mystical experience. Without access to transcendent states of consciousness, people search for meaning in life through addictions to drugs, crime, alcohol, and consumerism. To break this addictive cycle, Fox encourages people to embrace *panentheism*, a form of mysticism that finds divinity within everything in creation.

"Our denial of the mystic is evident in the way that we treat Mother Earth as [an] object," he writes in *The Coming of the*

*Cosmic Christ*. "Peace *on* earth cannot happen without peace *with* the earth and peace among all earth creatures. For humans to be part of the peace process, to cease being warriors against Mother Earth, a great awakening must take place. That awakening, I am convinced, will be an awakening in our mystical consciousness."

The rediscovery of our mystical traditions serves as a bridge to the new paradigm, Fox said. Mystical experience gives birth to transcendent feelings of awe and wonder, which connect us to the natural world and kindle our sense of ecojustice and environmental activism. No environmental movement worthy of the name can flourish, he said, unless we experience a rebirth of mysticism. And elders who expand their consciousness have a crucial role to play in this endeavor.

"A cadre of elders rediscovering their rootedness in the cosmos and in the Western mystical tradition can become a formidable force for an ecological revolution," Fox says. "For this to happen, elders should be reading, studying, and applying the teachings of the mystics. These profoundly visionary yet practical people provide us with the contemplative tools and inspiration to bring about a renaissance in Western culture."

## THE NEW WISDOM CULTURE

As Matthew Fox, Thomas Berry, and numerous other visionary thinkers have pointed out, the modern world is going through an unprecedented shift in premises and practices that will reweave humanity into the fabric of nature as its consciousness and guardian. This ecological sensibility inspires us to make political and consumer decisions with seven generations in mind. As elders make their inner riches available to the world, they can help midwife this process and safeguard the survival of the planet. Moreover, during this time of accelerated cultural transformation, elder wisdom can help heal intergenerational strife within the family and regenerate our social and political institutions. As spokespersons for Gaia and her many peoples, elders can "hold the field" for a world of sane consumption, social justice, and spiritual renewal based on celebrating the sacred within the natural world. In this way, the elders of the tribe can serve as leaders in giving birth to a more humane planetary civilization.

## Chapter 10

# *Spiritual Eldering Comes of Age*

Elders are the jewels of humanity that have been mined from the Earth, cut in the rough, then buffed and polished by the stonecutter's art into precious gems that we recognize for their enduring value and beauty. Shaped with patience and love over decades of refinement, each facet of the jewel reflects light that awakens our soul to intimations of its own splendor. We sense such radiance in our youth but we cannot contain it. It requires a lifetime's effort to carve out the multifaceted structure that can display our hidden splendor in all its glory.

In your mind's photo album, let me present a few snapshots of exemplary spiritual elders who reflect the light in this manner. Because they embody the elder archetype, they take pride in the fruits of old age, without hankering for the attractions of youth and middle age. Radiant, vital, and magnetic, they attract younger people who are drawn to their wisdom, inner strength, and uncanny ability to find equilibrium in the midst of life's unceasing change. Above all, they model lives that find validation, self-worth, and meaning from within. Using the last stages of life for removing the limiting filters of their social conditioning, they delight in an unbounded sense of freedom that comes from deepening their relationship with the Spirit.

Consider Lynn Radcliffe, a vivacious sixty-three-year-old woman from Dunedin, Florida, whose infectious smile and radiant sense of joy and inner peace attract people of all ages. Lynn, who attended my eldering seminar at Omega Institute in the summer of 1993, attributes her well-being to spirituality, which has become the central focus of her life in elderhood.

"I am a survivor, someone who lands on her feet despite life's adversities," she explains. "Young people admire this quality and ask me how they, too, can meet life's difficulties with a sense of optimism and equilibrium. I tell them in all honesty, 'I turn everything over to a Higher Power; I pray and meditate; I work on forgiving myself and all those who have injured me; and I cultivate a consistently positive attitude.' Young people frequently experience emotional crises, passionate uncertainties, and lack of balance. By my example, I try to show them that after the storms of youth and middle age have passed, they can look forward to a vibrant, fulfilling elderhood that's rooted in spiritual wisdom."

Lynn earned her serene attitude by meeting adversity with courage and perseverance. Early in life she seemed to have everything. As a traditional housewife married to a prestigious Philadelphia lawyer, she lived in a large house with a swimming pool and tennis court, drove a Mercedes, and sent her three daughters to private schools. Outwardly happy but inwardly in turmoil, Lynn became an alcoholic and eventually divorced her husband after seventeen years of marriage. She remarried precipitously, entering an ill-founded relationship that lasted for only six years, during which time she had two operations for breast cancer.

Using her encounter with cancer as an investigation into the unresolved pains of her life, Lynn awakened to the Spirit, becoming more compassionate, empathic, and less driven by traditional values. After working as a real estate agent and as administrative assistant for Planned Parenthood in West Chester, Pennsylvania, she moved to Florida for her health, where she now has her chronic emphysema under control. She goes to senior aerobics three times a week; volunteers at the Clearwater Marine Science Center, which rescues and rehabilitates marine animals, such as dolphins and turtles; and devotes a great deal of her time to spiritual practices. Cancer-free since 1979, she lives on Social

Security and disability income in a modest government-subsidized cottage where, to her amazement, she is "happy as a lark."

"Here I am, a former Philadelphia attorney's wife, accustomed to economic luxury, living on a fraction of what I used to consider necessary for the 'good life,' yet content, peaceful, and rich in friendships. I've simplified the clutter in my life so that I need fewer physical possessions for a sense of well-being. Yet I lack nothing! Because of my strong spiritual belief, I always feel provided for. As I tell my friends, spirituality is the most practical way I know for creating a happy, fulfilled, and loving life.

"By spirituality, I don't mean being zapped by a lightning bolt from God," Lynn adds. "I mean making the commitment in our everyday lives to practice compassion and forgiveness as our full-time job. Are you kind when you drive on the freeway? Can you forgive the grocery clerk for his temporary irritable behavior? Have you made peace with the members of your family? Such acts of kindness performed in daily life on a consistent basis go a long way toward healing the world."

Like Lynn, Leonard Gast, a seventy-four-year-old watercolorist who lives in Idyllwild, California, believes that elders perform a service to humanity by demonstrating how to live with joy in spite of the body's physical diminishments. Leonard, a former sales representative who sold industrial chemicals and photographic equipment, compares elders to salespeople whose "product" is the spiritual life. Since customers respond to the salesperson as much as to the product itself, they certainly might resist buying from someone who complains about life's inevitable aches and pains. The successful representative of spiritual life, therefore, needs to model a joyous, positive attitude, despite the physical and emotional losses that accompany old age.

Elders, he says, have a special vocation: to live in the Spirit and to show by example how to overcome the limiting beliefs and expectations that fill old age with needless suffering and negativity. For example, many of us worry excessively about our physical health. We identify so much with our bodies that we forget that there's another dimension to our being. In Leonard's view, spiritual insight can help mitigate the physical losses that we experience in later life.

"I think of the aging physical body as an automobile with a lot of mileage," he said. "Of course, we have to service it to maintain its longevity, and for this a healthy diet and exercise help. Sometimes we have to take it in for a major overhaul, such as an operation. Yet with all our maintenance, we need to recognize that we're the driver of the automobile, not the vehicle itself. With this understanding, even if the body slows down, we can connect with the Spirit, which is ageless, and experience zest in living."

Leonard, who kept up an active interest as an illustrator and painter during his career as a salesman, began working for Elderhostel at age sixty-nine as a watercolor instructor. Tall and thin, with a shock of curly gray hair, Leonard radiates so much vitality that often he is mistaken for a man in his late fifties or early sixties. To combat falling into stale, habitual ways of experiencing life, he counsels elders to practice a creative discipline such as painting. This forces us not only to look at, but to *see* the familiar objects in our environment with what Zen Buddhists call "beginner's mind," the open, wide-eyed, and curious mind that beholds all things as new and fresh.

"Our minds are so task-oriented, so driven by tunnel vision, that we rarely stop to appreciate the beauty of the world around us," he observes. "Elders can train themselves to look at the world in a fresh, childlike way. As we rediscover our ability to see more deeply into everyday life, we become creative, able to enter the moment with spontaneity and aliveness. In this way, we never have to dampen our curiosity as we age."

The world's spiritual traditions provide the contemplative tools that can help elders awaken to the miracle of everyday life, according to Ann E. Chester, a ninety-two-year-old Immaculate Heart of Mary Sister who lives in Detroit, Michigan. For example, meditation trains us to live *mindfully*, to bring our full attention to the tasks of the present moment with a deep, penetrating awareness that reveals the extraordinary in the ordinary, the sacred in the mundane. When we wash dishes, we just wash dishes, without racing through this somewhat tedious task in search of more pleasant and exciting experiences in the future. As we concentrate on our daily tasks, our minds become so absorbed in the present that we give up our restless search for happiness in the next moment. Effortlessly and spontaneously, we enjoy a deep sensory aliveness and a sense of inner joy that come from our newfound openness to everyday life.

When we are busy raising our families and working at our

careers, living mindfully often seems more like an ideal than a reality, Sister Ann points out. Because we tend to see the world in a task-driven, goal-oriented way, we don't always take the time to stop and smell the roses. But in retirement, when we become unmoored from our normal structures and we don't have to live according to rigorous schedules, mindful living can help reacquaint us with the joys that went unrecognized for so many decades.

"Retirement is like a spiritual discipline that enables us to become mindful and open to life as we were in childhood," says Sister Ann, who retired in 1985. "If we keep insisting on the old ways of perceiving and organizing life in elderhood, trying to control every minute in pursuit of our structured plans, we often cause ourselves pain and frustration. But we can discover a lot of unexpected delight by living in the present moment, which mystics around the world tell us is the gateway to eternity."

In her long and fruitful career, Sister Ann served as an English professor for twenty-seven years, as an educational administrator for eleven years, and as a tireless advocate of church renewal, specializing in the prayer ministry for thirty years. A robust, energetic woman who looks more like someone in her sixties than in her nineties, she recently rode a horse for the first time in her life. Following Teilhard de Chardin's prescription for remaining young, she assimilates and uses the diminishments of old age as part of the spiritual curriculum that evokes her full humanhood. In Teilhard's words, this keeps her "hopeful, energetic, smiling, and clear-sighted."

"The diminishments of old age school us in the art of humility and self-acceptance," she says. "They force us to surrender pride and to accept our human limitations, making us more open, humble, and childlike. Because we can't rely on our former attainments and on our physical strength, we must search more deeply within ourselves for a fund of inner strength and wisdom. Increased reflection and contemplation in elderhood, as taught by the world's mystical traditions, are invaluable in helping us befriend our hidden depths."

# HARBINGERS OF THE NEW ELDER

In the old paradigm of aging, with its negative stereotypes and expectations of later life, the three examples of spiritual eldering whom I have just presented stand out as exceptions to the rule of human development. They strike us as anomalies, who through good fortune or a sound genetic endowment somehow managed to avoid the debilitating and demeaning downside to old age that our culture mandates as "normal." In the new paradigm of aging, however, with its emphasis on lifelong learning, brain-mind development, and consecrated service to humanity, they are precursors of our full humanhood, models of a new and vital elderhood within nearly everyone's reach. With their magnetic personalities and positive attitudes, these pioneers call to us from the other side of aging's continental divide, tempting us to make the journey from middle age into the unknown, unstructured field of pure possibility that I call spiritual eldering.

Because of our extended life span, we need new maps and models for this journey. As we have seen, our culture has begun to reverse the negative stereotypes associated with old age through an activity-oriented approach called "successful aging." But in the words of Connie Goldman, a sixty-three-year-old independent public radio producer who specializes in aging issues, this approach doesn't really value aging at all. It essentially stresses extending middle-age values and preoccupations into elderhood.

"By making activity paramount in later life, we are popularizing a new cultural image that I playfully call the 'aerobic grandparent,'" says Goldman, who co-edited a book of interviews with admired elders called *The Ageless Spirit*. "Instead of feeling rested and whole in old age, aerobic grandparents feel compelled to be as busy, active, and involved as in middle age. Those elders who want to sit quietly, plant a garden, meditate, or walk on the beach can easily feel like failures if they aren't exhausting themselves in a frenzy of activity. The alternative is not to renounce activity, but to experience life *in praise of age* by mining the riches of old age and learning what it has to teach. Instead of lamenting the passing of our forties and fifties, why not accept where we are and explore it, rather than taking heroic measures to conform to earlier images of optimal functioning? The more we reject old age, the less opportunity we have to mine its intellectual and spiritual riches."

But how can we truly value old age when it lacks an overarching social and spiritual purpose? How can we live "in praise of age" when elderhood today appears devoid of meaningful roles? To help restore elderhood as a grand estate and to reinvest it with dignity and respect, I propose establishing a new role for today's elder citizens, which I call the *Western urban sannyasi*. This is the person of retirement age who adapts the best features of the Indian model of spiritual development to the uniquely challenging circumstances of Western industrial society.

As you recall from chapter 3, Indians conceive of life as a spiritual journey that is divided into four stages, or *ashramas*. In this system of life span development, after people pass through the student and householder stages, at around age fifty they begin detaching from their social identities in the forest-dweller stage by devoting greater amounts of time to spiritual development. Forest dwellers still fulfill their social obligations, but they begin to withdraw in stages from their work and family identities as they cultivate the awareness through meditation that the whole world is their family. In the final stage, called *sannyasa* or renunciation, which corresponds with retirement age in the West, they become wandering mendicants who devote all their time and energy to Self-realization. As citizens of the world who are beyond the pursuit of wealth, position, or power, they increasingly identify with the inner Self rather than their personas. Detached and emotionally unruffled by life's contingencies, they serve society by imparting wisdom to those in the other three ashramas.

The majority of modern Indians never reach the final two stages, choosing instead to spend their retirement in the family. But as a model that has guided spiritual aspirants since time immemorial, the traditional model has much to teach today's spiritual elder in training. First, it helps us conceive of life as a spiritual journey with certain identifiable stages that lead naturally and progressively to spiritual unfoldment. Second, it implies that old age offers the greatest opportunity for Self-realization than any of the other stages. Seen from this perspective, all of life is a preparation for old age and its crowning task of Self-development. Third, it encourages us to begin cultivating a spiritual life in middle age, so that when retirement detaches us from productive work in the marketplace, we don't fall into an abyss of emptiness and socially induced uselessness. We still have a full-time vocation that gives our lives meaning: developing wisdom and making it available for the well-being of society.

In adapting the Indian model to our industrialized society, we can take advantage of the Social Security and pension systems already in place that provide us with enough retirement income for our basic needs. Without having to become intinerant mendicants, we can create a modified fourth ashrama in our homes, where we can detach from the social roles and preoccupations of middle age, practice spiritual disciplines in earnest, and deepen our contact with Spirit.

Western sannyasis will not renounce the world as do their Eastern brethren. Rather, many will express their realization as spiritual social activists by working with AIDS patients, teaching and counseling inner-city students, working with alcohol- and drug-addicted youths, or volunteering in food shelters. Some sannyasis may do hands-on political work, while others with a less outgoing temperament may choose to express themselves through letter-writing campaigns. Since all the discoveries of elderhood need not express themselves in utilitarian action, some people may choose to focus exclusively on the contemplative arts in their single-minded pursuit of inner peace. Still others may bring a presence of peace into the hothouse of the modern family. No one way is superior to any other. Just as all roads lead to Rome, so there are many paths that lead to elderhood.

I believe that our increased longevity, the maturation of the baby boom generation, and the growing popularity of the new paradigm of aging are contributing to the emergence of the new sannyasi in a form that is appropriate to our age and social conditions. However, since the Western urban sannyasi represents a new shoot on the branch of contemporary spirituality, we cannot offer clear-cut prescriptive guidelines for how such a person will function. We have a lot of research to do in synthesizing the Eastern model with the social, political, and economic conditions of Western society. After several years of experimental trial and error, we will gather all the data, sift through it, and eventually come up with a comprehensive "job description" of the Western sannyasi.

Dr. Jag Deva Singh, a seventy-eight-year-old retired Indian linguistics professor who lives in Encinitas, California, endorses the current exploration under way in the West to create a spiritually meaningful old age. He and his wife live in a modest apartment near the Self-Realization Fellowship Retreat Center, which was founded by his spiritual preceptor, Paramahansa Yogananda. The spiritually uplifting atmosphere of the retreat center inspires him to practice yoga and meditation every morning and evening. During the day, he harnesses the energy and intuitive insight that come from his contemplative practices in writing his second book on Panini, the celebrated Sanskrit grammarian. He regards his spiritual practice and creative work as an integrated activity; in effect, spirituality and work have become one.

"As a teacher and scholar, I'm continuing my work into the fourth stage of life, in effect combining the renunciate phase with the student phase," Singh says. "It's so wonderful to be a continual learner! Because family life, work, and spirituality all keep me single-mindedly focused on my higher purpose, which is Self-realization, I call this a modified fourth stage life. I believe that it can be adapted without much difficulty here in the West."

As the summit and prime of life, he added, the new sannyasi lifestyle has many of the advantages of youth without its liabilities.

"As spiritual elders, we enter into an age of freedom in which we are not limited by the particularities of our personal history," Singh said. "We can quite literally be reborn into a new life. Once we've identified our purpose, we can pursue it passionately and unceasingly without worrying about supervisors, time clocks to punch, and obligations that sap our time and energy. Elderhood is the only time when we become truly free. And there's no limit to what we can achieve. People say that the sky is the limit; but in spiritual eldering, you can reach beyond the sky!"

However, to make sure that our reach does not exceed our grasp, Singh rightly points out that we need the support and encouragement that come from doing eldering work in a community of like-minded individuals. In fact, spiritual eldering initially is a search for companions, fellow travelers of this unexplored territory who share a compatible vision of human growth and lifestyle practices. One doesn't join a spiritual eldering center the way one joins a political party, with its ready-made organizational structure and its established litany of beliefs and practices. One has to search for spiritual companions, create a community around shared interests, and then develop a curriculum for continued growth based on the best knowledge available from the spiritual traditions, psychology, and other disciplines. As Singh says, "It's not an easy task because nothing is given. In many ways, you have to become a pioneer yourself."

## SPIRITUAL ELDERING RETREAT CENTERS

I believe that in the near future much of the pioneering work in spiritual eldering will take place in residential retreat centers that will combine the best features of Elderhostel, spiritual communities (called *ashrams* in the East), and humanistic growth centers such as Omega and Esalen Institutes. In these centers, retirees from across the country will take retreats for as short as a weekend and as long as six months in their pursuit of spiritual elderhood. Often located in rural settings, these holistic centers will provide restful, meditative environments to help people make the transition from the middle years into elderhood.

Spiritual elders, along with specialists in the emerging field of spiritual gerontology, will guide residents in putting their affairs in order, developing contemplative skills, harvesting life, and choosing a direction for future growth. Training also will include a preparation for service, with an emphasis on Earth stewardship and the well-being of future generations. Besides providing basic training for elders, facilities also will offer programs in preretirement planning and life review for people in midlife who are approaching the portals of elderhood. These centers also will provide householder training for young people who wish to apprentice themselves to spiritual elders who have graduated from the first two ashramas.

When elders complete their initial work at the retreat centers, they will return to their homes with the tools for continued growth. Some may join retirement villages that are dedicated to self-development, contemplative living, and community service. When middle-age people return home from these centers, they will have embraced the call for inner transformation prompted by the first appearance of thanatos. Having acquired the spiritual foundation to carry on their family and career responsibilities with greater poise, they will begin the work of individuation, the developmental curriculum of the second half of life.

Our culture, which emphasizes extroverted values, such as success, wealth, and productivity, would profit enormously from the residential eldering centers that I have described. In his essay "The Stages of Life," Carl Jung laments that because our culture lacks "colleges for forty-year-olds," people embark on the journey into the afternoon and evening of life wholly unprepared. He notes that many middle-age people fall prey to depression and emptiness when they face the realities of old age because they have devoted little or no time in developing an inner life.

The eldering centers that I envision will certainly address this problem. But as colleges in total life span development, they will help people of all ages—youth, midlifers, and elders—deepen their understanding of the aging process. They also will seed society with a model of spiritual development that reconceptualizes life from birth to death as a unified whole, a seamless journey with certain identifiable stages and activities. By providing the communal support, the knowledge, and the spiritual technologies to school people in their depths, these centers will initiate people into the profound mysteries of conscious aging.

Please keep in mind that we cannot assume the joys and responsibilities of elderhood without first going through a transformative process. If we work with the same ego motivations and ambitions that fueled our progress in the work world, we essentially will transfer our middle-age modus operandi into old age. Bedazzled by and addicted to the youth culture, we never will become true elders who have transcended the mentality of the workplace. To command the natural generational respect from which mentoring and Gaian leadership spring, we must come to terms with our mortality, set our emotional house in order, and reduce the pull of our personal egos, so we can serve others without being sabotaged by a hidden agenda of unfulfilled needs. To become sages, we must undergo an initiatory process, in which we learn to lead without dominating others, to make compassion the ruling principle of our actions, and to serve the whole with a multigenerational perspective. I believe that such a life-transforming process can best be accomplished in a supportive community with people who are committed to the same high aspirations.

## THE NEED FOR COMMUNITY

The personal transformation fostered by the growth of eldering retreat centers has profound social implications, given the aging of the baby boom generation and the graying of our society. By 2030, when the baby boom cohort is passing through old age, 61 million Americans—or nearly 20 percent of the population—will be over sixty-five, according to Carol Segrave, a gerontologist and managing director of Life Planning Management, a retirement education program in Idyllwild, California. Just ten years later, the figure could easily swell beyond 80 million. If these people are not trained to live effective, positive lives, the country will face social, economic, and psychological crisis.

"If we carry into the future our current mind-set—that aging brings planned obsolescence, painful physical diminishment, and a drain on economic resources—then our society, which is already strained to the limits, will be unable to handle the increased social, political, and economic strife that will result," she says. "Instead of becoming part of the problem, we can be educated and trained to become part of the solution. But we can't just snap our fingers and magically transform a large group of people into spiritual elders. We need to design an educational model of late-life development and explore it in residential training centers around the country."

Segrave is currently developing such a model, with the goal of bringing a holistic approach to aging into the mainstream. Over the next several years, she plans to assemble an eldering think tank that will design a spiritually based, multidisciplinary educational model of creative aging. After the model is popularized through proposed national conferences and an elder cable TV network, she then plans to create an educational center to train people in the nuts and bolts of spiritual eldering. At this short-term residential center, people will come for a weekend, a week, a month, or longer to deepen their understanding of the aging process, then return home to carry on their studies in local support groups. In the final phase of her project, elders will live in a full-time residential community devoted to spiritual self-development. Interdenominational, self-supporting through its cottage industries, and geared toward community service, this community could serve as a model of spiritual elders living and working together in a retirement community.

Funding for retreat programs in spiritual eldering would come from a four-way partnership among private corporations, government, insurance companies, and individuals. But why should public and private sectors of the economy foot part of the bill for these programs?

"Public policymakers, elected officials, and corporate leaders increasingly will realize that investing in healthier, happier, more fulfilled elders pays huge dividends to society," Segrave says. "On a practical level, for example, eldering programs would help reduce our staggering medical bills, ease pressure on our overburdened social service system, and promote intergenerational cooperation. Because of these and other intangible benefits, eldering programs should be part of everyone's lifelong education. Earlier in life, we consider education to be integral to a person's life, not a luxury. In the same way, we need to think of education for elderhood not as a luxury, but as a necessity for the health and well-being of our long-lived society."

The notion of pursuing late-life education in residential training centers should appeal to maturing baby boomers, many of whom explored communal lifestyles in the 1960s. Over the years, they have come to terms with their youthful idealism and naïveté by assuming the responsibilities of family life, careers, and political leadership. Yet their long, often tumultuous journey to maturity has not dampened their zeal for communal solidarity. It's quite possible that their generational craving for community, their refusal to accept the alienation of postindustrial society, will resurface in elderhood as part of the unfinished business of their youth.

"The need to create a new community is likely to become a permanent characteristic of [the] later stage in the life cycle," write Jerry Gerber, Janet Wolff, Walter Klores, and Gene Brown in *Lifetrends*. "Loneliness in aging is nothing new, but now that people are surviving into their later years healthier, less dependent, and in greater number than they used to, the possibilities of forging the spirit of community are becoming more realistic.... Current elders are laying the groundwork for a more communal old age, and of course the baby boomers are likely to be the elder community-builders par excellence."

In their youth, many boomers made passionate excursions into alternative spiritual paths, exploring the Eastern disciplines and humanistic therapies that form a part of what's called the New Age movement. The authors of *Lifetrends* suggest that if their questing spirit regerminates in the 1990s, elder boomers might give birth to a spiritual renaissance that took seed and sprouted three decades ago. "Such a birth," they write, "would require some of the same elements that spawned the youth culture of the 1960s: a sense of group cohesiveness, enough leisure and freedom from the pressures of daily life to follow where their instincts might lead, and at least a vague discontentment with the direction of their present lives." *Lifetrends*'s authors believe that the boomers are heading for a rendezvous with such a period, and I heartily concur.

But boomers are not moving in that direction alone. They have as traveling companions a large cohort of current elders who are dissatisfied with mainstream religion and who are seeking alternative paths to self-realization. According to Herbert Weiss, a writer who specializes in aging and health care issues, researchers estimate that 11 percent of the population makes up the New Age movement, with elders representing nearly half of this group. What this figure suggests is that older people are searching for the lifecraft that will enable them to create meaningful lives for themselves. Refusing to live as carbon copies of their parents, whose life spans many have already surpassed, these elders are flocking to workshops to acquire the skills for living with optimal physical, mental, and spiritual health.

Once we have set up retirement training centers around the country, boomers and elders will seek them out in pursuit of spiritual renewal and a holistic approach to aging. As the new paradigm of aging takes root in our culture, people will come to these educational centers to learn how to overcome the privatism and isolation fostered by the old paradigm. They will learn how to harmonize the needs of the individual with those of the greater community. They will practice lifestyles that stress cooperation rather than competition, Earth stewardship rather than mindless consumerism, and intuitive wisdom as a complement to our culture's one-sided rationalism. As spiritual elders in training, they will cultivate the awareness of being interdependent members of the greater web of planetary life that we call Gaia.

To make this vision a practical reality, Barry Barkan, an innovative gerontologist and pioneer in spiritual eldering, urges people to do the social planning, community building, and financial investment that will change the foundations of aging in America.

"To create a pro-elder society governed by more enlightened values, we need to dialogue with our spouses, friends, family members, colleagues at work, community organizers, and political leaders about how to create the institutions that will support us in old age," he says. "Holding a multigenerational perspective, we need to organize ourselves and design short-term and long-term strategies to make it happen. The first step is to create a healing community, a safe and supportive environment in which we can honestly explore the issues of aging. If we join together and train ourselves in the theory and practice of spiritual eldering, we will create the possibilities for unprecedented growth in our later years. We will ensure that when we are ready for old age, old age will be ready for us."

## THE ELDERING HMO

Let's look a little more closely at how we might prepare for old age in a spiritual eldering retreat center. I call such a center an "eldering HMO" because it offers the gerontological services of a number of specialists under the auspices of one organization. Imagine that you, the reader, decide to spend a month in elder training at the Seasons of Life Community, a 250-acre retreat center located in northern California. Nestled in a valley surrounded by rolling hills, the facility combines the secluded comfort of a health resort with the intellectual and spiritual vitality of a growth center.

Residents begin each day with a mind-body discipline, such as yoga, T'ai Chi, or meditative walking. During the morning and afternoon, they take classes and seminars on various aspects of eldering at educational centers that combine lectures with small-group experiential learning and interactive computer instruction. To deepen their connection to Spirit, residents receive guidance in the contemplative arts at meditation centers located throughout the facility. To evoke and explore their intuitive depths, they also take part in creative activities, such as music, dance, painting, and poetry.

In their free time, they relax at the spa complex, with its swimming pool, Jacuzzis, tennis courts, and exercise equipment. At the Mind-Body Health Center, residents "tune up" their bodies through a number of therapeutic approaches, including massage, acupuncture, bodywork, and nutritional counseling. In the evening, they gather in the center's auditorium, where they may attend concerts, view films, or enjoy special dramas about eldering that are written and performed by staff members and residents.

In general, the center provides a nurturing environment for body, mind, and spirit. In this low-stress setting, elders take a vacation from the frenetic pace of the workplace, give their bodies a much needed rest, and adjust to the natural rhythms of a contemplative lifestyle. They receive instruction from nutritionists in designing the optimal diet for their later years. They meet with elders involved in community service who give them the practical tools for launching their postretirement careers as wisdomkeepers working for the preservation of the Earth and the well-being of the next seven generations. While all this is going on, they learn how to take refuge in a delicious solitude from which spring the desire and the clarity to undertake life review. Through journal writing, meditation, and unstructured quiet time, residents befriend the Inner Elder, the presence that will accompany and guide them into the deeper mysteries of spiritual elderhood.

When you register at this eldering HMO, intake personnel evaluate your physical, emotional, intellectual, spiritual, and financial status to help you design an eldering curriculum tailor-made to your individual needs. A financial consultant helps assess whether your assets are sufficient for a comfortable retirement. A legal expert evaluates whether your will is in order and whether you have provided for the timely disposition of your estate. Staff members at the Mind-Body Health Center assess your medical status and design a specialized program of exercise and sound nutrition to increase your health and vitality in the elder years.

In classes or through one-on-one interviews, counselors and spiritual practitioners help you make an inventory of your inner life. In a climate of unconditional self-acceptance, you address questions such as, "What work do I need to do to complete my life's mission with a sense of peace and fulfillment? Whom do I need to forgive? What kind of contemplative life have I developed? How would I like to proceed with my spiritual development now?"

After the intake assessment has been completed, you and the staff collaborate in designing a personalized eldering program. What kinds of courses might you take during your month's stay?

Residential centers will offer a broad-based curriculum in the theory and practice of spiritual eldering, according to Carol Segrave. The program will include courses in the paradigm shift and aging, retirement planning, second career opportunities, community service options, eldering in the modern family, mentoring, death and dying, bereavement, exercise and nutrition, meditation, journal writing, and life review. Residents will familiarize themselves with a broad spectrum of subjects while they specialize more deeply in areas of pressing personal concern.

A person with arthritis might spend an entire week learning how to cope with the condition by culling the best knowledge from Eastern and Western medicine, Segrave says. A recently widowed person might spend a good deal of her time working on the grieving process. A recently retired person might spend a major portion of his time studying the retirement transition process, which includes financial and legal issues, housing and relocation, career choices, along with lifestyle options and the use of leisure.

"Eldering centers will help ensure that we no longer stumble blindly into our later years," Segrave says. "They will provide us with the vision and the practical tools to elder in grand style as spiritually radiant, physically healthy, socially involved leaders who are devoted to the welfare of society and the planet."

Besides helping older people make the transition into elderhood, these centers will attract midlifers seeking guidance in moving from the householder into the forest-dweller stage. Elders who already have made that transformation will stand as models and guides, showing people how deepening their spiritual orientation can help them begin disengaging from their pressure-cooker lifestyles. To prepare for elderhood, sannyasis can help midlifers reduce the pull of the social identities, work roles, and productive focus that occupy so much of early and middle maturity. By pursuing an eldering curriculum adapted to their needs, middle-age people will learn to fulfill their career and family responsibilities with greater poise and equilibrium as a prelude to moving more gracefully into the final stages of life.

Eldering centers also will attract young people seeking knowledge of how to construct workable lives. Imagine the potential for mentoring if college graduates apprenticed themselves to sannyasis before entering graduate school. Under our current arrangement, young people receive at best a haphazard training for adulthood, constructing their lives through inadequate, often painful trial-and-error methods. This picture will change when young people and sannyasis rub shoulders in spiritual eldering centers. Through direct contact with elders schooled in the wisdom of life, students will learn the lifecraft for building careers and taking on the responsibilities of marriage and family life—without losing sight of the deeper purpose of life, which is spiritual development.

When enough people "graduate" from spiritual eldering training programs, I believe that many of them will choose to continue their development in residential communities dedicated to the same values and lifestyle. Based on the eldering HMO model, these "urban ashrams," located in metropolitan areas across the country, will have all the amenities of gated retirement communities—and more. They will have individual homes and apartments, group dining, recreational facilities, in-house medical services, a long-term care facility—along with an educational complex and holistic health center where people can gather to do their eldering work in community.

Integrated with the outside community, urban ashrams will take part in community-based service, such as literacy training, Rent-A-Grandparent programs, and other volunteer activities. Some of the resident sannyasis will offer courses in spiritual eldering to people who live in the neighborhood. Others will do community outreach work, leading preretirement seminars and introductory courses in spiritual eldering in corporations, factories, colleges and universities, and senior centers. Still others will teach courses in the contemplative arts at local churches and synagogues. Living lifestyles dedicated to higher values and serving others through mentoring, counseling, and community service, urban sannyasis have the potential of regenerating our families, our neighborhoods, and ultimately society as a whole.

Living in spiritually based residential communities is not the only way to disseminate the message of spiritual eldering. With just a change of perspective, we can transform senior centers (now largely given to recreational and social purposes) into eldering centers. We can teach long-term eldering programs at colleges and universities and through their affiliated educational TV cable networks. We also can teach courses through the auspices of Elderhostel. Although many possibilities exist, let me tell you about the Elders Guild, an innovative approach proposed by Barry Barkan that I think has the potential of making a deep impact on aging in America.

## ENTERING THE PATH OF MASTERY

As envisioned by Barkan, the Elders Guild is an organizational model designed to create self-help communities that enable people to become spiritual elders by pursuing graded paths of learning that culminate in mastery and wisdom. Based loosely on the structure of the Masonic Order and the Boy Scouts, the Elders Guild will initiate members into the responsibilities of elderhood, then provide a curriculum for them to advance in stages from the rank of novice to master in specified fields of study. We need this kind of organization on a large scale, Barkan contends, to consciously reintegrate the wisdom of elders into our culture.

"Just as there is a preparation for life's earlier stages, there needs to be an initiation into and education for elderhood," he said. "Self-help communities devoted to personal growth and service provide a powerful foundation for empowering elders to change the world around them—beginning with themselves. I believe that a community of peers provides the best environment for older people to become a healing and visionary force within society."

The Elders Guild rests on three foundations: community, the gates to mastery, and service. We'll look at each of these in turn.

Like twelve-step programs, guild communities provide a democratic form of self-government that stresses equality and personal autonomy. Self-help groups typically provide networks of mutual support that do not depend on professional input. By giving and receiving help, members overcome the passivity and dependency fostered by reliance on professional caregivers and social workers. They also build up their self-esteem and take control of their lives. Thus when elders join a guild community, they embark on a lifestyle that fashions meaning and purpose in their lives. Guild communities sponsor activities such as potluck dinners, celebrations, cruises, family outings, athletic activities, matchmaking, memorial services, and fund-raising. Members visit the sick within their community and design ceremonies to initiate new members into elderhood.

Barkan conceives of the Elders Guild as a private organization, nationwide in scope, that will affiliate with a wide spectrum of organizations, such as churches and synagogues, corporations, as well as colleges and universities. Because of its broad-based approach, initiation into elderhood would depend on the setting and orientation of the sponsoring group. In some groups, initiates might read from the Torah. In other groups, they might go on a Vision Quest in the wilderness, take part in a multigenerational weekend experience with their families, attend Elderhostel programs, or take a one-week workshop sponsored by the Elders Guild or a spiritual eldering community. No matter what avenues people choose, their preparatory experience will culminate in formal initiation ceremonies marking their entry into the novice stage of elderhood.

At this point, initiates enter into the various gates of mastery, which are organized around key areas of knowledge and personal development. Progressing from novice to master, initiates who achieve mastery in a certain gate will have a comparable level of expertise as paraprofessionals (or in some cases even professionals) in a similar area. A nonexhaustive list of the gates includes health, arts, spiritual eldering, retirement, life cycle completion, family relations, financial management, legacy, and social change. Elders themselves will determine the content of the various gates and guide initiates in their progress to mastery. Guild members may choose to specialize in one area of study or attain mastery in several related areas.

"A woman with high blood pressure, breathing disorders, and a number of other physical ailments might enter the gate to health," Barkan explains. "She would enroll in a basic self-help program that specializes in holistic health, studying such subjects as mind-body medicine, stress management, nutrition, and meditation. This woman might spend three or four years investigating the principles of sound health and applying them in her life, eventually healing herself on a deep level. She would become a kind of folk healer, not someone who replaces the doctor, but who complements the practice of traditional biomedicine."

Someone specializing in the gateway of the soul would help people suffering with terminal illnesses prepare for a conscious transit at the time of death, he continues. Those who specialize in family relations would bring a healing balm of love and wisdom to parents and children at odds with each other because of unresolved family conflicts. Those skilled in the gateway of legacy would guide others in transmitting a financial, intellectual, artistic, and spiritual legacy to family members, the community, and the world.

As guild members attain mastery in their chosen fields, they will reach out to others through community service. Barkan foresees an Elders Guild Service Corps, a referral network and resource center that will link individuals with all areas of community life. They will work in schools and day-care centers, hospitals and nursing homes, prison rehabilitation programs, ecology projects, as well as in religious organizations. Although many people will work as unpaid volunteers, those who are not financially self-sufficient will receive stipends for their contributions.

"Because of their vast potential for community service, Elders Guilds might receive public funding for special projects, such as working with United Way to combat teen pregnancy or with local school boards to improve the quality of education," Barkan says. "All of society will benefit when we unleash and harness elders' natural desire to serve. In this era of unprecedented social and cultural change, our families, communities, and religious organizations need the participation of elders more than ever before. I believe that our ability to create a safe, prosperous, and optimistic global culture rests in large part on our ability to create meaningful roles for our elders."

## ENLIGHTENED NURSING HOMES

The Elders Guild is an extension of Barry Barkan's pioneering efforts to create an enlightened nursing home that enables elders to flourish even when suffering from physical and cognitive diminishment. He is the director of the Live Oak Living Center, an elder care facility in El Sobrante, California, that encourages growth in an institutional setting through the creation of what he calls a *regenerative community*. Like the traditional nursing home, the regenerative community provides standard medical care and rehabilitation services. But it also provides a nurturing environment in which residents can raise their consciousness and assume their rightful role as elders, worthy of dignity and respect despite being institutionalized.

"A regenerative community operates on the premise that no matter how infirm or cognitively debilitated someone is, there remains a part of that person that is still healthy and capable of growth and renewal," Barkan says. "In a supportive community that values people's autonomy and self-esteem, they can grow beyond previous conditioning and learn to be their best selves with one another."

Traditional nursing homes create sterile environments that are breeding grounds for the social diseases of isolation and neglect, he says. Once they are institutionalized, people lose the roles, relationships, and social support that sustained them over a lifetime. These losses are accompanied by a wrenching disconnection from the past and a sense of emptiness in confronting a nonexistent future. Dispirited and rendered passive by a system that attacks their dignity through rigid institutional regulations, they descend into a joyless, lethargic existence in which they are forced to endure ever increasing physical and spiritual diminishment.

By contrast, a regenerative community creates a culture within the nursing home that nurtures people's sense of connection with each other, Barkan explains. Life in such a community begins each day with a meeting in which all residents are invited to participate. Members recite the Live Oak Definition of an Elder, which is so crucial to spiritual eldering that it's worth repeating again. "An elder is a person who is still growing, still a learner, still with potential and whose life continues to have within it promise for, and connection to, the future. An elder is still in pursuit of happiness, joy, and pleasure, and her or his birthright to these remains intact. Moreover, an elder is a person who deserves respect and honor and whose work it is to synthesize wisdom from long life experience and formulate this into a legacy for future generations."

After reciting this elder credo, the community sings and exercises together, welcomes new members, and then discusses world events and issues that pertain to their daily lives in the institution. The community celebrates members who are recovering from illness or who are making progress in combating the negative stereotypes associated with old age. Unlike traditional nursing homes that make death a taboo topic, members of a regenerative community mourn the death of their friends through memorial services that make each resident's life precious and worthy of remembrance. Resident elders also have regular meetings with key staff and board members to air their opinions about problems that they face in the institution. According to Barkan, their individual and collective self-esteem grows as they challenge authority and catalyze institutional change.

In general, the consciousness raising that takes place in a regenerative community transforms the final stages of the aging process from a pathological condition into an extension of lifelong learning. It gives people a sense of connection to the past and future, as well an active, vital role in shaping the present. It also enables community members to share the knowledge, wisdom, and skills that otherwise would have a limited opportunity for expression.

Imagine, now, how the culture in nursing homes will change once this innovative approach to long-term care begins replacing the current one. Nobody looks forward to living in the sterile atmosphere of a traditional nursing home, especially if it's staffed by recalcitrant nurses and filled with overmedicated residents who are strapped into wheelchairs and left to vegetate in front of TV sets. But imagine what a nursing home would be like if residents had studied in spiritual eldering centers or Elders Guilds before losing the ability to live independently. Authentic community would provide people with the social nourishment necessary for their continued growth. They would continue mining and harvesting their lives as an extension of the contemplative disciplines they had been practicing since the onset of middle age.

Residents might meet in the morning for prayer or gather in a warm, indoor pool in the late afternoon for a group meditation.

During the day, these resident sages might counsel visitors from the community. Their mentees would receive profound teachings about how to face death with serenity from elders who were preparing for their conscious transition. In the evening, resident elders might enjoy a retrospective journey into nostalgia through music, literature, films, or TV programs. According to mind-body medicine, this excursion into the past perks up the immune system by increasing the production of antibodies that fight disease.

I believe that because spiritual eldering will affect all aspects of our lifestyle, it will revolutionize that most feared and despised institution, the nursing home. No longer will we think of the long-term care facility as a grim, dehumanizing terminus point, a dumping ground for people in the final stages of physical and mental deterioration. Rather, we will regard it as a center for advanced stages of spiritual eldering, a humane and loving extension of society's commitment to the self-realization ethic. In the words of Barry Barkan, "As the membrane between the community and the nursing home becomes permeable, healing will take place not only for residents living within alternative institutions, but for everyone who interacts with them."

## THE RISE OF ELDER CULTURE

As the spiritual eldering perspective takes root in our society, we will witness other fundamental changes in our lifestyles. The youth culture, with its glorification of the first half of the life cycle, will give way to an emphasis on life span development, with its new image of what gerontologist Robert Kastenbaum calls the completed person. An in-depth elder psychology, based on the input of humanistic and transpersonal psychologists, will popularize the image of the fully individuated older person whose development continues unabated through all the seasons of life. Such a psychology will address the issues that pertain to the transition from middle age into elderhood: changes in physical health and sexuality; retirement and the search for a new identity and life purpose; death of a spouse and bereavement; life review and legacy; the philosophic honing of values and the need for self-transcendence and community service; and preparation for one's own death.

"In the future, an increasing number of people will regard therapy as an essential part of spiritual eldering," says Hazel Stanley, a seventy-five-year-old bioenergetic analyst and dream educator who lives in Purchase, New York. "Elders will seek out therapists not only to treat pathology, but to unlock their inner potential that yearns to become self-actualized through career changes, rediscovered creative interests, or service to humanity. Therapists with a spiritual orientation can help elders undertake life review and resolve unfinished business while growing into the Spirit at the same time. As elders learn to return to center, they will discover a source of inner strength, wisdom, and cheerfulness that will see them through the stresses and strains of old age."

In providing the psychospiritual tools to acquaint people with their depths, spiritual eldering also will help in the renewal of our Western religious traditions. At the moment, many Jews and Christians, disaffected by the practice of mainstream religion, are rediscovering the mystical, contemplative practices in their traditions that for centuries guided seekers on the path to union with God. They are exploring the Christian mystical writings of St. John of the Cross, St. Teresa of Avila, and Meister Eckhart, as well as the profound forms of Western spiritual know-how hidden in the Jewish mystical teachings of the Kabbalah. These and other contemplative approaches, which are at the heart of spiritual eldering, will strengthen and accelerate the movement to rejuvenate Western religion.

As elders make use of the spiritual disciplines that in the past were reserved for only a handful of adepts, they will reintroduce their congregations to the authentic, life-transforming potential contained within their religious traditions. In alliance with spiritual eldering centers and Elders Guilds, churches and synagogues will educate their congregations in life span development that honors the elder as the crown and glory of creation. As we reinstate the biblical approach to gerontology, which respects age for its wisdom, we will give new meaning to Robert Browning's hopeful lines in "Rabbi Ben Ezra": "Grow old with me, the best is yet to be, the last of which the first was made." At the same time, we will stress that training in wisdom should begin at an early age. The growing influence of the new wisdom culture will give these lines from Proverbs renewed meaning: "Train the young man according to [wisdom's] way, so that even in old age it shall not depart from him." With spiritual eldering as the context for lifelong learning, we will help ensure that wisdom's way accompanies us through the entirety of the life cycle.

In propagating a revised and hopeful image of old age, the new elder culture will help break our automatic association of old age with physical deterioration and death. Scientific research and lifestyle changes that include exercise, a healthy diet, and stress management will postpone the onset of chronic disease and slow down physiological aging. Free from debilitating illness and filled with vigor, tomorrow's elder will enjoy an old age defined more by enjoyment and celebration than by gloomy inactivity and purposelessness. The growth of mind-body medicine, with its emphasis on attaining physical health through spiritual wholeness, positive mental attitudes, and healthy emotions, will play a crucial role in changing our expectations about old age. To escape from the prison of aging in which most of humanity has been chained, says Deepak Chopra, we need to overturn the beliefs that accelerate the body's preprogrammed deterioration.

"The decline of vigor in old age," he writes in *Ageless Body, Timeless Mind*, "is largely the result of people *expecting* to decline; they have unwittingly implanted a self-defeating intention in the form of a strong belief, and the mind-body connection automatically carries out this intention. Our past intentions create obsolete programming that seems to have control over us. In truth, the power of intention can be reawakened at any time. Long before you get old, you can prevent such losses by consciously programming your mind to remain youthful, using the power of your intention."

The new elder culture will encourage us to remain healthy, vigorous, and useful throughout our life span by disseminating positive images of old age in advertising, TV programming, and films. With the graying of the nation, elder boomers will demand to see role models in the media who reflect their commitment to lifelong learning and higher values. As creativity in the second half of life becomes more widespread, people will scarcely bat an eyebrow when told that Goethe completed *Faust* when he was eighty and Arthur Rubinstein performed at Carnegie Hall at ninety. "Of course they did," elders will say without that sense of disempowering awe that now accompanies anecdotes about long-lived elders, "and we have the very same potential."

Spiritual eldering also will help contribute to an improvement in the status of women. In popularizing the notion that menopause represents an intiation into elderhood, second-wave feminists will help dignify women's late-life passage as a time of spiritual fulfillment rather than physical decline and emotional barrenness. Instead of sinking into depression and social invisibility, older women will look forward to becoming crones, wise women who are valued for their spiritual wisdom, healing abilities, and leadership within the community.

"As role models [new elder women] can give younger women confidence to look forward to a life in which physical appearance is not the measure of their worth, and in which aging can be an asset," write Sara Arber and Jay Ginn in *Gender and Later Life*. "By asserting themselves as competent, strong, and resourceful, women can begin to reclaim their right to age without stigma."

When spiritual eldering transforms the very fabric of our family life, children and elders will spend time together as natural allies. Families will become natural environments of healing and reconciliation, and we will break the cycle of misery that has created our current epidemic of child abuse, drug addiction, and teenage suicide. As families experience real satisfaction, this sense of well-being will radiate outward in an ever-widening net of true community that will influence all our institutions and activities. By reintegrating elders into society and by reinvesting them with meaningful roles, we will meet the seemingly insoluble dilemmas of modern life with a fund of wisdom that the world needs not only to survive, but to prevail.

Where will we find this wisdom? Just look around you; it's in no short supply. You will find it in the hope-filled eyes of elders living in our homes, studying on Elderhostel campuses, volunteering in social service agencies, and attending spiritual eldering conferences. You will find it in the enchanted garden of your childhood memories when your grandparents gave you the love and encouragement that have blossomed into the fruits of your adult life. Most of all, you will find it inside yourself, in your soul's secret sanctuary, where the Inner Elder beckons you to take up the most rewarding work of a lifetime: becoming a sage. On this blessed and wonderful journey, so crucial to the survival of our beautiful planet, I wish each and every one of you Godspeed!

Appendix

# *Exercises for Sages in Training*

After reading this book and acquiring a theoretical understanding of spiritual eldering, you may wonder, "Where do I go from here?" The exercises in this appendix will help you get started in the practical work of translating theory into practice in the laboratory of your own life. These exercises serve as a soul and mind gym in which to flex and develop your eldering muscles. As you grow stronger in your determination to become an elder and as you become more skillful in harvesting the fruits of a lifetime, you will embark on an adventure in consciousness that will lead to a more noble, useful, and fulfilling old age.

To get started, I recommend setting aside specific periods of time for your eldering work in the same way that you schedule exercise into your weekly activities. There are no hard-and-fast rules as to the length and frequency of these eldering sessions. Some people may devote an hour each day to spiritual eldering, while others may work for half an hour or forty-five minutes three or four times a week. The important thing is to set aside quality time (when energy, awareness, and interest are at a peak) to ensure that you receive the maximum benefit from these exercises.

To avoid being distracted by the dual task of reading and responding to the instructions, you can record the exercises in your own voice or have a friend do it for you. When recorded in your own or a friend's voice, exercises have a certain immediacy and personal quality that invite you to internalize the various processes, in effect making them your own.

As part of your eldering tool kit, you might have a tape recorder on hand to preserve insights that arise as a result of these exercises. If you prefer to write down your insights and intuitions, then record them in a journal. For those who are computer literate, a word processor may serve as your journal. You can open directories on a wide spectrum of subjects, such as legal issues, health concerns, relationships, forgiveness work, recontextualizing experience, the philosophic homework, and mentoring.

Unless you have medical reasons to work at an accelerated pace, take your time in doing these exercises. Exploring them in an unhurried manner enables you to access information from the unconscious mind and to integrate it with your daily life. Some people may work through all the exercises in sequence and then repeat the process. Others may concentrate on an individual exercise, mining its depths slowly and thoroughly, before moving on to other exercises. Use your own judgment to determine how to proceed in your eldering work.

As an elder in training, you will need frequent sessions of solitude to do your contemplative homework. Distractions around the home easily can tempt you to cancel your appointment in self-awareness. Make sure, therefore, to handle potential distractions before each session. Turn on the telephone answering machine and hang a sign on your door: "Busy—Do Not Disturb. Eldering Work in Progress."

Because harvesting your life is a gift that you give yourself, please avoid approaching these sessions as a chore, like punching a time clock in the workplace and "putting in your time." If, for example, you feel one day that the time is not propitious for your eldering work, then by all means make an appointment with yourself for another day. You need not "grin and bear it" to win some sort of imagined spiritual eldering merit badge.

On the other hand, doing these exercises will not always leave you feeling happy and upbeat. From time to time you may wander into territory that arouses enough anxiety to dissuade you from continuing, and it will require commitment and discipline to keep your appointment. Distractions such as television, food, or phone calls to friends temporarily may lure you away from your session for reasons that seem quite reasonable. If at these times you choose to confront yourself rather than flee into various diversions, taking a mini-retreat in solitude can provide the uninterrupted concentration needed to work through the temporary impasse. The rewards of such self-confrontation are great, because every step forward, every victory over the forces of nescience, counteracts the downward pull of aging and contributes to the ascending process of spiritual eldering.

When you have finished your exercises for the day, plan to do something pleasant to reward yourself. For example, you might listen to some of your favorite music, take a meditative walk, or treat yourself to a tasty snack. This rhythm of inner work followed by an anticipated reward helps you look forward to life harvesting as a gift rather than a burdensome chore.

As you continue with these exercises, certain indicators will mark your success as an elder in training. You will feel more energy and a renewed zest for life as you practice forgiveness and recontextualize difficult and disappointing experiences, finding the pearl of wisdom within them. Depressions will lift, and you will anticipate the future with greater excitement. You will meet people with a more open heart, and they will greet you with greater respect as the sage begins to peek out through your eyes. As you continue your eldering work, you may attract to yourself a whole new cast of people and circumstances to make the last stage of life an experience of inestimable meaning and beauty.

One last bit of advice: Approach these exercises with openness and a lightness of spirit. Be gentle with yourself and lighten up your expectations as to what kind of elder you "should" be. Do you know why the angels fly? Because they take themselves lightly! If you apply this attitude to your own eldering process, you will have a more enjoyable journey through elderhood.

## ***Exercise 1:*** *Approaching Elderhood*

Oftentimes we unthinkingly accept the images of aging propagated by our culture, seeding our bodies and minds with the expectation of sliding into a weak and socially useless old age. In the first exercise, we will unearth the sources of our aging images (both negative and positive) and then reprogram our consciousness with the expectation of a vital and meaningful old age.

**1.** Prepare to write in your journal by sitting in a comfortable chair, closing your eyes, and relaxing your body. Take several deep breaths, emptying your lungs completely after each inhalation. Remain in a meditative state as you become quiet and centered.

**2.** Spend some time exploring the question, "How do I feel about aging?" What do you look forward to and what do you fear? In this regard, you may want to consider these questions in terms of your profession, family life, finances, health, intellectual life, and spirituality. Write naturally without censoring yourself, telling the truth in your own language. Remember that there are no "right" or "wrong" answers in this exercise.

**3.** Now list negative models of aging that you have internalized from our culture from sources such as literature, films, television, advertising, religious instruction, your family life, and older people you have known. Be specific in describing traits and attitudes that may be influencing your own aging process.

**4.** List positive models of aging that have influenced you. Have you acquired any traits and attitudes that are helping you become an elder?

**5.** In your mind's eye, make a composite of the good models and imagine what it feels like to walk in the shoes of such an elder. Do you have a useful role in society? Are you earning respect and recognition for your wisdom? Is growing older a blessing or a burden?

**6.** Visualize going through a routine day as your ideal elder, feeling confident, respected, and socially useful. Be as concrete and detailed as possible in imagining encounters with colleagues at work, loved ones, friends and associates, and mentees. Know that by envisioning a positive future, you are seeding consciousness with the expectation of your own potential growth.

7. To end this exercise, read the Elder Creed:

> An elder is a person who is still growing, still a learner, still with potential and whose life continues to have within it promise for, and connection to, the future. An elder is still in pursuit of happiness, joy, and pleasure, and her or his birthright to these remains intact. Moreover, an elder is a person who deserves respect and honor and whose work it is to synthesize wisdom from long life experience and formulate this into a legacy for future generations.

Write in your journal any insights or questions that occur to you after reading the Elder Creed. Are you in the process of becoming this kind of elder? What personal and social forces could prevent you from claiming your full stature as an elder?

## **Exercise 2:** *The Cycles of Your Life*

All of us experience dramatic changes as we move through childhood, adolescence, first maturity, middle age, and elderhood. However, grasping the larger pattern that unites these diverse stages of life often eludes us. The following exercise helps us to perceive the "pattern that connects" by partitioning the continuum of our lives into seven-year cycles in an attempt to discover how the parts are related to the whole. In general, memory becomes sharper and clearer when it's associated with partitioned time. Telling someone to remember the past in general terms usually does not yield good results; targeting a specific period of time works far better. When we ask someone to remember what happened during the April of his life from ages 22 to 28, a person may respond, "When I was twenty-eight, I bought my first home and celebrated the birth of my second child." Focusing on specific periods of time acts like a magnet in the psyche, bringing to awareness all the "filings" (the experiences) that we need to recover our past and harvest our lives.

Once we have assembled the raw data of our experience, we can grasp the overarching pattern that was struggling to express itself through the ups and downs, the successes and failures that make up the rich texture of our lives. Seeing which experiences remain incomplete, we can take measures to express the unlived life that beckons from within. Perceiving the larger pattern of our lives, we can gain insight into how to harvest our lives and bring them to completion. Besides showing us directions for future growth, this exercise can help us cultivate an appreciation for all that we have had and enjoyed, even if our means were only modest by the world's standards. We can say, "I experienced friendship, a home and family, a useful career, and I grew in maturity over my life span." If we encountered sorrow and suffering, we can affirm, "By bearing these burdens, I grew in inner strength. I did something heroic."

**1.** Down the left side of a large piece of paper, list the seven-year cycles of your life: January, 0–7; February, 8–14; March, 15–21; April, 22–28; May, 29–35; June, 36–42; July, 43–49; August, 50–56; September, 57–63; October, 64–70; November, 71–77; December, 78–84 (and beyond).

**2.** Across the top, divide the remainder of the paper into three sections in which you write answers to the following questions for each of the 12 periods:

a) What were the significant moments and events of each phase of life?

b) Who were the people who guided and influenced you during each period?

c) What did each phase contribute to the continuum of your life?

**3.** To deepen your memory of people and events, you may want to devote a separate page or more to various time periods. You can enhance your memory by attaching photos to the paper, making sketches, writing little poems that evoke the era, or making a collage of newspaper and magazine clippings. Be creative in calling forth and harvesting the experiences of a lifetime.

**4.** Use this exercise to help recover memories of experiences that remain incomplete and that you can bring to completion as part of your eldering work. You also can use the exercise for working on forgiveness, recontextualizing difficult outcomes, mining the past for its untold riches, and discovering a future direction for growth.

## *Exercise 3: Turning Points*

Like the preceding exercise, "Turning Points" helps you survey your life with panoramic vision. By revisiting some of the highlights of our personal history, we can contemplate the unfolding pattern of our life. Once we move from the past to the present with an awareness of the larger panorama, we can reach toward the future with a greater sense of optimism and confidence. Because we can perceive a direction toward which our life has been moving, we can address the question, "Where would I like to be in five years?" without giving way to paralyzing anxiety. By contemplating the past, we consciously can begin shaping our future without conforming to external goals and standards. We can follow the promptings that come from within, constructing a life based on self-knowledge and the hard-earned autonomy we have developed over a lifetime.

**1.** Sit in a comfortable chair, relax your body, and prepare to write in your journal. Take several long, deep breaths to put yourself in a meditative state of mind.

**2.** Write down your earliest memories of your . . .
—first Holy Day
—first day in school
—first love; first kiss
—first and most recent experience of illness
—high school
—college
—first job
—first significant achievement
—first failure
—career changes

—marriage
—children (including births and weddings)
—first and most recent experience with death (including your ideal departure)

**3.** On a piece of paper, make a time line on which you place the significant turning points of your life. Begin with your birth on the far left and fill in the experiences until you arrive at the present time.

**4.** Place a point beyond the present time to indicate the near future. Now ask yourself the question, "Where do I want to be in five years?" Using your imagination, project yourself into the future and see yourself living your ideal life as a fulfilled elder. Where do you live? What is the quality of your relationships? What activities give your life meaning?

**5.** Spend some time in your journal exploring the life that you envision for yourself as an elder. Because you are dealing in the realm of possibility, you may want to return to this exploration on a number of occasions until a clear sense of purpose and direction emerges.

## ***Exercise 4:*** *Journey to Our Future Self*

Many perplexing questions confront us as we make our way through the unexplored terrain of spiritual eldering: How should I plan my retirement? What lifestyle should I choose? How should I grow intellectually and spiritually? What is the meaning of my life? For insight into these questions, we should seek out the most reliable and knowledgeable sources, including books, magazines, continuing education classes, and retirement counselors. But as elders in training, we also need to contact an inner source of wisdom to receive guidance from our spiritual Self. In meditation we can make an appointment to visit our Realized Self, the Inner Elder who is already enlightened and who can inspire us with compassionate wisdom to carry on our struggles for self-knowledge. This enlightened Self dwells beyond space and time yet has an intimate relationship with our personality. Establishing a permanent relationship with the Inner Elder can provide us with guidance for all aspects of daily life.

**1.** Sit quietly, close your eyes, and for a few moments follow the inflowing and outflowing of your breath as you become calm and centered.

**2.** Count slowly from your actual age to 120, the biblical age of accomplished wisdom. At the same time, visualize in your mind's eye walking up a set of stairs leading to the door of your Inner Elder. When you knock on the door, your realized Self, the embodiment of boundless compassion and wisdom, greets you with a warm embrace. As you gaze into the Inner Elder's eyes, you feel unconditionally loved and reassured about your progress so far.

**3.** As a pilgrim confronting the highest, most all-embracing source of wisdom, ask the Inner Elder for guidance about an issue that you have been puzzling over. The guidance that you seek can range from practical concerns ("Should I continue working at my present position or take early retirement?") to the most metaphysical inquiries ("What is the meaning of my life? Is there continuity of life after physical death?"). After posing your question, remain in a state of receptivity, allowing an answer to imprint itself in your consciousness as a sign, symbol, or an inner sense of knowing.

**4.** When you receive your answer, rest in the silence for a while. Then, as you look again into the eyes of your enlightened Self, you receive these parting words of encouragement: "Journey on with confidence and with blessings as you proceed on your path. Visit me again whenever you need further guidance."

**5.** With deep gratitude, take leave of your Inner Elder and with joy and confidence walk down the stairs to your point of departure. Sit quietly for a few moments, slowly open your eyes, and return to normal consciousness.

**6.** Record your impressions and intuitions in your journal. As you establish a long-term relationship with your realized Self, over time you will begin to trust the guidance that comes from within and begin incorporating it in your everyday life.

## ***Exercise 5:*** *Healing a Painful Memory*

Life review sometimes involves reaching back into the past to repair events and relationships that caused us pain or disappointment. We can mend our personal history because time is stretchable and therefore subject to reshaping through the use of contemplative techniques. To heal the part of ourselves that is still imprisoned in the past, we can return to the scene of a questionable decision or a bruised relationship and apply the balm of our more mature consciousness. In this way, we can forgive ourselves for actions undertaken without the benefit of the more enlightened awareness we now have. By recontextualizing the past, we can release the defenses that obstruct the expression of our natural love and spontaneity and recover a sensitivity and sense of innocence that we may have lost in becoming our mature selves.

**1.** Sit in a comfortable chair, close your eyes, and begin breathing in a slow, rhythmic manner. With each breath, feel yourself reaching further and further into the past until you return to a time of emotional turmoil and pain. Do not resist the memory; with all your strength and awareness, make contact with your younger self who felt alone, misunderstood, unconsoled, or hurt.

**2.** Now let your elder self reach back with reassurance from the present and hold your anxious younger self in its arms. Visualize this embrace in your mind's eye as your mature self blesses the younger self that is smarting with pain and self-doubt about its present course of action.

**3.** Reaching through the fog of anxiety, the elder self says, "I come with assurance from the future. You are going to make it. You lived through this difficulty, healed from it, and learned important lessons that matured into wisdom. You acted courageously, you grew in strength and character, and in the end everything worked out well. Be at peace: Even though it seems impossible now, unforeseen blessings will result from your present course of action."

**4.** Still feeling the embrace of your elder self, let go of the cramp around the pain. Reach into the pain, hugging, consoling, and finally sanctifying it by offering it as a sacrifice for the good of all humanity. In this way, you elevate and ennoble that which you took to be worthless and ignoble.

**5.** As you let go of the burden of the past, focus your attention on your breathing and become aware of the increased energy, the buoyancy of feeling, and the sense of courage that are now available to you. Breathe in a sense of well-being and give thanks for having rescued and harvested a holy spark of your life.

**6.** Sit quietly for a few moments and then record your observations in your journal. Instead of writing, you may prefer to paint a picture, write a poem, play some music, or go for a meditative walk in nature.

## **Exercise 6:** *Giving Yourself the Gift of Forgiveness*

Because all of us have unhealed scar tissue from past relationships, practicing forgiveness plays a major role in spiritual eldering work. When we heal our major woundings, along with the minor bruises that accompany intimate relationships, we release feelings of anger and resentment that armor our heart with defensiveness, drain our energy, and reduce the level of our vitality. Forgiveness work has two dimensions. First, we need to take responsibility for initiating acts of forgiveness. This means overcoming our passive attitude that makes forgiveness dependent on the other person's apology. Second, we need to forgive ourselves for our contribution to the misunderstanding.

Because this kind of enlightened behavior does not come easily to us, we need to train ourselves in this noble and beneficial practice. By gaining proficiency in the art of forgiveness, we can learn how to transmute our sorrows into the capacity to love, enabling us to reach out to others with a spontaneity and openness that will add emotional richness and enjoyment to our lives. As you practice the following exercise, you will discover through firsthand experience why forgiveness is one of the greatest gifts that we can give ourselves.

**1.** Sit quietly and take a few deep breaths to center yourself.

**2.** In your mind's eye, visualize being in the presence of someone toward whom you have unresolved anger or resentment, someone who has wronged you and toward whom you harbor a grudge. As you contemplate this person's actions, consider how your lack of forgiveness keeps you chained to this relationship, drains your energy, and disturbs your emotional equilibrium.

**3.** Place yourself in your adversary's shoes for a moment and investigate whether your own unacknowledged needs and expectations or a misunderstanding in communication contributed to the upset or rupture in your relationship.

**4.** Allow your awareness to move back and forth between yourself and the other person, giving you an enlarged perspective and an objectivity with which to view the relationship.

**5.** Imagine that the two of you are bathed in a ray of golden sunlight that melts your resentment and allows forgiveness to take root within your heart. Rest in the warmth of this sunlight for a while.

**6.** With a sincere desire to mend the relationship, say, "I forgive you with all my heart and wish you nothing but unalloyed goodness. And I forgive myself for my complicity in creating this misunderstanding. May neither of us have to suffer any further painful consequences from our past encounter."

**7.** Now visualize being in the presence of your former antagonist and mending your relationship with kind words and gestures. As you contemplate this auspicious encounter, feel how a great weight is being lifted from you and how a sense of inner peace is replacing it.

**8.** Slowly open your eyes and relax for a few moments. When you return to everyday awareness, record your observations in your journal.

## ***Exercise 7:*** *A Testimonial Dinner for the Severe Teachers*

This exercise uses the broad perspective of time to reframe hurtful relationships and situations. With this perspective, you welcome people back into your life, thanking and blessing them for the unexpected good fortune that resulted from the apparent injustice that was inflicted upon you. Besides coming to terms with these "severe teachers," we can use this exercise to investigate how our own behavior unconsciously may have contributed to our victimization. As we witness our behavior from an objective platform that was unavailable earlier in life, we can take responsibility for actions on our part that unwittingly led to personal suffering. In this way, we can end the blame game and reclaim a sense of personal empowerment.

**1.** Sit in a comfortable chair, relax your body, and take some long, rhythmic breaths to center your mind.

**2.** Divide a piece of paper into three columns. In the first column, list the guests whom you are inviting to this testimonial dinner, those who have wronged you in some significant way. In the second column, describe the apparent injustice that was inflicted on you. In the third column, describe the unforeseen benefits, the unexpected good that resulted from their actions.

**3.** Using the broad perspective of time, say to each of the offending parties, "I understand now that you did me a great deal of good by your actions when you did ______ for which I want to thank you. I understand now that it was difficult for you, *and* it was difficult for me. But now that I forgive you, I am grateful for your contribution to my life."

**4.** As you consider how each of the offending parties treated you, ask yourself, "What part did I play in being victimized? Did I have an unconscious program that made me an unwitting collaborator in this scenario?" If you uncover ways in which you sabotaged yourself, extend the same courtesy to yourself that you just extended to your severe teachers. Forgive yourself. As you free yourself from the blame game and take responsibility for yourself, you can release the energy that has been tied up in resentment and redirect it into your conscious growth as an elder.

## ***Exercise 8:*** *Doing Your Philosophic Homework*

In addressing the philosophic homework, elders work on synthesizing wisdom from long life experience. Contemplating the past as well as the future, they seriously investigate the "big questions" that have occupied humanity's greatest thinkers since time immemorial: Where do we come from? Why are we here? Where do we go after we die? What is our purpose? What is our place in the universe? To whom are we answerable? Is there inherent in life a way of being harmonious with it? In doing your philosophic homework, you confront these questions not as an interesting intellectual exercise, but as an impassioned examination of your ultimate values and commitments. In the following exercise, you will use socialized meditation to investigate one of the issues that humanity has wrestled with for millennia. Sitting in spiritual intimacy with a trusted friend, you will induct yourself into a state of deepened awareness and attempt to gain clarity on this major philosophical question.

1. Sit quietly with a friend who has agreed to work with you on the philosophic homework. Both of you should close your eyes for a few moments and take long, deep breaths to quiet and center yourselves.

2. When you open your eyes, your partner will pose a question to you, such as, "What do you believe about the soul and the afterlife?" or "What is the purpose of your life?"

**3.** As your partner listens in silence, providing a safe, supportive field of attention for the exploration to take place, speak from your heart about this subject without censoring yourself. Explore your thoughts and feelings without trying to impress either your friend or yourself. Forget about what Socrates, Jesus, Confucius, and Mohammed have to say about this issue; speak from the immediacy and the authority of your own experience. Continue for ten minutes or so and then close your eyes and return to silence.

**4.** When you open your eyes, pose the same question to your partner and listen attentively as he or she wrestles with the issue. When your friend has finished, close your eyes and be silent for a few moments.

**5.** Now write in your journal whatever insights emerge from this session. You also might want to paint a picture, sculpt, or express your discoveries through any of the expressive arts. You also can use your insights as a launching point for further solo meditation.

## ***Exercise 9:*** *Scripting Your Last Moments on Earth*

A major task of spiritual eldering involves coming to terms with our mortality. One way we can reduce our fear of dying is by rehearsing our own physical death. When we courageously confront the reality of our finitude, we convert the energy that normally goes into repressing death into an increased appreciation for the richness of our lives. In the following exercise, we will attempt to familiarize ourselves with the reality of physical death by envisioning our final moments on Earth. As we rehearse our deathbed scenario we not only take steps to reduce the terror associated with death, but enhance our capacity to experience vitality and joy in the present moment.

**1.** Prepare to write in your journal by getting comfortable, relaxing your body, and taking several long, deep breaths.

**2.** Using your imagination, experience your final moments on Earth in the most ideal manner possible:

a) What music would you like to hear as you are dying? What poems, prayers, or sacred texts would you like recited?
b) What would you like to taste? What scents would you like to smell? What objects would you like to have near you to touch and appreciate?
c) What kind of physical surroundings would you like?
d) Whom would you like to be present?
e) Whom would you definitely not invite to celebrate your departure from the Earth?
f) What would you like to say to those who have assembled around your deathbed? What would you like to have them say to you?
g) How do you imagine the moment of your actual death?
h) How would you like to have your body disposed of?

**3.** Record your responses in your journal. Read over what you have written several days later and then write a follow-up entry to see whether this exercise has made you more accepting and less squeamish about the reality of your physical demise.

**4.** As another follow-up exercise, you may want to write your own epitaph or obituary. By increasing your familiarity with the reality of physical death, exercises like these will put you on better terms with thanatos, the Completing Instinct, and facilitate the process of life harvesting.

## *Exercise 10: Letters of Appreciation*

As elders, we often feel the desire to express our heartfelt appreciation to those people who have helped us on our life journey. We may have had a brief encounter with someone who changed our perspective at a crucial turning point in our youth. We may have felt uplifted by someone's wise counsel when we were going through a life-threatening illness. Or we may remember a brief but intense love affair that nourished us during a difficult transitional period in our lives.

We can write letters to such people expressing our gratitude and appreciation. By writing "How wonderful it was to have a friend like you" or "You mean a lot to me, even though we haven't communicated to each other for some time," we acknowledge our interconnectedness with the many people who have contributed to the inner richness that we now feel as elders. As elderhood takes root in our psyches, we increasingly need to communicate what people really mean to us, how they have nourished our lives, and how we have benefited from knowing them. By sending letters of appreciation to our children, spouse, close friends, relatives, neighbors, and the spiritual teachers who have influenced our development, we gain closure in our relationships while widening the circle of our compassion.

Make a list of people whom you would like to invite to a Thanksgiving Reunion of the Benevolent Teachers. These are the people to whom you will write letters of appreciation. In writing each letter, try to communicate the essential qualities that make the person unique and the ways in which you have grown because of your association with him or her. Don't hold yourself back: Express the "mushy" sentiments that you may have avoided articulating over the years. Now is the time to open your heart and to speak with unadorned simplicity and straightforwardness. When the letters are written, you may choose to mail them or to have them mailed posthumously. (Because of unique circumstances in relationships, some people may prefer to wait until after their deaths before having their letters sent.) In either case, your actions not only will bring closure to your relationships, but strengthen the social web that is in danger of being fragmented and atomized by the exigencies of modern life.

## **Exercise 11:** *Acting as an Elder of the Tribe*

Like tribal elders of the past, today's spiritual elders are wisdomkeepers entrusted with the responsibility of maintaining the well-being of our families and communities. When they serve in the public sphere, elders bear witness to enduring values that transcend shortsighted political partisanship. Motivated by broad cultural and planetary concerns, elders call into question our overreliance on consumerism and our continued assault on the planet's ecological health. Guided by an ecological sensibility, they urge us to make political and consumer decisions with the long-term consequences of our actions in mind. Serving as stewards of the community and the environment, they champion the causes of sane consumption, social justice, and cross-cultural understanding and cooperation.

The following exercise will help you get in touch with the sage within yourself who longs to make a contribution in the public sphere. By exercising your responsibility as an elder, you can serve as a leader in rebuilding our fractured communities and in safeguarding the health of our ailing planet Earth.

**1.** Sit in a comfortable chair and relax body and mind by taking a few deep breaths.

**2.** Think back to all the animated conversations you have had with your children, relatives, friends, and colleagues at work in which you voiced solutions to world problems or to problems closer to home. Recall those occasions in which you spoke with such passion and clear-sighted vision that had you been a political leader, you would have inspired people to pursue an enlightened course of action on issues of local, national, or international importance.

**3.** Now imagine that you are addressing a Parliament of World Leaders. Standing at the podium, you speak fearlessly and eloquently, expressing your concerns about ecology, world hunger, the deprivation of civil liberties around the globe, religious and political intolerance, or any other issues that deeply move you. Invoking your authority as an elder, rebuke these leaders for failing to serve the interests of the planet and the next seven generations, who may inherit a severely compromised environment and a world divided by political, economic, and religious differences.

**4.** Still in touch with your moral and political convictions, open your journal and consider ways in which you can express your wisdom as an elder in the public sphere:
a) How can you best serve the planet?
b) How can you serve the nation?
c) How can you serve the community?

d) How can you be of service to your family?
e) How can you best serve those who are in the process of becoming elders?

**5.** As a further step in priming the pump of your awakened activism as an elder, you might want to write letters to your elected officials or to newspapers about issues that concern you. You also might consider joining organizations dedicated to protecting the environment such as the Sierra Club or Friends of the Earth.

# Bibliography


Adams, Kathleen. *Journal to the Self: 22 Paths to Personal Growth*. New York: Warner Books, 1990.

Augros, Robert, and George Stanciu. *The New Story of Science*. Lake Bluff, Illinois: Regnery Gateway, 1984.

Ansley, Helen. *Life's Finishing School*. Sausalito, California: Institute of Noetic Sciences, 1991.

Arber, Sara, and Jay Ginn. *Gender and Later Life*. London: Sage Publications, 1991.

Assagioli, Roberto. *The Act of Will*. Baltimore, Maryland: Penguin Books, 1974.

Baldwin, Christina. *Life's Companion: Journal Writing as a Spiritual Quest*. New York: Bantam Books, 1991.

Becker, Ernest. *The Denial of Death*. New York: Free Press, 1973.

Berman, Phillip, and Connie Goldman, eds. *The Ageless Spirit*. New York, Ballantine Books, 1992.

Berry, Thomas. *The Dream of the Earth*. San Francisco: Sierra Books, 1988.

Berry, Thomas, and Brian Swimme. *The Universe Story*. New York: HarperCollins, 1992.

Bianchi, Eugene. *Aging as a Spiritual Journey*. New York: Crossroad Publishing, 1982.

———. *On Growing Older: A Personal Guide to Life After 35*. New York: Crossroad Publishing, 1986.

Bolen, Jean. *Goddesses in Everywoman*. New York: Harper & Row, 1984.

Capra, Fritjof. *The Turning Point*. New York: Bantam Books, 1982.

Chinen, Allan. *In the Ever After: Fairy Tales and the Second Half of Life*. Wilmette, Illinois: Chiron Publications, 1989.

———. *Once Upon a Midlife: Classic Stories and Mythic Tales to Illuminate the Middle Years*. Los Angeles: Jeremy P. Tarcher, 1992.

Chopra, Deepak. *Ageless Body, Timeless Mind*. New York: Harmony Books, 1993.

———. *Quantum Healing: Exploring the Frontiers of Mind/Body Medicine*. New York: Bantam Books, 1989.

Cole, Thomas. *The Journey of Life: A Cultural History of Aging in America*. New York: Cambridge University Press, 1992.

Cole, Thomas, David Van Tassel, and Robert Kastenbaum, eds. *Handbook of the Humanities and Aging*. New York: Springer Publishing, 1992.

Davis, Richard. *Television and the Aging Audience*. Los Angeles: Ethel Percy Andrus Gerontology Center, University of Southern California, 1980.

de Beauvoir, Simone. *The Coming of Age*. New York: G.P. Putnam's Sons, 1972.

de Ropp, Robert. *Man Against Aging*. New York: Arno Press, 1979.

Doore, Gary, ed. *What Survives? Contemporary Explorations of Life After Death*. Los Angeles: Jeremy P. Tarcher, 1990.

Dychtwald, Ken, and Joe Flower. *Age Wave*. Los Angeles: Jeremy P. Tarcher, 1989.

Elgin, Duane. *Awakening Earth: Exploring the Evolution of Human Culture and Consciousness*. New York: William Morrow, 1993.

———. *Voluntary Simplicity*. New York: William Morrow, 1981 (rev. ed., 1993).

Erikson, Erik. *Childhood and Society*, second edition, revised and enlarged. New York: W.W. Norton, 1963. [Note: the original edition was published by Norton in 1950.]

Erikson, Erik, with Joan Erikson and Helen Kivnick. *Vital Involvement in Old Age*. New York: W.W. Norton, 1986.

Evans, William, and Irwin Rosenberg. *Biomarkers: The 10 Keys to Prolonging Vitality*. New York: Simon & Schuster, 1991.

Feinstein, David, and Peg Mayo. *Rituals for Living and Dying*. New York: HarperCollins, 1990.

Fitch, Victoria. "The Psychological Tasks of Old Age." *Naropa Institute Journal of Psychology*, 1985, V3: 90–106.

Foos-Graber, Anya. *Deathing*. York Beach, Maine: Nicolas-Hays, 1989.

Fowler, Margaret, and Priscilla McCutcheon, eds. *Songs of Experience: An Anthology of Literature on Growing Old*. New York: Ballantine Books, 1991.

Fox, Matthew. *The Coming of the Cosmic Christ*. New York: Harper & Row, 1988.

Francis, Polly. *Songs of Experience*, Margaret Fowler and Priscilla McCutcheon, eds. New York: Ballantine Books, 1991.

Friedan, Betty. *The Fountain of Age*. New York: Simon & Schuster, 1993.

Gerber, Jerry, et al. *Lifetrends: The Future of Baby Boomers and Other Aging Americans*. New York: Macmillan, 1989.

Gerzon, Mark. *Coming into Our Own*. New York: Delacorte Press, 1992.

Goldman, Connie. *The Ageless Spirit*. New York: Ballantine Books, 1992.

Greer, Germaine. *The Change: Women, Aging and the Menopause*. New York: Alfred A. Knopf, 1992.

Gutmann, David. *Reclaimed Powers: Toward a New Psychology of Men and Women in Later Life*. New York: Basic Books, 1987.

Harman, Willis. *Global Mind Change*. Indianapolis: Knowledge Systems, 1988.

Heard, Gerald. *The Five Ages of Man*. New York: Julian Press, 1963.

Heschel, Abraham. *The Insecurity of Freedom*. New York: Farrar, Straus & Giroux, 1966.

Hessel, Dieter, ed. *Maggie Kuhn on Aging*. Philadelphia: Westminster Press, 1977.

Houston, Jean. *Life Force: The Psycho-Historical Recovery of the Self*. New York: Delacorte Press, 1980.

———. *The Possible Human*. Los Angeles: Jeremy P. Tarcher, 1982.

Imara, Mwalimu. *Death: The Final Stage of Growth*, Elisabeth Kübler-Ross, ed. Englewood Cliffs, New Jersey: Prentice Hall, 1975.

Johnson, Robert. *Inner Work: Using Dreams and Active Imagination for Personal Growth*. New York: Harper & Row, 1986.

Jung, C.G. *Memories, Dreams, Reflections*. New York: Vintage Books, 1965.

Kapleau, Philip, ed. *The Wheel of Death*. New York: Harper & Row, 1971.

Kastenbaum, Robert, and Ruth Aisenberg. *The Psychology of Death*. New York: Springer Publishing, 1972.

Keen, Sam. *Fire in the Belly*. New York: Bantam Books, 1991.

Keleman, Stanley. *Living Your Dying*. New York: Random House, 1974.

Kemper, Donald, et al. *Growing Wiser: The Older Person's Guide to Mental Wellness*. Boise, Idaho: Healthwise, 1986.

Kessler, Julia. *Getting Even with Getting Old*. Chicago: Nelson-Hall, 1980.

Kramer, Kenneth. *The Sacred Art of Dying: How World Religions Understand Death*. New York: Paulist Press, 1988.

Kübler-Ross, Elisabeth. *Death: The Final Stage of Growth*. Englewood Cliffs, New Jersey: Prentice Hall, 1975.

———. *On Death and Dying*. New York: Macmillan, 1969.

Kushner, Harold. *When Bad Things Happen to Good People*. New York: Schocken Books, 1981.

Lefevre, Carol and Perry Lefevre, eds. *Aging and the Human Spirit: A Reader in Religion and Gerontology*. Chicago: Exploration Press, 1981.

Leonard, George. *Mastery: The Key to Long-Term Success and Fulfillment*. New York: New American Library/Dutton, 1991.

Levine, Stephen. *Who Dies? An Investigation of Conscious Living and Conscious Dying*. New York: Anchor Press/Doubleday, 1982.

Levinson, Daniel. *The Seasons of a Man's Life*. New York: Ballantine Books, 1978.

Luce, Gay. *Longer Life, More Joy*. North Hollywood, California: Newcastle Publishing, 1992.

Luke, Helen. *Old Age: Journey into Simplicity*. New York: Parabola Books, 1987.

Macy, Joanna. *World as Lover, World as Self*. Berkeley, California: Parallax Press, 1991.

McLeish, John. *The Ulyssean Adult: Creativity in the Middle and Later Years*. New York: McGraw-Hill Ryerson, 1976.

Miller, Ronald. *As Above, So Below: Paths to Spiritual Renewal in Daily Life*. New York: Jeremy P. Tarcher/Putnam, 1992.

Miller, Stephen, et al. *Conquest of Aging*. New York, Macmillan, 1986.

Minois, Georges. *History of Old Age: From Antiquity to the Renaissance*. Cambridge, England: Polity Press, 1989.

Monroe, Robert. *Far Journeys*. Garden City, New York: Doubleday, 1985.

———. *Journeys Out of the Body*. New York: Free Press, 1973.

Moody, Harry. *Abundance of Life: Human Development Policies for an Aging Society*. New York: Columbia University Press, 1988.

Moody, Raymond. *Life After Life*. New York: Bantam Books, 1975.

Nouwen, Henri, and Walter Gaffney. *Aging: The Fulfillment of Life*. New York: Doubleday, 1976.

Nuland, Sherwin. *How We Die: Reflection on Life's Final Chapter*. New York: Alfred A. Knopf, 1994.

Owens, Claire Myers. *Old Age on the New Scene*, Robert Kastenbaum, editor. New York: Springer Publishing Company, 1981.

Pearce, Joseph. *Evolution's End: Claiming the Potential of Our Intelligence*. New York: HarperCollins, 1992.

Penfield, Wilder. *The Mystery of the Mind*. Princeton, New Jersey: Princeton University Press, 1975.

Perry, John Weir. *Lord of the Four Quarters*. New York: George Braziller, 1966.

Ram Dass. *Journey of Awakening: A Meditator's Guidebook*. New York: Bantam Books, 1978.

Ring, Kenneth. *Heading Toward Omega: In Search of the Meaning of the Near-Death Experience*. New York: William Morrow, 1984.

Russell, Peter. *The Global Brain*. Los Angeles: Jeremy P. Tarcher, 1983.

Samuels, Mike, and Nancy Samuels. *The Well Adult*. New York: Summit Books, 1988.

Schachter-Shalomi, Zalman. *Paradigm Shift*. Northvale, New Jersey: Jason Aranson, 1993.

———. *Spiritual Intimacy: A Study of Counseling in the Hasidic Tradition*. Northvale, New Jersey: Jason Aranson, 1991.

Scott-Maxwell, Florida. *The Measure of My Days*. New York: Viking Penguin, 1979.

Skinner, B.F., and M.E. Vaughan. *Enjoy Old Age: A Program of Self-Management*. New York: W.W. Norton, 1983.

Sogyal Rinpoche. *The Tibetan Book of Living and Dying*. New York: HarperCollins, 1993.

Teilhard de Chardin, Pierre. *Let Me Explain*. New York: Harper & Row, 1966.

———. *The Future of Man*. New York: Harper & Row, 1964.

Thompson, William Irwin. *Passages About the Earth*. New York: Harper & Row, 1973.

Vaughan, Frances. *Awakening Intuition*. New York: Anchor Press/Doubleday, 1979.

Walker, Barbara. *The Crone: Woman of Age, Wisdom, and Power*. New York: Harper & Row, 1985.

Wall, Steve, and Harvey Arden. *Wisdomkeepers: Meetings with Native American Spiritual Elders*. Hillsboro, Oregon: Beyond Words Publishing, 1990.

White, John. *A Practical Guide to Death and Dying*. Wheaton, Illinois: Theosophical Publishing House, 1980.

# About the Authors

Zalman Schachter-Shalomi is a preeminent rabbi, teacher, and Professor Emeritus at Temple University. His belief in the universality of spiritual truth has led him to study with Sufi masters, Buddhist teachers, Native American elders, Catholic monks, and humanistic and transpersonal psychologists. He is the founder of the Spiritual Eldering Institute in Philadelphia, which sponsors workshops nationwide that provide the psychological and spiritual tools for people of all ages to grow into elderhood.

Ronald S. Miller, an award-winning journalist, is the former health editor of *Senior World* and the author of *As Above, So Below: Paths to Spiritual Renewal in Daily Life*. He has taught courses in human development, transpersonal psychology, and stress management at universities and growth centers across the country. He lives in San Diego with his wife and son.

# About the Spiritual Eldering Institute

Located in Philadelphia, the Spiritual Eldering Institute provides workshops nationwide that guide elders in reviewing their lives, harvesting the wisdom of their years, and transmitting a legacy to future generations. The institute encourages the formation of local spiritual eldering groups. Led by trainer facilitators, these groups provide ongoing community support for those pursuing the path of spiritual elderhood. The institute also provides a Leaders Training Program for those seeking to enhance their professional skills as facilitators of spiritual eldering groups and workshops. For information, contact the Spiritual Eldering Institute, 7318 Germantown Avenue, Philadelphia, PA 19919; (215) 248-9308, our toll-free number is (888) ELD-RING; FAX: (215) 247-9703.

# INDEX